Peace or Violence

Religion, Education and Culture

Series Editors:
William K. Kay (University of Wales, Bangor, UK),
Leslie J. Francis (University of Wales, Bangor, UK) and
Jeff Astley (University of Durham, UK)

This series addresses issues raised by religion and education within contemporary culture. It is intended to be of benefit to those involved in professional training as ministers of religion, teachers, counsellors, psychologists, social workers and health professionals, while also contributing to the theoretical development of the academic fields from which this training is drawn.

Peace or Violence

The Ends of Religion and Education?

Edited by

JEFF ASTLEY, LESLIE J. FRANCIS and MANDY ROBBINS

on behalf of the International Seminar on
Religious Education and Values (ISREV)

UNIVERSITY OF WALES PRESS
CARDIFF
2007

© The Contributors, 2007

All rights reserved. No part of this book may be reproduced, stored in a retrieval system, or transmitted, in any form or by any means, electronic, mechanical, photocopying, recording or otherwise, without clearance from the University of Wales Press, 10 Columbus Walk, Brigantine Place, Cardiff, CF10 4UP.
www.wales.ac.uk/press

British Library Cataloguing-in-Publication Data
A catalogue record for this book is available from the British Library.

ISBN 978-0-7083-2078-5

The rights of the Contributors to be identified separately as authors of this work have been asserted by them in accordance with sections 77 and 79 of the Copyright, Designs and Patents Act 1988.

Typeset by Florence Production Ltd, Stoodleigh, Devon
Printed in Great Britain by the University Press, Cambridge.

Contents

Preface		vii
The editors and contributors		viii
Introduction JEFF ASTLEY		1
1	Militant piety: violence as a sacred duty GARETH LLOYD JONES	6
2	The peace that passes all secular understanding: facing religion and ourselves JACK G. PRIESTLEY	30
3	The education of the religious fanatic JOHN M. HULL	46
4	Hospitality and the voice of the Other: confronting the economy of violence through religious education ANDREW WRIGHT	64
5	Power, force and violence GABRIEL MORAN	81
6	Developing an ethos of anti-violence: the role of Christianity in Africa EUNICE KARANJA KAMAARA	90
7	Education for peace: a multidimensional approach KARL ERNST NIPKOW	110
8	Does public religious education imply 'symbolic violence'? In search of a political theory of religious education ELISABET HAAKEDAL	131

9	Public and personal peace in life, religion and education: an exercise in ordinary theology JEFF ASTLEY	151
10	Violence for political purposes: the case of the London bombings WILLIAM K. KAY	174
11	Education for peaceful coexistence in the Israeli state Jewish school system YAACOV J. KATZ	195

Name index   208

Subject index   213

Preface

Since its inception in 1978, the International Seminar on Religious Education and Values (ISREV) has been a key meeting-place for religious educators across the world. In two recent conferences, one held in Jerusalem and one in Philadelphia, members of this Seminar addressed the themes of peace, violence and terrorism, and the role of religion and religious education in both their promotion and their prevention. Updated and edited versions of a number of the papers presented at these conferences, together with some additional material, have now been brought together to be offered to a wider audience.

This book will be of value to teachers, scholars and students in religious education, religious formation, theology and religious studies, as well as to those who work in more general areas, such as politics and social ethics. It should be of particular interest to religious leaders and religious commentators who are concerned with questions of inter-religious dialogue, tolerance, faith schools and general education, and to every citizen who cares about the cohesion of society and the welfare of all humankind.

Our thanks are due to the authors for making their essays available in this way, and to staff at the North of England Institute for Christian Education and the Welsh National Centre for Religious Education, two Church-related foundations committed to research and development in religious education in schools and churches, for preparing the manuscript for publication. In this regard, we are particularly grateful for the work of Evelyn Jackson, Carol Roberts and Susan Thomas.

Jeff Astley
Leslie J. Francis
Mandy Robbins

The editors and contributors

The Revd Professor Jeff Astley is Director of the North of England Institute for Christian Education, and Honorary Professorial Fellow in Practical Theology and Christian Education, University of Durham, England.

The Revd Professor Leslie J. Francis is Director of the Welsh National Centre for Religious Education, and Professor of Practical Theology, University of Wales, Bangor, Wales.

Dr Elisabet Haakedal is Associate Professor of Religious Education, Agder University College, Kristiansand, Norway.

Professor John M. Hull, the General Secretary and Co-founder of ISREV, is Emeritus Professor of Religious Education at the University of Birmingham, and Honorary Professor of Practical Theology in the Queen's Foundation for Ecumenical Theological Education, Birmingham, England.

The Revd Professor Gareth Lloyd Jones is Emeritus Professor of Theology and Religious Studies, University of Wales, Bangor, Wales.

Dr Eunice Karanja Kamaara is Senior Lecturer/Researcher in Religion, Department of Religion, Moi University, Eldoret, Kenya, and Affiliate Professor, Indiana University, Indianapolis, USA.

Professor Yaacov J. Katz is Professor of Education at the School of Education, Bar-Ilan University, Israel.

The Revd Dr William K. Kay is Reader in Practical Theology and Director of the Centre for Pentecostal and Charismatic Studies, University of Wales, Bangor, Wales.

Professor Gabriel Moran is Professor of Education and Director of the Program of Philosophy of Education, New York University, New York, USA.

Professor Karl Ernst Nipkow is Professor of Religious Education emeritus in the Faculty of Protestant Theology, and Co-opted Member of the Faculty of Social and Behavioural Sciences, University of Tübingen, Germany.

Dr Jack G. Priestley is Honorary Research Fellow, School of Education and Lifelong Learning, University of Exeter, England.

Dr Mandy Robbins is Lecturer in the Department of Theology and Religious Studies, University of Wales, Bangor, Wales.

Dr Andrew Wright is Senior Lecturer in Religious and Theological Education and coordinator of the Centre for Theology, Religion and Culture, King's College London, England.

Introduction

JEFF ASTLEY

Do religions and religious education intend peace or do they intend violence, and – whatever the intention – which of these ends (peace or violence) do these activities really promote?

The editors of this volume, before boarding an El Al flight to Israel for a conference of the International Seminar on Religious Education and Values, were subjected to the usual security questioning by airline officials. On learning that this conference would involve representatives of several religions from many different countries who were coming together to discuss the theme, 'Religion, education and peace', one official asked: 'Do you think that that is a good idea?'

Along with the other contributors to this collection, the editors continue to believe that discussions focused on issues of peace and violence should be of central concern to all those who teach and explore religion and its communication. Many would claim that religion is itself at least partly responsible for some of the major outbreaks of terrorism and warfare that currently poison the peace of peoples and nations. Honesty forces us to agree. A few would even seek a moratorium on religious education, as a necessary preliminary to creating a peaceful society. Here we disagree, and it is this debate that the present volume seeks to address. While much has been written from within the disciplines of theology and religious studies on the attitudes to peace and violence of the religions of the world,[1] few contributions have so far been made on this topic from the field of religious education.[2]

In chapter 1, 'Militant piety: violence as a sacred duty', Gareth Lloyd Jones begins the book by concentrating on some of the religious sources of the debate over peace and violence. He examines how Jews and Christians have interpreted and employed passages from the Hebrew Bible/Old Testament that sanction violence, and suggests some ways of preventing scripture from becoming a paradigm for those who preach a militant piety. He offers examples of the way in which passages that stress the superiority of the Israelites, call for the ethnic cleansing of Canaan, or advocate a theology of dispossession have been utilized, arguing in each case that dogmatic considerations disable the reading of biblical texts and influence their application. He then discusses interpretative strategies that take the scriptures of ancient Israel seriously but deny them a moral authority that would allow later generations to commit atrocities in God's name.

In chapter 2, 'The peace that passes all secular understanding: facing religion and ourselves', Jack Priestley begins with an alternative reading of religion, treating peace as the basis of the religious quest and arguing that its realization should also be the primary focus of religious education. To this end, religious education should be 'largely, if not primarily, a study of the attitudes, behaviour and relationships which make for peace and harmony'. In order to deliver this, however, we should concern ourselves not only with what it means to think religiously, but also with what it means to 'teach through our actions as much as by our words' by facing ourselves more honestly.

John Hull follows this with a provocative essay on religious fanaticism. In chapter 3, he attempts first of all to define fanaticism and to explore both its affective and its cognitive aspects, before exploring the problems and possibilities of 'the education of the religious fanatic' in a world in which the phenomenon has become increasingly widespread. He then proceeds to analyse the significant part that religious education may play in deepening respect for religion without encouraging fanaticism.

Andrew Wright takes a rather different position in 'Hospitality and the voice of the Other: confronting the economy of violence through religious education' (chapter 4), arguing that a religious education that encourages pupils to identify the commonalities that exist between different faith traditions runs the risk of distorting the self-understanding of such traditions. It does this by forcing them into a common framework in a manner that threatens to be colonial and imperialistic. Wright therefore proposes an alternative model, in which the identification of difference is given priority over the assertion of sameness, so as to establish mutual respect and thereby enhance the possibility of a move towards the cessation of violence. A 'host–guest' model of religious education is proposed as a means of overcoming the limitations of the dominant 'identity–sameness' model.

Gabriel Moran's succinct discussion, entitled 'Power, force and violence' (chapter 5), offers the reader a subtle linguistic analysis of these three related concepts. 'The real paradox of power', Moran insists, 'is that power can be almost the exact opposite of force.' He argues that the misunderstanding of these terms has led to confusion and blindness regarding our definition of, and reaction to, terrorism. In particular, this American scholar concludes, the 'war on terrorism' is a nonsensical phrase.

The nature of power is also explored in chapter 6, by Eunice Karanja Kamaara, a Christian educator who writes out of an African context. In 'Developing an ethos of anti-violence: the role of Christianity in Africa', she treats ethnic conflict and violence towards women as a preliminary to identifying the interpretation and use/abuse of power as key factors behind African violence. The role of Christian religious education in Kenya is then rehearsed, and the author describes the significance of the biblical understanding of power as servanthood, in contrast to the notion of power as mastery over resources. 'The tragedy for Africa', Kamaara writes, 'is that our leaders claim to be Christian . . . they love power, but have little understanding of the power of love.'

Karl Ernst Nipkow next seeks to develop a theory of peace education that recognizes the harsh confrontation between a religious view and the sober facts of human life. In chapter 7, 'Education for peace: a multidimensional approach', he addresses the daunting anthropological question of how human nature is as it is, acknowledging an alliance between the realistic but disillusioning stories of the Hebrew Bible and those based on the data of evolutionary research. Nipkow draws on both sources, as well as on the history of reflection on peace in theology, philosophy and education, to develop a more realistic understanding of the nature of a proper religious education into peace, justice and tolerance.

In chapter 8, Elisabet Haakedal draws on the concept of 'symbolic violence' (as it is understood by the French sociologist Pierre Bourdieu) as a platform for discussing some basic issues in anthropology and epistemology that are relevant to a political theory of pluralistic religious education. She argues that public religious education need not be symbolically violent, proposing 'symbolic competition' as a bridge to an alternative understanding of the subject.

Jeff Astley's 'Public and personal peace in life, religion and education: an exercise in ordinary theology' (chapter 9) explores these two categories of peace language in everyday English. The concept of personal peace is then briefly traced in Christian scripture, spirituality and experience, and with reference to the psychology of religion. The relationship between this spiritual state and the practice of peacemaking is discussed, and some reflections offered on the implications for the nature of religious education interpreted as an 'education in peaceable perception'.

On 7 July 2005, suicide bombers attacked the transport system in London. One of the most shocking elements in the situation was that the alleged bombers were British Muslims. Arguing in 'Violence for political purposes: the case of the London bombings' (chapter 10) that suicide bombers could be drawn from the overlap between two sets of people, those who use violence for political purposes and those who commit suicide, William K. Kay interrogates a database of young people aged 14 to 20 for the light it might throw on these issues. After examining sociological and psychological variables, the author concludes that a small segment of young people are ripe for recruitment as suicide bombers but that they are not necessarily drawn from one particular religious, or non-religious, group. Rather, they are conformist young people with poor family relationships and high psychoticism scores.

In the final chapter of the book, Yaacov Katz explores the nature of peace education within Israel, a society that includes numerous heterogeneous ethnic and national groupings, along with different religious sectors. Katz's essay recounts what has been done to promote peaceful coexistence among the two major Jewish sectors in the Israeli state education system: pupils attending state religious and state secular schools. He acknowledges, however, that little has been attempted as yet to promote coexistence between pupils belonging to these sectors of the school population and to the minority Arab Muslim, Christian and Druze population groups. But the educational system is now beginning to develop programmes to promote more widely those values that are vital for cohesion and coherence throughout Israeli society – and, indeed, for the welfare of all humankind.

Notes

1. See, for example, the material collected and the literature cited in Jeff Astley, David Brown and Ann Loades (eds), *War and Peace: A Reader*, London, T. and T. Clark/Continuum, 2003; and the collection of essays in Gerrie ter Haar and James J. Busuttil (eds), *Bridge or Barrier: Religion, Violence and Visions for Peace*, Leiden and Boston, Brill, 2005.
2. But see also Padraic O'Hare (ed.), *Education for Peace and Justice*, San Francisco, Harper & Row, 1983; and Karl Ernst Nipkow, *God, Human Nature and Education for Peace*, Aldershot, Ashgate, 2003.

1
Militant piety: violence as a sacred duty

GARETH LLOYD JONES

In any detailed study of the Old Testament, a concern which frequently comes to the fore is the applicability of its directives to later generations. Do the ordinances of God, given in the distant past to ancient Israel, apply to Jews in the twenty-first century? Are they to be regarded by Christians as divinely inspired commandments valid for all time? Naturally the concern is not with the Ten Commandments and with laws that define an ideal world in which there would be no poor. The problem arises when the reader is confronted with what any civilized society would regard as morally reprehensible passages. How are faithful followers of the God of the Bible to react to xenophobic directives which call upon the Israelites to commit appalling atrocities on fellow human beings? Can anything be learned from the misinterpretations of the past? To what extent can authority be granted to abhorrent texts? How are commands to commit genocide in God's name to be interpreted today? In a word: How does one handle a holy book? In an attempt to address these questions, we consider first the way in which dogma has influenced the understanding and application of the biblical text.

The dictates of dogma

Chosen people
There is a saying in South Africa: 'When the white man came to our country he had the Bible and we had the land. The white man said to us, "Let us pray." After the prayer, the white man had the land and we had the Bible.' Black South Africans recognize the crucial part played by the Bible in their exploitation by white colonialists. For the indigenous population, conversion to Christianity meant embracing a book which very quickly became an instrument

of oppression. This view is substantiated when we consider the use which the Dutch Reformed Church (DRC) made of Scripture to justify its policies with regard to the black population. In 1948, the year when apartheid became the official policy of the state, the DRC proudly proclaimed: 'As a Church, we have always worked purposefully for the separation of the races. In this regard apartheid can rightfully be called a Church policy' (quoted in Boesak, 1983: 6). It could be 'rightfully' so regarded because, according to the DRC, it could be justified theologically. 'Although theology has not been the main source of apartheid, it can by no means be understood without a knowledge of the way in which Afrikaners experience and worship God. In this context the "apartheid bible" played a significant role' (Loubser, 1987: xviii). The divine sanction for apartheid came predominantly from the Old Testament, especially from the book of Deuteronomy.

Deuteronomy, which purports to be God's instructions given by Moses in a series of sermons to the Israelites before they invaded Canaan, is a book of contradictions. On the one hand it is a positive and irenic document. The numerous laws concerning those who live a marginal existence have made a favourable impression on most exegetes. They regard its humanitarian concern for widows, orphans, slaves and resident aliens to be worthy of commendation. The book marks the highest point in the history of Israelite religion because it is designed to announce a utopia by making poverty history. Its laws call for empathy with fellow human beings. As Moshe Weinfeld has shown, it is one of the great repositories of humanistic values in Scripture (1972: 282–97).

On the other hand, Deuteronomy is extremely xenophobic. Because the Israelites are a minority in Canaan and constantly at risk from forces beyond their control, the choice between survival or annihilation, life or death, is forever before them. Foreigners who co-inhabit the promised land will jeopardize the chosen people's survival. They must be given the inferior status of hewers of wood and drawers of water (Deut. 29: 11). The nation's inability to insulate itself from such a potentially harmful influence makes it highly intolerant of outsiders. The word 'enemies' occurs over twenty-five times in thirty-four chapters. When God delivers the surrounding hostile nations into his people's hands, Moses gives explicit instructions to Israel how to deal with them, instructions which must be observed faithfully if the nation is to preserve its purity:

> You must exterminate them. You must not make an alliance with them or spare them. You must not intermarry with them ... You are to devour all the nations which the Lord your God is giving over to you. Show none of them mercy. (Deut. 7: 2–3, 16)

The divinely inspired mission of the Israelites must be one of destruction.

This spirit of xenophobia is given added impetus by the doctrine of election. The nation is reminded time and again that it is a people 'holy' to the Lord, who chose it 'out of all the peoples of the earth to be his special possession' (Deut. 7: 6). The choice is ratified by means of a covenant, which promises deliverance from danger, victory over enemies and a land the Israelites could call their own. The inference is clear. God has his favourite 'chosen' nation; all other peoples are of lesser importance. The elect possess a unique spiritual destiny, which emphasizes their singular righteousness and their superiority over adherents to other religions. The corollary of such favouritism is suffering, which the 'not chosen' are destined to endure. This belief in divine election is characteristic of adversary situations and small sects. It justifies the rejection, and even destruction, of all that threatens the purity or sanctity of the group. In the words of Michael Wyschogrod: 'If God elects one individual or group, there is someone else whom he does not elect and that other is left to suffer his exclusion' (1983: 60).

When the theologians of the DRC in South Africa sought to defend apartheid during the first half of the twentieth century, they had recourse to Deuteronomy. Its description of ancient Israel was relevant to their social situation and suited their vested interests. Boer Calvinism was based on the plain sense of the Bible, uninfluenced by any critical handling of the text. In sermons and official Church statements, the laws of Deuteronomy were related directly to the South African situation. 'A naïve reading and application of concepts from the book of Deuteronomy' provided the scriptural basis for the policy of apartheid (Deist, 1994: 26). Three examples must suffice of how the Torah supplied norms and principles for rulers who sought to organize society along the lines of 'separate development'.

First, the division of the nations. 'When the Most High gave each nation its heritage, when he divided all mankind, he laid down the boundaries for peoples' (Deut. 32: 8). This was taken to mean that separation between different peoples is divinely ordained. God was the 'Great Divider', as the story of Creation in Genesis 1: 3–19 demonstrates. Because apartheid is of God, humans must not seek to unite what the Creator has divided. The separation of peoples is based on the Bible, whereas equality is a human invention. So, instead of equality the DRC spoke of pluriformity.

Second, the legality of discrimination. 'You must not eat anything that has died a natural death. You may give it to aliens residing among you, and they may eat it, or you may sell it to a foreigner; but you are a people holy to the Lord your God' (Deut. 14: 21). For members of the DRC, this was biblical proof that people are unequal. The same deduction is made on the basis of the law which allows the charging of interest on loans to foreigners, but not to a fellow Israelite (Deut. 23: 20).

Finally, the recognition of natural distinctions. 'You are not to plough with an ox and a donkey yoked together. You are not to wear clothes woven with two kinds of yarn, wool and flax together' (Deut. 22: 10–11). The original idea in these verses seems to be that natural distinctions should not be disregarded. The DRC interpreted them as a prohibition against mixed marriages. If the Bible teaches that divisions exist in nature, how much more does this apply to people? This text, together with the law against intermarriage between Israelites and Canaanites (Deut. 7: 3), was the basis for the Immorality Act, which prohibited marriage between blacks and whites. Like the Israelites, the Afrikaners had to be kept pure.

The policy of separate development legitimized by the state and supported by the Church was dictated by dogma, which in turn was founded upon the scriptural concept of election. The Dutch Calvinists who arrived in South Africa in 1652 identified themselves with ancient Israel: they regarded themselves as God's chosen people. Consequently, the biblical narrative became meaningful and relevant. Like the Israelites who went from Palestine to Egypt to escape famine, they went from Europe to Africa to escape persecution. Like the Hebrew slaves in Egypt suffering under foreign rule, they suffered when the British captured the colony in 1806. Like the Israelites in the desert seeking a haven from oppression, the Boers went on the Great Trek to find a promised land in the north, beyond British administration, because they were disgusted at Britain's abolition of slavery. Like the people of Israel, the white South Africans would achieve their goal only by violent means. In the words of Alan Boesak, writing during the apartheid era: 'We still have, in South Africa, a system of racism that is maintained by violence . . . the systemic violence inherent in apartheid society' (1986: 43–4).

Like Israel in Canaan, a faithful minority whose religion was threatened by paganism, the Boers kept themselves apart from the 'Kaffirs' (that is, heathen) who surrounded them.

> The Dutch settlers regarded the indigenous peoples as culturally inferior heathen destined by God to be the 'hewers of wood and the drawers of water' for their superior masters. The settlers prospered; the indigenous peoples and imported slaves suffered. The Christian faith seemed to provide the rationale necessary to justify the situation.
> (de Gruchy, 2004: 172)

The Boers were angered not only at the freeing of the slaves, but also because the indigenes were

> being placed on an equal footing with Christians, contrary to the laws of God and the natural distinction of race and religion, so that it was intolerable for any decent Christian to bow beneath such a yoke; wherefore we withdrew in order to preserve our doctrines in purity.
> (MacCrone, 1937: 126, quoting Anna Steenkamp)

And, as in the case of the Israelites, the preservation of racial and religious purity depended on strict adherence to the laws of God, as interpreted by their own theologians. It was assumed that God would reward and protect those who kept the command to exercise separate development, because such a policy reflected his wisdom and will.

Holy war

On 13 September 1993, President Clinton introduced the Israeli premier, Yitzhak Rabin, and the Palestinian leader, Yasser Arafat, to a waiting world. The occasion was hailed as a breakthrough. The image of the two leaders shaking hands on the White House lawn is probably etched on the memory of many. Both pledged to work for a peace shaped by the values of the Qur'ān and the Bible. According to the *Washington Post*, Clinton had been unable to sleep the previous night because he was worried that his speech was not up to scratch. He got up at 3 a.m. and opened his Bible. He read the whole of Joshua and parts of the New Testament before going back to sleep. His speech the following morning contained a mixture of biblical exhortations and clever political moves. We do not know whether or not he suffered nightmares after reading one of the most blood-curdling narratives in the history of civilization, but there must surely be more appropriate literature for an influential world leader who cannot sleep.

Joshua is presented in the book named after him as Moses's successor, appointed by God to complete his mentor's work. The first half of the book (2:1–12:24) describes the conquest of Canaan. In accordance with the rules of Holy War, the key cities were 'put to the ban': that is, they were completely destroyed and all their inhabitants slaughtered. The final editor sums up the campaign in a matter-of-fact way:

> The Israelites ... put every living soul to the sword until they had destroyed everyone; they did not leave alive anyone that drew breath. The Lord had laid his commands on his servant Moses, and Moses laid these same commands on Joshua, and Joshua carried them out. Not one of the commands laid on Moses by the Lord was left unfulfilled. (Joshua 11: 14–15)

In his attempt to ethnically cleanse Canaan, Joshua was only obeying orders: so was Moses.

In his farewell address shortly before his death, Joshua reminded the people why they had engaged in Holy War. He justified his acceptance of the mandate for genocide given in Deuteronomy 7: 1–3 on two grounds. First, in order to provide a safe haven for the Israelites after their escape from Egyptian bondage, God himself had driven out the indigenous population in order to give Israel a home: 'he dispossessed them to make way for you, and you occupied their land' (Josh. 23: 5). Canaan supplied *Lebensraum* (living room) for the liberated slaves. In this promised land they would be expected to live as the covenant community in accordance with the precepts of the Torah.

Second, the ethnic cleansing of Canaan would ensure that the Israelites did not commit apostasy. Because syncretism threatened 'to destroy Israel's identity as the people of Yahweh ... the suppression of apostasy' was viewed as 'an act of national self-preservation' (Patrick, 1985: 107). Anyone who encouraged or was engaged in prohibited religious practices must be purged from the land (Deut. 13: 1–18; cf. Exodus 22: 20). This was necessary because pagan neighbours would draw the children of the Israelites away from worshipping Yahweh (Deut. 7: 4) and teach them to imitate their abominable practices (Deut. 20: 18). In the words of R. E. Clements:

> The particular horror of the Deuteronomists was that vestiges of the beliefs and practices of the pre-Israelite inhabitants of Canaan should continue. These are made the object of the strictest prohibitions because of their offensive nature, and any participation in them is made a capital crime. It is on this account that the pre-Israelite inhabitants are threatened with extermination. (1968: 35; see also Stern, 1991: 221)

Genocide was a precautionary measure against idolatry: it was the only way of preserving religious purity. Should some Canaanites escape annihilation and continue to live in the land, Joshua warns the Israelites that any association with them will bring severe penalties. If you

> associate with them and they with you, then be sure that the Lord will not continue to drive out those peoples from before you. They will be snares to entrap you, whips for your backs, and barbed hooks in your eyes, until you perish from this good land which the Lord your God has given you. (Josh. 23: 12–13)

President Clinton was not the only influential American to read the scriptural account of the Holy War waged by Israel against the Canaanites at a significant moment in world history: the early Puritans also found it relevant. The first settlers had come to North America to escape religious persecution in England. They identified themselves with the people of Israel and applied biblical texts describing the conquest of Canaan to their own situation. They justified their actions by means of analogies from the Old Testament. Like the Israelites, they needed *Lebensraum* and dreamed of a promised land; they embarked on 'an errand in the wilderness' to find 'a Western Canaan', as they called the New World, where they could practise their religion without censure. But between the dream and its realization were the Indians. As God's chosen people, the Puritans believed that they had a divinely appointed destiny to convert the indigenous population. But although the missionaries had some success in New England, on the whole the Indians resisted evangelization (Noll, 2002: 36). Like the Canaanites in the time of Joshua, those who persisted in their paganism were regarded by the Puritan preachers as 'snares . . . whips . . . and barbed hooks'. They were begotten of Satan. 'In Joseph Mede's view, America was uniquely the land of the devil, so the Indians were a satanic parody of the Puritans, the Chosen People of the devil as the Israelites, and then the Puritans, were the Chosen People of God' (Silverman, 1985: 239). God's elect had no option but to annihilate them.

On 1 September 1689, Cotton Mather preached a sermon in the Old North Church, Boston, where he served as assistant pastor to his father, Increase. The younger Mather was an influential champion of the Congregationalist cause in New England, and would have been an outstanding individual in any era.

> He was ostentatiously pious, shamelessly self-promoting, overbearingly moralistic, and his 469 separate books and pamphlets suggest that he never had a thought he felt unworthy of publication. (In fact, however, his largest work, a massive reference work and commentary on the Bible, has never been published.) Yet superficial treatments do not take the measure of this extraordinarily learned and preternaturally active clergyman. (Noll, 1992: 87)

Mather's congregation on that September morning consisted mainly of soldiers fighting the native inhabitants of New England. In a sermon entitled 'Souldiers Counselled and Comforted', the preacher told his listeners that they should think of themselves as Israel in the desert confronted by the Amalekites, the descendants of Esau, who first resisted the Israelite invaders on the borders of the promised land. Because of their hostility they were singled out for destruction by God. As soon as the Israelites entered Canaan they 'must without fail blot out all memory of Amalek from under heaven' (Deut. 25: 19).

The soldiers listened with rapt attention as Mather identified his congregation as the New Israel of God, and the Indians who refused to convert with the Amalekites, 'a treacherous and barbarous enemy ... the veriest tigers'. He exhorted the troops to exterminate them:

> Turn not back until they are consumed; wound them that they shall not be able to arise. Though they cry, let there be none to save them. But beat them small as the dust before the wind and cast them out as the dirt in the streets. (Silverman, 1985: 237)

The genocide of the Indians is justified not only on practical grounds, because they murder Christians, but also on dogmatic grounds. Those who resist the gospel must be disinherited to make room for God's elect. Mather had no difficulty at all applying the method of Joshua to his own situation, because he believed that the policy of the Puritans had divine approval. The drive by God's people to find a new land where it could preserve its purity had its paradigm in Scripture and was dictated by dogma.

Promised land

On 25 February 1994, Dr Baruch Goldstein, an ultra-orthodox Jew of American extraction, entered a mosque in his home town of Hebron in Israeli-occupied territory carrying a machine gun. Before he was overpowered and beaten to death, he had shot twenty-nine Muslim worshippers as they knelt in prayer. Today the assassin's grave in a park outside Hebron looks like a garden of remembrance. His massive gravestone, illuminated at night by ornamental lights, refers to him as a saint. The inscription reads: 'Having given his life on behalf of the Jewish people, its Torah and its ancestral homeland, he was an innocent, pure-hearted individual.' Pilgrims hold services and light memorial candles. Supporters kiss the tomb and stop to pray. At his funeral, Rabbi Jacob Perrin commended his action by stating in his widely reported sermon that 'one million Arabs are not worth a Jewish fingernail'. Another religious leader described him as a 'royal martyr'. When Goldstein's son became a bar mitzvah two years later, the officiating rabbi said to him: 'Jacob Jair, follow in your father's footsteps. He was a righteous man and a great hero' (*Jerusalem Report*, 12 December 1996: 10).

The British Chief Rabbi, Jonathan Sacks, condemned the massacre in no uncertain terms by declaring that 'violence is evil.

Violence committed in the name of God is doubly evil. Violence against those engaged in worshipping God is unspeakably evil.' Reflecting on Sacks's reaction, Rabbi Norman Solomon commented thus:

> The problem with Sacks' position is that, much as we may concur with the sentiment, and however many Biblical and talmudic citations we may amass in praise of peace, we are left with numerous texts that *do* summon us to violence in the name of God, and this makes it difficult to argue against Perrin and the like on purely *textual* grounds. (1997: 8)

Goldstein and his supporters justified the massacre on the grounds that the Palestinians should not be occupying land which God gave to Jews. Palestine was by divine right a Jewish birthright. But when Theodor Herzl insisted that the only solution to the plight of European Jews was the recovery of their national identity, his concept of a Jewish state was based on nationalism, rather than religion. During the First Zionist Congress of 1897 he spoke of the distinctive nationality of the Jews, not of their divine right to a piece of land. Nevertheless, there are biblical overtones in what he said. For example, he recognized that the notions of a chosen people and of a return to the promised land were potent factors in mobilizing support. Furthermore, like Joshua, he gave no consideration to the rights of the indigenous population. In his diary he wrote:

> When we occupy the land we must expropriate gently the private property on the estates assigned to us. We shall try to spirit the penniless population across the border by procuring employment for it in the transit countries, while denying it any employment in our own country. Both the process of expropriation and the removal of the poor must be carried out discreetly and circumspectly. (Patai, 1960, vol. 1: 87–8)

The needs and rights of the native population were to be ignored.

Initially, Herzl's dream was firmly rejected by orthodox Jews on religious grounds. The return to Zion could be accomplished only by the Messiah, who would come in God's good time. Autoemancipation contradicted the religious tradition and therefore violated the Torah. But during the second half of the twentieth century, after the Holocaust and the wars of 1967 and 1974, Zionism became a compelling alternative, even for the orthodox.

By now the occupation of Palestine has strong support because it is viewed as being consistent with Torah and prophecy. Zionism has been given a theological foundation.

The great majority of orthodox rabbis in Israel have denounced the so-called 'peace process' between Israel and the Palestinians because they recognize that the Bible, in Ben Gurion's famous phrase, is their 'sacrosanct title-deed' to the land. They now accept that the Bible legitimizes the Jewish state, not only by establishing its borders (Genesis 15: 18–20; cf. Deut. 1: 7), but also by stating that the exiled Jews will again live within them. The map reading provided in Genesis 15: 18–20 is unambiguous: the promised land will one day extend from 'the river of Egypt to the Great River, the river Euphrates'. It was to this land that God would bring back the Jews of the Dispersion, an assurance repeatedly given by the prophets: 'I shall take you from among the nations, and gather you from every land, and bring you to your homeland' (Ezekiel 36: 24, cf. 20: 42; Jeremiah 29: 14; Zechariah 10: 10).

An influential colonizing group is Gush Emunim (Block of the Faithful) formed in 1974. Their interpretation of the Bible, 'which equates the present-day Arab inhabitants of the Land with the Amalekites ... who lived there in Moses's and Joshua's day, has seeped into current ultra-orthodox theology' (Landau, 1993: 159). An example of the extreme measures they advocate against Palestinians is to be found in an article published in a student newspaper in 1980 by Rabbi Yisrael Hess, a former campus rabbi of Bar-Ilan University in Tel Aviv. Entitled 'The commandment of genocide in the Torah', the article states: 'The day is not far when we shall all be called to this holy war, this commandment of the annihilation of the Amalekites' (quoted in Masalha, 1997: 208).

The commandment to which Hess refers is Deuteronomy 25: 19, which is highlighted by Samuel in his instructions to Saul: 'Go now, fall upon the Amalekites, destroy them ... Spare no one; put them all to death, men and women, children and babes in arms, herds and flocks, camels and donkeys' (1 Samuel 15: 3). The rabbi regards the Palestinians as the 'Amalekites of today'. Like their ancient forebears, they should be shown no mercy. But even if the modern Amalek is not annihilated, Jewish extremists, to quote Hess, will seek to 'settle a million Jews on the West Bank before the turn of the millennium so that territorial compromise becomes impossible and eventual annexation becomes the obvious conclusion'. The Palestinians' claims to land they have occupied for centuries are dismissed out of hand on the basis of a fundamentalist reading of Scripture.

Zionist-Orthodox Jews also believe that a third temple, reconstructed on the site of the first two, is essential as a necessary prelude to the coming of the Messiah. The rebuilding will actually hasten his arrival; if they build, he will come. Zealous extremists believe that their action will force God's hand. But before the rebuilding can begin, the Islamic presence must be removed. The Messiah cannot come to a site which is 'polluted' by a Muslim shrine. Gershon Salomon, founder of the 'Temple Mount and Land of Israel Faithful Movement', is clear about his goal: 'Our vision is to move the mosque, move the Dome of the Rock, and have them rebuilt in Mecca. The mount must become again the centre of the Israeli nation' (quoted in Mairson, 1996: 30).

In 1990, Salomon attempted to do just this. He led a group of his followers to the Mount to lay a cornerstone for the third temple. A crowd of about five thousand Muslims gathered to defend the site. Israeli soldiers sent to control the situation left at least seventeen dead and hundreds wounded. Yehuda Etzion, the leader of an underground Jewish movement, is quoted as saying that he hopes that the Muslim shrine and mosque will not have to be blown up. Nevertheless, he said: 'these buildings will have to go. That's clear. Their removal is the jewel in the crown in the process of Jewish redemption' (quoted in Landau, 1993: 195).

Once the site is cleared and the temple built, the religious ceremonies will be conducted in the appropriate manner and by suitable personnel. The Temple Institute, a group of researchers and craftsmen dedicated to promoting the restoration, has already drawn up blueprints for the new building. Under the leadership of Rabbi Chaim Richman, an American Jew who came to Israel in 1982, students are taught the elaborate details of temple ritual. Sacred vessels, vestments and implements are being manufactured in readiness for the resumption of the daily sacrifice.

On the issues of land ownership and the rebuilding of the temple, many Christians, especially America's New Religious Right, join forces with Jews in what is theologically a most improbable alliance. The Zionist-Orthodox claim that the right of the Jews to the land rests on the authority of Scripture is supported by pre-millennial dispensationalists. These are Christians who believe that Christ will soon return to earth to inaugurate a new era, or dispensation, and reign for a thousand years. In Christian fundamentalist thought, the return of the Jews to Palestine is crucial, because it is a sure sign of the end of the world and of the second coming of the Messiah. Only when the Jews are back in their ancestral home and have converted to Christianity can the Messiah and his saints begin their thousand-year rule. The reoccupation of the land is one of the last pieces in the jigsaw.

Given this theological understanding, it is not surprising that the Jewish homecoming in 1948 was a cause of jubilation among fundamentalists. The prominent American televangelist, Jerry Falwell, founder of the Moral Majority, claims that since the ascension of Jesus 'the most important date we should remember is May 14, 1948', because the formation of the state of Israel is 'the single greatest sign indicating the imminent return of Christ' (Boyer, 1992: 189). The Six Day War of 1967, when the Israelis captured the Old City of Jerusalem and occupied the West Bank, was of even greater significance. This was the beginning of the territorial expansion, promised in Genesis and Deuteronomy, which would end with modern Israel being twenty times larger than it was initially. The argument was incontrovertible, because the title-deeds of the enlarged state were in God's handwriting: the Bible was the mandate for expansion.

Though Christian fundamentalists disagree with the Zionist-Orthodox about the significance of a rebuilt temple, they enthusiastically support its restoration. They believe that the Temple Mount is where the world as we know it will end and the new age will begin. The restoration will force God's hand and kick-start the apocalypse. They also believe that together with the Jews they are doing God's will by fulfilling an ancient prophecy. They interpret Ezekiel's vision (in chapters 40–8) of a rebuilt temple as referring to the millennial temple. The programme is therefore in keeping with God's intention for the end-time. One of the most influential pre-millennialist authors, Hal Lindsey, highlights the issue thus:

> There is only one place that this Temple can be rebuilt, according to the law of Moses. This is upon Mount Moriah. It is there that two previous Temples were built ... There is one major problem barring the construction of a third Temple. That obstacle is ... the Dome of the Rock. This is believed to be built squarely in the middle of the old

temple site. Obstacle or no obstacle, it is certain that the Temple will be rebuilt. Prophecy demands it. (Lindsey, 1977: 45–6)

The fact that any attempt to take over one of Islam's principal sacred sites might unleash a third world war cuts no ice with premillennialists. The reconstruction of the temple must be regarded as an absolute necessity because 'prophecy demands it'.

The same appeal to prophecy was made when President Carter, in his concern for human rights, shocked American fundamentalists by using the words 'Palestinian homeland' in a speech about the Middle East in 1977. Shortly afterwards a full-page advertisement appeared in leading newspapers, signed by prominent evangelicals. Under the title 'Evangelicals' concern for Israel', the statement read: 'The time has come for evangelicals to affirm their belief in biblical prophecy and Israel's divine right to the Holy Land' (*Christian Science Monitor*, 3 November 1977).

While every Christian has abandoned certain demands of the Torah, such as circumcision, kosher food and the death penalty for cursing one's parents, all of which express the revealed will of God as much as any other commandment, many still justify the appropriation of Arab land by Israel on purely biblical grounds. The theology of dispossession carries the seal of divine approval. Ultimately, this standpoint, to use a phrase attributed to Hannah Arendt, engenders a 'God-like certainty which stops all discussion' (quoted by Ellis, 1997: 7). Among Christians, as among Jews, the drive to dispossess the Palestinians is based on an idiosyncratic interpretation of the Scriptures and is dictated by dogma.

Rehabilitating the Bible

The use to which Scripture has been put to endorse exploitation, genocide and the appropriation of land has important implications for biblical exegesis. Recognition of the damage done by narratives which legitimize violence in God's name poses a fundamental moral problem for those who accept such narratives at face value. It is difficult to reconcile a God who commands and gloats over the destruction of whole communities with a God of justice and compassion. The Bible loses respect as a guide for human life when the message found in parts of it is, to say the least, morally questionable.

The above examples of the reception history of specific passages demonstrate how readers in various periods of history interpret the Scriptures, and how perpetrators of violence are inspired by religious ideals. They are not interested in what the laws, stories and prophecies meant in their original context. They believe that the Bible is a divinely given guidebook containing subtle allusions to future events. They make no distinction in the text between the *pre*scriptive and the *de*scriptive: the message is eternally relevant. What *they* say the Bible means becomes what it means. This inevitably raises the question: how is the Bible to be interpreted in a way which will negate its authority for those who use it to legitimize oppression? For the remainder of this essay we will note two ways of minimizing the damage done by an irresponsible and uncritical reading of Scripture.

Historical criticism

Until recent times, the traditional view of the biblical narratives was that they were genuine historical documents, the products of reliable historians, which recorded actual events. Scholars who wrote histories of Israel and Judah considered that the Scriptures provided a firm factual foundation for their endeavours. Consequently, they produced volumes which were little more than a paraphrase of the biblical text. Those who regard the biblical account of Joshua's exploits as historically accurate accept the biblical claim that such drastic action was necessary in order to root out the pernicious influence of the pagan population (Josh. 23: 12–13). The renowned twentieth-century archaeologist W. F. Albright took this view:

> From the impartial standpoint of a philosopher of history, it often seems necessary that a people of markedly inferior type should vanish before a people of superior potentialities, since there is a point beyond which racial mixture cannot go without disaster ... Thus the Canaanites, with their orgiastic nature worship, their cult of fertility in the form of serpent symbols and sensuous nudity, and their gross mythology, were replaced by Israel, with its pastoral simplicity and purity of life, its lofty monotheism, and its severe code of ethics. (1957: 280–1)

The Lord's own people must avoid contamination with any others. Drastic measures were needed to safeguard the future of the elect, and through them God's blessing to all humanity. The only possible course of action was the extermination of the Canaanites.

For some, this is a satisfactory explanation of the ethnic cleansing of Canaan, because it not only allows Joshua's account, with its frequent references to the 'abominations' of the Canaanites, to stand, but also exonerates the perpetrators. Genocide, terrible as it is, may be regarded as legitimate when undertaken to eliminate a greater evil. However, extra-biblical sources provide no evidence of unusual wickedness within Canaanite culture. In fact, a recent study paints a far more positive picture of life in Canaan than has been hitherto recognized. Closer scrutiny of ancient Near Eastern documents, coupled with a fresh assessment of the value of the Bible for historical analysis, has called into question 'the supposed difference between what may be termed genuine Israelite and genuine Canaanite society and culture' (Lemche, 1990: 20).

But Albright's description of the Canaanites as immoral and sensuous, and his justification of their wholesale slaughter on grounds of inferiority, has further ramifications. Keith Whitelam regards it as 'an outpouring of undisguised racism which is staggering . . . It is a characterization which dehumanizes, allowing the extermination of native populations, as in the case of Native Americans' (1996: 84). As we noted above, such a racist attitude is typical of the colonialist enterprise, which believed that the 'superior' peoples of the west had the right to expel and even exterminate indigenous populations.

During the past three decades, biblical scholarship has questioned the reliability of Scripture as a historical record. The majority of commentators no longer accept that it contains a factually accurate portrayal of the past. They believe the biblical narrative to be religiously motivated and to represent the ideology of a later age. They maintain that the Israelite redactors had political and didactic reasons for the way in which they represented the early period in their nation's history. They regard the literary nature of the biblical account of Israel's beginnings, as it appears in Genesis to Judges, to be folklore, epic or legend, rather than history.

T. L. Thompson (1974) and J. van Seters (1975) have vigorously challenged past efforts to establish the historicity of the patriarchs based on extra-biblical literature, arguing that they were fictional characters created by a much later age. According to Finkelstein and Silberman, archaeology does not support the biblical account that the invading Israelites ethnically cleansed Canaan in a matter of months (2001: 105–22). Apart from the witness of Scripture, there is no evidence that a Hebrew conquest, as described in Joshua 1–12, ever took place. Norman Gottwald has put forward persuasive arguments in favour of regarding the Israelite occupation of Canaan as a peasant revolt, rather than a massive onslaught by desert tribes under Joshua's leadership (1979). The origins of Israel were inside Canaan, not outside it. Norman Cantor states the current position clearly:

> Until the glorious day dawns of archaeological verification for the line of Abraham, we have to stipulate that all of Jewish history of the first millennium BCE and some of it for a century after that, as told in the Bible, is one of the great masterpieces of imaginative fiction or artfully contrived historical myths of all time. From empirical evidence, it did not happen. (1995: 5)

The view that the biblical narratives are inaccurate representations of ancient Israel, retrojections of a later period which are divorced from historical reality, have led to a heated debate about the authority of Scripture and about the relation of archaeology to the Bible.

If the biblical texts are not straightforward descriptions of what actually happened, how are they to be understood? It is now commonly accepted by modern scholars that Deuteronomy and the Deuteronomistic History (Joshua to 2 Kings) were written several centuries later than the period of which they purport to tell. This view inevitably questions the value of the source as an accurate historical description of an earlier period. Deuteronomy is regarded as a seventh-century work, composed in the wake of the Assyrian conquest of the Northern Kingdom of Israel in 722 and linked to the reform of King Josiah (2 Kings 22–3). Critical investigation suggests that the book, or at least parts of it, was written to legitimate Josiah's attempts to reform the Jerusalem cultus and reassert a sense of identity among his subjects after a century of oppression. Any practice that did not conform to Deuteronomic orthodoxy was condemned.

It may, therefore, be argued with some plausibility that the authors of Deuteronomy and Joshua were not recording history. They were using the term 'Canaanites' to indicate those who opposed Josiah's reforms. Lori Rowlett points this out:

Although the Canaanites are the ostensible victims in Joshua, the goal is not to incite literal violence against a particular ethnic group. The text of Joshua is concerned with voluntary submission to a set of rules and norms; it is directed primarily at Josiah's own subjects, not at real (ethnic) outsiders, but at insiders who pose a threat to the hierarchy being asserted. The message is that the punishment of Otherness is death, and that insiders can easily become outsiders (Others) by failure to submit. (1996: 183)

Though, prima facie, Joshua tells the story of a foreign nation conquered by the early Israelites, the motive of the seventh-century author is to show dissenters within his own camp that the religious authorities will not tolerate disobedience. In doing so he resorts to the violent ideology of the Assyrian oppressors.

The recognition that the biblical authors fabricated Israel's past, for ideological reasons, should cancel out the use made of the Bible by oppressive regimes to legitimize the appropriation of land and the expulsion of its inhabitants. It should undo the damage which a literalist reading of the text has done. If the authors' intention was didactic, rather than factual, how can their words be used to support a standpoint which requires its justifying text to be historical? Michael Prior asks pointedly:

Do texts which belong to the genre of folkloric epic or legend, rather than of a history which describes what actually happened, confer legitimacy on the 'Israelite' possession of the land and on subsequent forms of colonialism which looked to the biblical paradigm, understood as factual history, for legitimization later? Does a judgement which is based on the premise that the genre of the justifying text is history in that sense not dissolve when it is realized that the text belongs to the genre of *myths of origin*, which are encountered in virtually every society, and which ... were deployed in the service of particular ideologies? (1997: 252)

Historical and literary investigations should invalidate the claims made by erroneous interpretations.

Ethical critique

The biblical critics of the nineteenth century placed great emphasis on the antiquarian setting of the text. They concentrated on trying to discover the meaning intended by the author at the time of writing. They studied Scripture in its original context and made an invaluable contribution to its understanding, but they went no further. They did not recognize the challenge of the text for themselves, and therefore did not seek to discover its contemporary relevance in matters of faith. They asked what it *meant*, but not what it *means*. The impact of the Bible, for good or ill, on personal and social morality was not on their agenda. They did not evaluate its message.

The past three decades have witnessed a very different approach to biblical study. The relevance of the critical enterprise for the believer has been questioned, and the discipline found to be wanting. In any study of the text, the role of the reader has now become significant, and has revolutionized our approach to Scripture. Members of any particular group or movement want to know how the Bible addresses their situation. They ask: How does Scripture apply to us where we are? How does the text address current issues? Does our understanding of the Bible lead to socio-political transformation? This is usually referred to as the 'reader-response' approach to Scripture.

When we study the reception history of the Bible, we see how its message has been read into the cultural context in which the readers find themselves. We discover how it has been interpreted in order to justify what in any civilized society is unjustifiable. This highlights the necessity to evaluate the text. Since divine approval of violence has clearly provided militants with dangerous encouragement, explanation or comment is not sufficient. Confronted with morally dubious passages which have been put to the kind of use noted above, we must apply an ethical critique. But, as David Clines points out, this is something that biblical scholars are loathe to do. They are eager to be called upon to explain and interpret the text, but they draw the line at evaluation. However, if it is to be regarded as an academic discipline, 'biblical studies has to be truly critical, critical not just about lower-order questions like the authorship of the biblical books or the historicity of the biblical narratives, but critical about the Bible's contents, its theology, its ideology' (1997: 25).

Commenting from the perspective of black South Africans, Takatso Mofokeng claims that 'the Bible itself is indeed a serious problem to people who want to be free', because 'there are texts, stories and traditions in the Bible which lend themselves to only oppressive interpretations and oppressive uses because of their inherent oppressive nature' (1988: 38). In a discussion of Native American liberation theology, R. A. Warrior makes the same point. He insists that knowledge of the historical background, however illuminating it may be, does not alter the inferior status of the Canaanites in the biblical text and the theology which has developed from it:

> The research of Old Testament scholars, however much it provides an answer to the historical question – the contribution of the indigenous people of Canaan to the formation and emergence of Israel as a nation – does not resolve the narrative problem. People who read the narratives read them as they are, not as scholars and experts would *like* them to be read and interpreted. History is no longer with us. The narrative remains. (1997: 280)

Read through the eyes of the Canaanites and their descendants – the marginalized in every age – the Bible is hardly 'the good news of God's love'. It is more likely to be regarded as 'an ideological instrument of colonization, oppression and exploitation' (Mofokeng, 1988: 34).

Referring to the 'ethical consequences of the biblical text and its subsequent interpretations', Elizabeth Fiorenza, a leading feminist theologian, writes:

> If scriptural texts have served – and still do – to support not only noble causes but also to legitimate war, to nurture anti-Judaism and misogyny, to justify the exploitation of slavery, and to promote colonial dehumanization, then biblical scholarship must take responsibility not only to interpret biblical texts in their historical contexts but also to evaluate the construction of their historical worlds and symbolic universes in terms of a religious scale of values. If the Bible has become a classic of western culture ... then the responsibility of the biblical scholar cannot be restricted to giving 'the readers of our time clear access to the original intentions' of the biblical writers. It must also include the elucidation of the ethical consequences and political functions of biblical texts and their interpretations. (1999: 28)

Clearly, ethical critique, however necessary it may be, threatens to undermine the authority of Scripture. Appeal is made to the Bible because it is believed to reflect God's will. Those who regard the Bible as divinely inspired and inerrant will criticize the interpreters, rather than the text. In an essay in which he recognizes 'the dangers of Deuteronomy', F. E. Deist exonerates the biblical authors and blames the commentators: 'Perhaps Deuteronomy *does* contain dangerous ideologies and therefore might very well *be* a dangerous book. But the greater danger lies in its (uncritical) *readers*' (1994: 28–9). But the issue is more complex. It is not simply one of interpretation: it involves the actual words of Scripture. A xenophobic text will never be changed by interpretations of it. It will still speak clearly of slaughter.

Those who find it difficult to engage in an ethical critique of Scripture might find it helpful to recognize the different standpoints represented within the canon. Evaluation can be justified on an inner-biblical basis. The Bible itself contains 'a hermeneutic of suspicion'. In the words of E. W. Davies:

> The biblical authors themselves frequently exercise a critical role, questioning past beliefs and querying past judgements. Far from accepting passively the values that they had inherited, their strategy was to probe, question, modify and even reject some of their inherited traditions ... The Hebrew Bible comes to us bearing clear traces of its own critique of tradition, and thus provides the contemporary reader with a warrant to dissent from its teachings and to question (and perhaps even reject) some of its ethical injunctions. (2005: 221)

It is not difficult to demonstrate the existence of conflicting opinions within Scripture. A balanced reading would probably cancel out all biblical claims, simply because each one has its opposite somewhere in the text. For example, the Torah states that Canaan belongs to the Israelites in perpetuity. But according to Jeremiah 7: 15, the gift of land has been forfeited many times by Israel, on ethical grounds: 'Because you have done all these abominations, says the Lord, I shall fling you away out of my presence.' The xenophobic elements in the Torah are contradicted by the universalism of Ruth, Jonah and Isaiah. The divinely ordained onslaught on the Canaanites (Deut. 7: 1–6) can be balanced with the command to love one's neighbour and to be concerned for the welfare of foreigners (Leviticus 19: 18; Exodus 22: 21). The author of Job disagrees with the concept found in the book of Proverbs, namely that suffering or misfortune is an infallible index to a person's character. Some see in Amos's oracles against the nations (1: 3–2: 5) a trenchant critique of the horrors associated with war. The clash of opinion appears even within individual books. Mention has already been made of Deuteronomy, where the portrait of a militaristic and racist deity is balanced by that of God as a merciful and loving father. Confronted by these differing viewpoints, readers of Scripture may choose to question its teachings and become ethical critics in their own right.

The issue of the authority of the Bible in the context of ethics is addressed by Tom Deidun in an essay which deserves careful attention. He believes that the problem of the relation between the Scriptures and Christian ethics is derived from a preoccupation with biblical authority, a preoccupation born of theological controversies embedded in past cultures. But this emphasis may not be the way forward now. Instead of referring to the authority of the Bible, Deidun suggests that we think of its 'potency' or 'fecundity'. He promotes an approach to the text which will be

> free and unpredictable ... versatile and imaginative ... It will be disdainful of biblical one-liners, and suspicious of 'favourite' texts or 'themes' ... Because it will want to take biblical writings seriously, it will not use them woodenly. It might on occasion put forward the opinion that the ethical insight of this or that biblical writer is wonderfully intuitive, while accepting with perfect equanimity that this or that other biblical writer's ethical stance is irrelevant or distasteful. (1998: 31)

We must take responsibility for the moral and political results of accepting without question the violent passages in Scripture and refusing to assess them. We must recognize not only the ideological distortions of certain passages in promoting violence and injustice, but also their very nature. We must accept that there is much in the Bible which is not worthy to serve as a model for imitation: it is not an infallible guide to complex ethical questions. In our attempt to handle our holy book responsibly, we might begin by considering how the actions of those who read the Bible without evaluating its message have affected their fellow human beings.

References

Albright, W. F. (1957). *From the Stone Age to Christianity: Monotheism and the Historical Process*, New York, Doubleday.

Boesak, A. (1983). 'He made us all, but ...', in John de Gruchy and Charles Villa-Vicencio (eds), *Apartheid is a Heresy*, Guildford, Lutterworth, pp. 1–16.

Boesak, A. (1986). *Black and Reformed*, New York, Orbis.

Boyer, P. (1992). *When Time Shall Be No More: Prophecy Belief in Modern American Culture*, Cambridge, MA, Harvard University Press.

Cantor, N. (1995). *The Sacred Chain: A History of the Jews*, London, HarperCollins.

Clements, R. E. (1968). *God's Chosen People*, London, SCM.

Clines, D. J. A. (1997). *The Bible and the Modern World*, Sheffield, Sheffield Academic Press.

Davies, E. W. (2005). 'The morally dubious passages of the Hebrew Bible: an examination of some proposed solutions', *Currents in Biblical Research*, 3, 2, 197–228.

Deidun, T. (1998). 'The Bible and Christian ethics', in B. Hoose (ed.), *Christian Ethics: An Introduction*, London, Cassell, pp. 1–33.

Deist, F. E. (1994). 'The dangers of Deuteronomy: a page from the reception history of the book', in F. Garcia Martinez, A. Hilhorst, J. T. A. G. M. van Rutten and A. S. van der Woude (eds), *Studies in Deuteronomy in Honour of C. J. Labuschagne* (supplement to *Vetus Testamentum*, LIII), Leiden, Brill, pp. 13–29.

Ellis, M. (1997). *Unholy Alliance: Religion and Atrocity in our Time*, Minneapolis, MN, Fortress.

Finkelstein, I. and Silberman, N. A. (2001). *The Bible Unearthed: Archaeology's New Vision of Ancient Israel and the Origin of its Sacred Texts*, New York, Free Press.

Fiorenza, E. S. (1999). *Rhetoric and Ethic: The Politics of Biblical Studies*, Minneapolis, MN, Fortress.

Gottwald, N. K. (1979). *The Tribes of Yahweh: A Sociology of the Religion of Liberated Israel 1250–1050 BCE*, Maryknoll, NY, Orbis Books.

de Gruchy, J. W. with de Gruchy, S. (3rd edn, 2004). *The Church Struggle in South Africa*, London, SCM.

Landau, D. (1993). *Piety and Power: The World of Jewish Fundamentalism*, London, Secker & Warburg.

Lemche, N. P. (1990). *The Canaanites and their Land*, Sheffield, Sheffield Academic Press.

Lindsey, H. (1977). *The Late Great Planet Earth*, Grand Rapids, MI, Zondervan.

Loubser, J. A. (1987). *The Apartheid Bible: A Critical Review of Racial Theology in South Africa*, Cape Town, Maskew Miller Longman.

MacCrone, I. D. (1937). *Race Relations in South Africa*, Oxford, Oxford University Press.

Mairson, A. (1996). 'The three faces of Jerusalem', *National Geographic*, 184, 4.

Masalha, N. (1997). *A Land without a People: Israel, Transfer and the Palestinians 1949–96*, London, Faber & Faber.
Mofokeng, T. A. (1988). 'Black Christians, the Bible and liberation', *Journal of Black Theology in South Africa*, 2, 1, 34–42.
Noll, M. A. (1992). *A History of Christianity in the United States and Canada*, Grand Rapids, MI, Eerdmans.
Noll, M. A. (2002). *The Old Religion in a New World*, Grand Rapids, MI, Eerdmans.
Patai, R. (ed.) (1960). *The Complete Diaries of Theodore Herzl*, 5 vols, New York, Herzl Press.
Patrick, D. (1985). *Old Testament Law*, Atlanta, GA, John Knox.
Prior, M. (1997). *The Bible and Colonialism: A Moral Critique*, Sheffield, Sheffield Academic Press.
Rowlett, L. L. (1996). *Joshua and the Rhetoric of Violence: A New Historicist Analysis*, Sheffield, Journal for the Study of the Old Testament, suppl. 226.
Silverman, K. (1985). *The Life and Times of Cotton Mather*, New York, Columbia University Press.
Solomon, N. (1997). 'Jewish sources for religious pluralism', unpublished lecture delivered in Amman in November 1997.
Stern, P. D. (1991). *The Biblical Herem: A Window on Israel's Religious Experience*, Atlanta, GA, Scholars Press.
Thompson, T. L. (1974). *The Historicity of the Pentateuchal Narratives: The Quest for the Historical Abraham*, Berlin, de Gruyter.
Van Seters, J. (1975). *Abraham in History and Tradition*, New Haven, Yale University Press.
Warrior, R. A. (1997). 'A Native American perspective: Canaanites, cowboys, and Indians', in R. S. Sugirtharajah (ed.), *Voices from the Margin: Interpreting the Bible in the Third World*, London, SPCK, pp. 277–85.
Weinfeld, M. (1972). *Deuteronomy and the Deuteronomic School*, Oxford, Clarendon.
Whitelam, K. W. (1996). *The Invention of Ancient Israel: The Silencing of Palestinian History*, London, Routledge.
Wyschogrod, M. (1983). *The Body of Faith: Judaism as Corporeal Election*, Minneapolis, MN, Winston.

2
The peace that passes all secular understanding: facing religion and ourselves

JACK G. PRIESTLEY

Introduction

When Israeli forces crossed through the United Nations' lines into the Lebanon in 1982 their tank commander at the time was reported to have greeted the helpless blue-helmeted troops with the traditional Jewish greeting of 'shalom' – 'peace'. This irony, I want to argue, is at the heart of all religion. That greeting could just as well have been 'salaam', 'hello', or simply the putting together of the palms and a lowering of the eyes. Even the wave of the hand to display an open palm was originally a demonstration that no weapon was held but, in the course of time, has become a military salute, held to or above the head.

'Shalom', we tell our pupils and students, simply means 'peace'. But it has that meaning at the very deepest level. It represents the arrival point of the religious quest. It marks the summation of all our spiritual striving, the ultimate end of the creative process, the point of arrival at perfection. It really belongs among a cluster of similar words in other religions, not all of which are used as casual greetings, such as 'moksha', 'nirvana' or 'Kingdom of Heaven'. The religious quest is, above all else, a quest for peace.

It is hardly surprising, then, that for many people in our world today, the words and the claims of religion are seen as offensively hypocritical. For in many instances it appears that religions, far from seeking peace, are the progenitors of war, with the result that the secular world sees in us only hypocrisy of a high order. To face ourselves, we have to admit to but not to be overwhelmed by this, for there is plenty of hypocrisy in the secular world as well. Nevertheless, we have a problem, indeed, many problems, but perhaps one above all, namely, that within our scriptures we often find that the very exhortations to find peace are couched in the language and imagery of conflict. My own religion of Christianity itself provides plenty of examples.

There is much evidence to suggest that it was originally pacifist, certainly in the first century and a half of its existence, and probably until it was adopted by Constantine for the Roman Empire, after which things changed dramatically, so that it remains a moot question as to whether Christianity converted Rome or vice versa. But in those early years the language of St Paul, later to be enshrined as the earliest scriptures, was full of mixed metaphors, in which peacemaking was couched in the warlike imagery of swords and armour and the rest (see, for example, Ephesians 6: 10–17). It was, of course, only a matter of time before that idea of 'fighting for peace' became transferred into action: and where later an enemy was found in Islam, the cross, itself the symbol of a willingness to die rather than to kill, became the predominant banner of the Crusades – a concept which, even in our present irreligious age, still finds currency and causes offence.

Peace and tranquillity for ourselves have, throughout history, been bought at the expense of that of others: and here lies a key dilemma of all religions in our modern age. They each have their origins within a narrower territorial context than that in which we live today. But to dismiss such conflicts and aspirations as the results of 'tribal religion', as, for example, in the recent genocide in Rwanda (when, incidentally, 160 times as many people were killed than in the Twin Towers disaster) does not progress the argument very far. All too often we merely extend the notion of tribe or nation and create new divisions. The history of Britain can provide many good illustrations in this respect.

A few years ago I was attending a small conference at a centre in the grounds of Windsor Castle. In the course of it we attended evensong at St George's Chapel. No building could more represent the inseparable mixture of Church and state. There lie many of the kings and queens of England, with Henry VIII and the beheaded Charles I together under the same stone slab in the central aisle, with evidence of other royal and military figures all around them. The service was being held in the choir, and as I looked around I could see the individual stalls behind the pews, all carved with the coats of arms and the insignia of past knights.

The iconography was almost all in the form of weaponry – swords and shields, spears and daggers, balls and chains. Then at the last minute, to add to the atmosphere, in marched an army cadet corps group dressed in full military uniform. We came to the point in the liturgy when we chanted those words from the song of Mary: 'He has brought down the mighty from their seats and has exalted the humble and meek' (Luke 1: 52). And, as Kierkegaard might have added – indeed, did add on a rather similar occasion in the cathedral in Copenhagen (Vidler, 1961: 208) – 'and nobody laughed'!

Not, of course, that it is always like that. That same Church is itself only too well aware of such irony, witnessed in recent years by the stand-off between Prime Minister Margaret Thatcher and Archbishop Ronald Runcie when the latter insisted that prayers be said for both sides in the Argentinian conflict, and more recently when the present Archbishop of Canterbury, Rowan Williams, rejected the clamour of some for a victory celebration after the military victory in Iraq.

Peace, I am suggesting, is the agreed aim of all our religious quests. It is the end of all our strivings, and the imagery which accompanies them reflects that, represented in our literatures with images of gardens and still waters, of angels with harps, of clear skies and total relaxation. But that very word, 'striving', itself rather gives the game away. It comes, of course, from the same root as the word 'strife', which the *Oxford English Dictionary* defines as 'angry and bitter disagreement over fundamental issues; a synonym of conflict'. Striving does not have to result in strife: the athlete can strive against past performance, for example. But all too often it does. Nowhere is this expressed more forcefully than in those lines from a Christian hymn: 'The strife is o'er, the battle done. Now is the victor's triumph won.' Indeed, a high proportion of the imagery in Christian hymnology is expressed in such militant terms, from 'Fight the Good Fight' to 'Onward Christian Soldiers'. But, of course, the hymn writers take it all from the Scriptures themselves, so that we are faced with a deeper problem – that of how we read, interpret and teach our own religious texts and those of others (for the battle imagery is by no means contained only within western religions).

All of this, it seems to me, is the stuff of religious education. If the core aim of all religion is that of trying to arrive at a state of peace, then it surely follows that religious education should be primarily focused on what makes for that. But a look at many of our syllabuses shows, I think, that most of the time it remains a peripheral issue. It is all too easy for us to convince ourselves as scholars that we can somehow stand outside the drama of the real world, assuming the role of directors or producers as if from behind the stage, and avoid being part of the action. But from time to time we come face to face with a reality we cannot avoid. The disaster of 9/11 (to use the American way of dating) was obviously one such event. Meeting Frederick Mwesigwa was another.

Mwesigwa and 'we' or 'they'

The Revd Dr Frederick Mwesigwa is a priest in the Church of Uganda, and currently Head of the Department of Education and Senior Lecturer in Religious Education at the new Christian University of Mukono. When I first met him, he was in England at one of our major northern universities just completing his doctoral thesis (Mwesigwa, 2003), and our conversation concerned the fact that he had come to a different conclusion from the one he had been expecting to reach. He was looking for peace and he was looking for it in the context of a country and, for him, a lifetime riddled with conflict. His concern was the role of religious education in that task, because it was religious differences which had, in Uganda's more recent history, taken the place of earlier tribal divisions. Uganda is predominantly divided into three groups, two Christian and the other Muslim. The older of the Christian groups is Roman Catholic, the result of the work of French missionaries in the middle years of the nineteenth century. The Protestant group came later in the same century, with the advent of the British colonial service and the Church Mission Society. While smaller than the Roman Catholic population, it has been more powerful in terms of political and social influence. The Muslim group is smaller still, but it is also the oldest of the imported religions, having come with Arab merchants, including slave traders, at the beginning of the nineteenth century. And underlying all of them, of course, is the deep and continuing foundational core of traditional African religion.

Mwesigwa's problem was straightforward enough. Growing up at the time of Idi Amin he knew all about conflict and violence.

He had himself, as a young child, been hidden away and had escaped detection when soldiers had ransacked his home. Subsequently, having become a priest in the Church of Uganda, he was searching, as a religious educator, for the common ground which could be shared between these groups, through what he anticipated would be some sort of adaptation of a modern British multi-faith syllabus – based, as such syllabuses are, on an assumed vantage-point of neutrality, standing outside all faiths.

In his thesis, it did not work out. The problem was that Ugandans were more religious than British children, and both pupils and teachers were unable sufficiently to detach themselves from their faith to share a middle or neutral position. He had become sensitive to the subtle but highly significant shift from the use of the first person, 'we', in Uganda's religious education syllabuses to the more common third person, 'they', in Britain. He had concluded, therefore, that the answer lay in what he termed 'a single-faith syllabus with a multi-faith element'. In other words, it was more productive when individuals and communities had to find the peace teachings within their own religion and to bring those to the fore, rather than to look for some sort of common, or neutral, ground. Religious education, he argued, must consist primarily of self-discovery and not study *about* religions, as if the secular ground of the social scientist was superior to that of genuine religious commitment. The aim of promoting any understanding of one's own religion, he argued, needed to take precedence over exploring the comparative element. It followed, therefore, that the twofold aim of the Islamic religious education syllabus, for example, was, first 'to teach us how to be good Muslims' and, secondly, to specify 'the development of respect and tolerance for other people's religions' (2003: 91–2). Mwesigwa's key point was that religious education exists in order that religion might be understood, but that any notion of understanding must acknowledge its particular vantage-point. In arguing this he endorsed Jackson's comment that 'multi-faith RE is a continuing and emergent field – an ongoing debate and a discipline, rather than a body of factual information – and each debate is sure to reflect the historical and political situation of the society in which it takes place' (Jackson, 1997: 141).

The point that was being made was a valid one. It is all too easy to assume with secularists that religion has been a major cause of conflict, and that the simple solution is to abandon it in search of a more neutral position. But a single line of argument quickly starts to undermine that position.

There have been four major holocausts or acts of genocide during the past eighty years (five if we include Rwanda). In the middle of the First World War, while the major nations of the western world were looking elsewhere, the then Turkish rulers organized the removal and large-scale massacre of the Armenians. Most of us in the west remain ignorant of this even today, though its effects have come to the fore again quite recently in the situation in northern Iraq. Then there were Stalin's purges, beginning in the 1920s and continuing into the 1950s, on either side of the Nazis' attempted genocide of the Jews. More recently there have been Pol Pot's massacres in Cambodia.

The point I want to make about all these is a very simple one. It is that they were all driven by secularists. Religion played no explicit part in them, although Hitler's pogrom is sometimes interpreted that way. In fact, he explicitly instructed the SS that it did not matter whether a Jew was religious or atheist, intellectual or illiterate, rich or poor, or of any particular nationality. And a large proportion of those few who had changed their outward religious adherence by being baptized found that it made no difference. The aim of the Nazis was the obliteration of a race. As it was for Frederick Mwesigwa in Uganda, so it was for any Jew in Nazi-occupied Europe between 1933 and 1945: there was no luxury of a neutral ground on which to stand and be detached. It was always a 'we' situation, never a 'they' situation. This is a vital distinction to which perhaps we do not always give as much attention as we should.

There are other dangers, too. Detachment of any sort, and scholarly detachment is no exception, is a way of separating ourselves from the subject matter so that it becomes, again in the words of Kierkegaard, 'a monstrous abstraction'. Such an abstraction is a child of the Enlightenment, and a very necessary one for any sort of scientific investigation, but it has its dangers, and they are very real in our contemporary world. Once human beings become objective their attitude to the human condition can change subtly but significantly: they (that is, 'we') become objects too. In battle, soldiers no longer kill other soldiers: they 'take out' a tank, 'shoot down' an aeroplane or sink a ship. The whole process becomes depersonalized. It is no accident that, for all the slaughter of the 1914–18 world war, only some five per cent of the dead were civilians. By the war of 1939–45 and the development of air power, that figure had grown to around forty per cent; by the time of the Korean conflict it was touching sixty per cent; and in Vietnam it was nearer ninety per cent. No one has yet added up the figures in Iraq, but then the distinction between civilian and military has perhaps started to disappear altogether: we simply categorize 'casualties'.

It would seem to follow, therefore, that if peace is the ultimate end and central purpose of all religion, religious education should be largely, if not primarily, a study of the attitudes, behaviour and relationships which make for peace and harmony. But we immediately run into the irony which characterizes this whole discussion at every level. To attempt to discuss peace, we have to examine violence. When the University of Bradford introduced the first degree-course in Peace Studies in England, the new department faced an immediate problem. From where would they get external examiners? The answer eventually lay in an unexpected place. The syllabus of the Army officers' Royal Military Academy at Sandhurst, with its highly international intake, was discovered to be the closest to that proposed at Bradford. To study what makes for war is *ipso facto* to discover what might make for peace.

Facing ourselves

This is part of the basic rationality of a school curriculum project that had its origin in the United States during the presidency of Jimmy Carter in the 1980s and is now, over twenty years later, spreading to parts of Europe. It is a project simply called 'Facing History and Ourselves'. Its basic philosophy is to look at war in order to promote peace. Its subject matter is two of those holocausts that I referred to earlier on, namely those associated with Atatürk[1] and Adolf Hitler, which it looks at in stark detail to study how they came about as well as to study their consequences, and for students to be sensitized as to how these events were able to happen. It involves looking especially at the turning points, the small simple things, as they appeared at the time, but from which led a road to absolute disaster. The project asks if we are not, in fact, looking at the past, so much as at ourselves and the present. For history is not just about 'them' then, it is equally about 'us' now. We have to face the mirror and confront the possibility that we would have made the same decisions or allowed the same things to happen. Indeed, in many instances we can come to see that we are making the same decisions now and that future disasters will come from them.

As one American teenager put it: 'What makes the course special for me is the connection it makes between past and present. As someone said in class today, the past should not be a refuge for us but rather a reflection on what is to come' (Strom and Parsons, 1982: 23). Two or three simple examples serve to illustrate the point. Take, for example, the beginning of Reading 14 in the course:

> Hitler learned from the failure of the 1923 uprising [the Munich beerhall putsch which landed Hitler in jail for five years] that an open physical attack was foolish. 'Democracy', he then declared, 'must be defeated with the weapons of democracy.' His revolution would have to wait until after he came to power *legally*. (ibid.: 83)

Or note Reading 23, quoting verbatim from Hitler's address to his generals when giving the orders to march on Poland. Observe how he had learned from other tyrants and the reaction of people to them.

> Our strength is in our quickness and brutality. Genghis Khan had millions of women and children killed by his own will and with a gay heart. History sees only in him a great state builder. What weak Western civilisation thinks about me does not matter . . . I have sent to the east only my 'Death Head Units' with the order to kill without mercy all men, women and children of Polish race and language. Only in such a way will we win the vital space that we need. Who talks nowadays of the extermination of the Armenians? (ibid.: 97)

Well, who indeed does talk nowadays about Atatürk and the Armenians? Hitler was looking back only twenty years to Atatürk – his pogrom forgotten – but today, of course, its effects are still there in northern Iraq.

But the crucial point of all this for us as educationalists is to ask: Is this sort of curriculum appropriate for teenagers? There is, of course, a natural human tendency to shield young people from the real horrors, and we assume that the gory details are unsuitable for children. That is less possible than previously, perhaps, now that the full gory details come straight into our living rooms. But perhaps there they are muddled with fiction, with horror movies, unreal and exaggerated. Do we deal with the reality of such events in school? Soon after this programme first appeared, I happened to be spending four months in Boston. It came to my attention because of reports in the press that young adolescent males in some of the city's rougher schools (and they are pretty tough in downtown Boston) had been tearing Nazi insignia off their leather jackets as a direct result of this curriculum initiative, with comments such as, 'I know I'm bad Miss, but I'm not like that.'

All that is about history teaching. I deliberately subtitled this essay 'Facing religion and ourselves', in order to ask the same questions about religion and education. Can we face the truth about the real religious picture in the world today and confront it in our teaching? Have we the courage to take on, not the people, but the distortions that are being presented to the world as 'real' religion, under the guise of which conflict and violence are breaking out all over the world? For the past fifty years we have prioritized the idea of harmony and understanding, and nothing could be more admirable, but have we, at the same time, neglected the causes within religion of disharmony and misunderstanding? We are being presented with conflicts between Jews, Muslims and Christians; but in our religious education it seems to me that we hold back, often for the best of reasons, from confronting the real issue within all of our faiths. It is all too easy to produce syllabuses along the lines of 'Muslims believe that . . .' and to show some sort of common ground between the *hajj* and Christian pilgrimage, or the importance of the Western Wall to Jews. But meanwhile we often avoid or pass over the real and threatening factors within all our religions. I am sure that there was much merriment and exchange of jokes among sophisticated, cultured and well-educated Germans in the 1920s about this little Bohemian corporal who had tried to start a revolution in the beer-halls of Munich. But the laughter had dried up a decade later.

That is what the 'Facing History and Ourselves' project is all about – confronting issues and at the same time confronting our reactions to them: like Mwesigwa, turning a 'them' situation into a 'we' situation. It is as much about the 'how' of teaching as about the 'what' of exploring, between and within ourselves, hostile attitudes towards others and their justification and rationality. The key words in this sort of education are not just 'teaching and learning', which we hear like a daily mantra from our politicians, but words such as 'imagining, appreciating, reflecting', which include not just our intellectual responses, but emotional ones as well.

Fundamentalism

Such words, of course, take us back into the realm of the arts rather than into the sciences. They belong to the study of texts and the way in which we cope with them. For the issue that we as religious educators have to face today, and from which we all too often turn away, is that which passes under the name of fundamentalism. And fundamentalism is, as has often been said, the result of an educational failure. Often it arises from the way in which religious education has been taught and the fact that we continue not to confront it, for fear of showing divisions within our respective faiths. But it seems to be the case that at the heart of every conflict in the world today there lies some reference to fundamentalism. What exactly is it, and how has it come about?

Karen Armstrong's book, *The Battle for God* (2000), subtitled *Fundamentalism in Judaism, Christianity and Islam*, will be referred to elsewhere in this book. Armstrong's pedigree is impressive (recorded in her more recent autobiography, 2004). After spending seven years as a Roman Catholic nun, she left her order and took a degree at Oxford. She then taught at the Leo Beck College for the Study and the Training of Rabbis and Teachers, and in 1999 was awarded the Muslim Public Affairs Council Media Award for her public insights into Islam.

Fundamentalism has been related to many causes, but her suggestion is simplicity itself. It is that, when they come to religions, growing numbers of people in the modern world cannot distinguish between 'mythos' and 'logos'. And they cannot do so because they have not been taught how. Myth, as Armstrong says, was never intended to be taken literally: it is related more to psychology than to history; its insights are similar to those of art, music, poetry or sculpture. 'Logos', by contrast, is rational, practical and scientific.

It looks outward rather than inward, forward rather than backward. We know all this, of course, but somehow, as religious educators, we have failed to communicate it. Others have been more successful. While the population at large can distinguish between imagery and fact in secular, modern literature – indeed, fantasy novels and films are becoming among the most popular – many appear unable to do so with religious texts. We, on our part, have treated this phenomenon with a mixture of amusement and derision, but the effects are dangerous and the results devastating. And it bears directly on this whole question of religion and violence: religious education is right at the heart of the matter. A quotation from the opening paragraph of Armstrong's introduction makes the point.

> Fundamentalists have gunned down worshippers in a mosque, have killed doctors and nurses who work in abortion clinics, have shot their Presidents and have even toppled a powerful government (Iran) ... Fundamentalists have no time for democracy, pluralism, religious toleration, peacekeeping, free speech, or the separation of church and state. Christian fundamentalists reject the discoveries of biology and physics about the origins of life and insist that the Book of Genesis is scientifically sound in every detail ... Muslim and Jewish fundamentalists both interpret the Arab–Israeli conflict, which began as defiantly secularist, in an exclusively religious way. (Armstrong, 2000: ix)

Armstrong then traces the historical steps by which this has come about, since the traumatic events in Spain in the year 1492. The first three months of that year saw the Christian standard raised over the Muslim stronghold of Granada on 2 January and the edict for the expulsion of all Jews pronounced on 31 March. The notion of Christendom was established. It is worth noting that no fewer than 50,000 of Spain's Jews fled to the Muslim Ottoman Empire and were given a warm welcome. (Also, it was, of course, in August of that same year that Columbus sailed from adjacent Portugal to look for a western route to India and 'discovered' America on the way.)

Karen Armstrong gives us the whole scenario across three Mediterranean religious developments in awe-inspiring factual detail, as she argues that the key to the issue of modern fundamentalism is simply that of the inability to distinguish between different literary forms of truth and, in particular, the dangers of failing to recognize the true value of indirect communication, as well as direct.

I well remember the very first lecture in religious education that I ever heard as a student at a teacher training college. It was a simple invitation to shelve the sixty-six books of the Christian Bible (derived, of course, from the plural *biblia*, not the singular *biblos*) according to the type of literature involved, as if for library shelves. Were they history or poetry or saga? Were they fantasy, parable, letters or biographies, etc.? It was certainly an oversimplified exercise as we took our sixty-six matchboxes and tried to arrange them, acknowledging as we did so that many of them were composite works anyway. But one thing stuck – simply that the truth can take many forms and that most spiritual truths can only be communicated indirectly, and not directly. In short, we had begun a pursuit that is wholly engaging and knows no end. It is perhaps that of much Jewish rabbinical training: that the text is a living thing to be engaged and argued with.

Extreme fundamentalists simply refuse to accept that basic fact. Certainly, for vast numbers of Christians it seems today as if a whole century of biblical scholarship, from the 1850s until the 1950s, might never have been, and it seems to me that that is in itself an educational failing. I know that this is far from any joking matter. Simply to read Armstrong's spine-chilling account of influential bodies actually promoting and looking forward to a nuclear Armageddon is to realize that such groups are not lightly to be dismissed.

So where have we gone so wrong? As I listen to the continuing debate on religious education in my own country one thing strikes me above all others, and that is that our concern over the 'what' far outweighs our concern for the 'how'. By that, I mean that we do not concern ourselves nearly enough with what it means to think religiously. For centuries we were unable to do science because we were unable to think scientifically, so that in retrospect we can now laugh at our historical stupidities or empathize with the overwhelming sadness of the story of Galileo, as told in Dava Sobel's historical novel *Galileo's Daughter* (1999), which so vividly and sympathetically sees the conflict through real human beings who wanted to be both scientifically honest and religiously loyal but were caught up in unnecessary confrontation.

But is it not the case that future generations might look back similarly at societies which are irreligious in much the same way that we were all formerly unscientific – that is to say, that the vast majority of people no longer know how to do religion? They are just unaware of the appropriate questions to ask in a western world which is so scientifically oriented that it seeks to do religion by scientific methods alone. Ludwig Wittgenstein admitted to the fact that he was not a religious man, but commented that he could not help seeing every question from a religious point of view, adding: 'the religious thinker seems like a tightrope walker: he looks as if he is standing on nothing but air but there is something there' (1980: 73). We must, I think, as religious educators, ask what such statements might mean. What is there, and how does it hold up? Religious thinking and scientific thinking must surely complement each other. To put those two processes in contention is no longer just a category error. It is one of the major causes of physical conflict within our contemporary world. And it serves only to make us miss some of the great religious insights of the past that still retain their power today.

To return to the literary scene. One has heard, for example, of expeditions to the eastern Mediterranean to see if whales could once have existed there. At the same time, I have yet to hear of any widespread awareness of the fact that the book of Jonah, together with the other immediate post-Exilic books of Nehemiah, Ezra and Ruth, are, in different literary formats, directly concerned with the whole question of the relationship between the return of Israel and what has, for three millennia, been called the 'people of the Land'. The literal or fundamentalist position is akin to searching for Robinson Crusoe's island or the site of George Orwell's *Animal Farm*.

Fact or fantasy

What is interesting is that a counter-culture is already well under way, but one which, by and large, has not found its way into religious thinking or religious teaching. I refer, of course, to the current box office and publishing resurgence of fantasy. We all know that the great battles of Tolkien's *The Lord of the Rings* (1954–5) trilogy are battles of the mind, not to be taken literally as if they were ever history. The same is true of Pullman's 'His

Dark Materials' (1995–2000), where, interestingly, he attacks the religion in which he was brought up, not by historical criticism, such as was evident during the nineteenth and much of the twentieth century, but rather by counter-fantasy. In both of these examples, it is the world of the spirit which is being explored, rather than the world of physical reality. Ironically, it is just that spiritual world which much of western religion and religious teaching has vacated over two centuries, centring instead on the empirical and the historical. Many such discoveries have, of course, proved of enormous value, but there is a price to pay for what we ignore in other literary forms where the violence is a symbolic, not an actual violence. Warnings of confusing the two, of contending 'not against flesh and blood but rather against principalities and spiritual powers' (Ephesians 6: 12) go back, certainly as far as Christianity is concerned, to the very beginning. I could well imagine that a phrase like 'war on terrorism' might well have been used by the likes of St Paul, but the weapons he would have selected would surely have been those he listed in his Letter to the Ephesians, although, as there, they would be images and metaphors apt for exploration – not intended as literal fact.

The 'Facing History' project added the all-important phrase 'and Ourselves'. This raises the question that Fred Mwesigwa is also asking in present-day Uganda. It is the question many of us like to avoid. But, again, it is a question as well answered in the classroom through fantasy as through fact. The Taoist writer Ursula Le Guin tackled just this issue in *A Wizard of Earthsea* (1968), where Ged, the sorcerer's apprentice, releases into the world a great evil, a huge shadow, which he cannot name as it pursues him over sea and mountain. And yet he must name it if he is to overcome it. He reverses the pursuit, knowing that this may lead to his own extinction, and at the very last second, as he himself is about to be destroyed, the name comes to him. It is, of course, his own – 'Ged'. He utters it and he is free.

Le Guin was writing in the 1960s, but, of course, the tradition of religious fantasy goes back a long way. It is just that in recent years we have seen a tremendous growth in this form and style. All of it is related to moral issues and much of it to religious ones, and the popularity with children and young people is huge – in fact, it has its appeal right across the age range, jovially recognized by well-dressed business executives reading Harry Potter novels on the way to and from the office. There are perhaps not many religious undertones in Potter; they are stronger in Tolkien's *Lord of the Rings* trilogy and quite explicit, of course, in Pullman's 'His Dark Materials'. And in the midst of all this we have to take into account Salman Rushdie's *The Satanic Verses* (1988), which was intended for adults and contains his disastrous attempt to make humorous the suggestion that the Holy Qur'ān might contain even the smallest clerical error. All are challenging 'spiritual wickedness in high places', while questioning the value of literalism in the process.

Pullman is an example of an extreme religious antidote to a fundamentalist approach to religion. As he said in conversation in 1997, he is 'an atheist' – before going on to add, 'but a Church of England atheist'. His overt intention, again in his own words, was, 'to do Milton's *Paradise Lost* for teenagers' (cited in Sampson, 2000: 78–9).

The battles of 'His Dark Materials', like the battles of *The Lord of the Rings* are, of course, battles of the mind and the spirit, and everybody who reads and watches them senses that. The question for us is why that is not equally evident to many who come to the first eleven chapters of Genesis, to the visions of Ezekiel with his fiery horses and chariots with wheels within wheels, to Jonah and his big fish, and to a Nineveh ten days' journey across, to say nothing (and we usually do say nothing) about John the Divine's revelatory visions of the new heaven and the new earth?

Conclusion

'The essence of fundamentalism', wrote the Quaker Robin Hodgkin, 'is that it gives a false, inflated emphasis to the words of the text and discourages us from exploring the metaphorical depth and meaning.' Those metaphors, he added,

> often run in harmony with the stories the sciences are telling: about the creation (the big bang), about the origins of life, of evolution and ancient history. The truth often lies in the depths (yes, *that* kind of fundamentalism) but is scarcely ever revealed by the unquestioning acceptance of surface language. (2002: 9)

But at the end of the day, if we really want to confront the whole issue of religion and violence, we are compelled to teach through our actions as much as by our words. Whether it be the Buddha, the Christ, the prophets or *the* Prophet (about whom it is always said 'peace be upon him'), or more modern exponents like Gandhi or Martin Luther King, with their non-violent action designed to destroy violence by bringing it upon themselves until it is exhausted, we have all the role models that we need. We can face religion as experts quite easily but, as with Ursula Le Guin's Ged, it is facing ourselves that is the difficult bit.

Note

[1] It is usually overlooked that at the time of the Armenian holocaust Atatürk was a serving military officer under military discipline and orders from above. When he became the elected Dictator of Turkey in 1924, his very different personal attitude came to the fore, as is evidenced in his personal wording on the war memorial to both sides in the conflict at Gallipoli.

References

Armstrong, K. (2000). *The Battle for God: Fundamentalism in Judaism, Christianity and Islam*, London, HarperCollins.
Armstrong, K. (2004). *The Spiral Staircase*, London, Harper Perennial.
Hodgkin, R. (2002). 'Fox and the fundamentalists', *Friend*, 160, 4, 9.
Jackson, R. (1997). *Religious Education: An Interpretive Approach*, London, Hodder & Stoughton.
Le Guin, U. (1968). *A Wizard of Earthsea*, New York, Parnassus Press.
Mwesigwa, F. S. (2003). 'Religious pluralism and conflict as issues in religious education in Uganda', unpublished Ph.D. thesis, University of Leeds, UK.
Pullman, P. (1995–2000). *His Dark Materials*, London, Scholastic Children's Books.
Rushdie, S. (1988). *The Satanic Verses*, London, Viking.
Sampson, F. E. (2000). 'Surprisingly good: images of the numinous in children's novels', unpublished MA thesis, University of Plymouth, UK.
Sobel, D. (1999). *Galileo's Daughter*, London, Fourth Estate.
Strom, M. S. and Parsons, W. S. (1982). *Facing History and Ourselves: Holocaust and Human Behavior*, Watertown, MA, Intentional Publications.
Tolkien, J. R. R. (1954–5). *The Lord of the Rings*, London, Allen & Unwin.
Vidler, A. R. (1961). *The Church in an Age of Revolution*, Harmondsworth, Pelican.
Wittgenstein, L. (1980). *Culture and Value*, Oxford, Blackwell.

3
The education of the religious fanatic

JOHN M. HULL

Defining fanaticism

The word 'fanatic' comes from the Latin *fanum*, meaning a temple or the precincts of a holy place. The Temple of Fortune was known at the *Fanum Fortunae*, and the person devoted to the temple was the *fanaticus*.

In the sixteenth century, the Anglicized form of the word was used to describe someone who was possessed or inspired by a divine frenzy, and so emerged the more modern meaning of fanaticism as the 'actions, attributes, etc.' of persons insofar as these are 'characterized, influenced, or prompted by excessive and mistaken enthusiasm, especially in religious matters' (*Oxford English Dictionary*, 1989). In the second half of the seventeenth century theologians of the Church of England described the dissenting or nonconformist clergy as fanatics.

The scope of the word seems gradually to have widened, until by the late eighteenth century it could refer to a passionate or one-sided enthusiast, a person utterly devoted to a single idea. Sometimes it seems to suggest a lack of empathy or understanding of other points of view. By the mid-nineteenth century, the word was often used in a milder, often slightly amusing way to describe anyone who was preoccupied with an activity, for example someone who was a bit of a fanatic about music or sport. The word 'fan' is an abbreviation of 'fanatic'. It is an Americanism first used in the mid or later nineteenth century to describe enthusiastic followers of baseball: hence we speak today of the fan club and fan mail.

In Britain an enthusiast for a particular sporting club or for the sport as a whole would be called a 'supporter'. The word 'fan' is usually reserved for devotees of popular cult figures, such as musicians or film stars. So you might be a fan of David Beckham, but be a supporter of Real Madrid.

Christians would not describe themselves as fans of Jesus Christ, and the idea of being a fan of Allah would be absurd or even preposterous. This is because the idea of turning an object of such profound and ultimate concern into an enthusiastic preoccupation, such as one might have for a hobby, is almost blasphemous. In a similar way, if you were said to be a fan of a certain political party, this would imply a slightly amused and perhaps condescending attitude which was short of committed membership. It would also suggest that the political party in question was not worthy of serious affiliation.

This, then, is the religious problem: how to find the golden mean. In connection with one's religious faith one must neither be a fan nor a fanatic. To be a fan is to trivialize faith; to be a fanatic is to be obsessed by a narrow-minded, rigid and exclusive devotion. Can an intermediate state between the fan and the fanatic be imagined?

Understanding fanaticism

Some research problems

The meaning of the word points to what might be a research difficulty. The word 'fanatic', like 'fundamentalist', is pejorative. It suggests that the researcher has already decided that the belief, emotion or action is excessive, inappropriate and mistaken. We must ask whether such a biased expression has any place in a professional or academic enquiry, which is supposed to be conducted along scientific and phenomenological lines.

This difficulty is fully discussed in the literature on fundamentalism (Küng and Moltmann, 1992; Marty and Appleby, 1995), where it is generally accepted as referring to an object of legitimate academic enquiry. 'Fundamentalism' is useful in describing a cross-cultural phenomenon, the reality and importance of which is undeniable, and one has to call it something. Moreover, there are other examples of pejorative expressions used in the social sciences, for example the word 'racist' is pejorative. Those who are thought of by others as being racist do not see themselves in that way. Similarly, the fanatic never regards himself (most fanatics are male) as being excessively and mistakenly devoted. On the other hand, when we consider the curious beliefs of many of the Ranters in seventeenth-century England (Hill, 1972; Smith, 1983), or the strange delusions of the people described in the posthumously published papers of Hannah Whitall Smith (1928), or the religious obsessions of the mental patients described by Moshe Halevi Spero (1996), there can be no doubt that religion is capable of exciting some of the strangest and darkest aspects of human belief and behaviour. With the resurgence of conservative religion in the last three or four decades and the appearance of extremist groups in all major religions, and finally with the appropriation by these groups of modern armaments, explosives and even weapons of mass destruction, the phenomenon of religious fanaticism demands examination (Juergensmeyer, 2000).

The problems of research and education in this area go beyond the mere meaning of the word. Fanaticism itself is highly ambiguous. Although 'fanatic' – and to a lesser degree 'fundamentalist' – are pejorative expressions, not all fundamentalists by any means are fanatics, nor are all conservatives fundamentalists. In any religious faith, those who conserve are as important as those who innovate or transform. In recognition of this, thoughtful conservatives and responsible innovators may respect each other's contribution.

The prophet Joel called upon his fellow believers to rend their hearts and not their garments (Joel 2: 13). Mere lip devotion is never thought of as an adequate expression of genuine religious faith. A formal and routinized devotion is not acceptable, and we must also bear in mind the fact that, in a secular and largely pleasure-seeking society, those whose first commitment is to religious faith may always seem to be somewhat fanatical. It is in this sense that the Christian ethical philosopher Stanley Hauerwas (2000) writes in defence of fanaticism, slightly tongue in cheek. What to the outsider appears to be fanaticism is to the insider a fully justified zeal. Was not Muhammad (peace be upon him) fanatical when he destroyed the idols in the Kaaba? Was not Jesus fanatical when he overturned the tables of the moneylenders and drove them out of the temple with a whip? When the disciples of Jesus tried to understand his actions, they remembered the words from the Hebrew Bible: 'The zeal of thy house hath eaten me up' (John 2: 17). On the other hand, the archetypal zealot is Phinehas, who killed a fellow Israelite who had formed an attachment to a foreign woman. The tradition commends him for this act of fidelity to his faith (Numbers 25: 6–13).

Fundamentalism, as a distinctively modern form of religious conservation, may occupy a significant place in a religious faith, especially if it is a tradition exposed to threat. Is there a point at which the religious conservative becomes fundamentalist? If so, why does this occur with some conservatives but not others? Can the circumstances of this change be described? Similarly, is there a moment when certain fundamentalists become fanatical? And why only some? It would not be correct to regard these characteristics as different stages in an inevitable development, although it is undeniable that this sometimes happens. If we reply that fanaticism appears when unreasonable religious beliefs are held with excessive fervour, we will probably be along the right lines; but when do beliefs become irrational, and how are we to judge when commitment and fervour have become disproportionate? We can answer this partly in clinical terms and partly in social or political terms. From a clinical point of view, when a religious belief is so strange or held with such zeal that the individual is unable to find employment, to maintain human relationships and to live an independent life, we may regard such a person as requiring therapy as a fanatic. Two points, however, must be borne in mind. The first is that very few religious fanatics experience internal suffering or distress. If they feel unusual or even abnormal, this is explained as a mission or a calling. Fanatics never seek healing or believe they need it. The other point is that there is a kind of cold, efficient, administrative fanaticism which is consistent with living a perfectly normal private life.

The social and political criteria point towards injury done to others, and here we come to the typical contemporary religious terrorist organization. It must be emphasized that not all fanatics are injurious to society. There is an overlap between the saint and the fanatic (James, 1985), and no doubt many great creative geniuses have possessed more than a touch of fanaticism (Van Gogh?). The Fundamentalism Project suggested four types of fundamentalist group: the world conqueror, the world transformer, the world creator and the world renouncer (Almond, Sivan and Appleby, 1995), and we may similarly distinguish between the inverted fanaticized personality and the aggressive, socially oriented one. We are concerned here with education for the public good, not with the psychotherapy of the individual, so it is the socially aggressive world-conquering type of fanatic that we are most interested in.

Of course, not all terrorists are religious, just as not all religious fanatics are terrorists. I would, however, insist that at least some terrorists are correctly described as being religious fanatics. Let us take the case of the notorious Islamic terrorist. Some people say that we should not use the word 'Islamic' or 'Muslim'. Richard Harries, the Bishop of Oxford, argued in a BBC Radio 4 broadcast on the 'Today' programme (on 3 May 2004) that this is to malign Islam in general, since the description tends to overlook the fact that the vast majority of Muslims are not terrorists. Harries suggested 'anti-western terrorists'. The question, to my mind, is whether the terrorist professes a direct connection between commitment to acts of terror and religious faith. Here the analogy often alleged between Muslim terrorist groups and the IRA in Northern Ireland breaks down. No Northern Ireland terrorist ever claims that the acts of violence are carried out in the name of the Blessed Virgin Mary, but some of the anti-western terrorists do claim to have acted precisely in the name of Allah. By the same token, the anti-abortion fanatics in the United States who have assassinated doctors and nurses running abortion clinics, and have done so in the name of Jesus Christ or in claimed obedience to the God of life, may reasonably be called Christian terrorists. No doubt such acts of terror are distortions of both Islam and Christianity, deviations so extreme that the mainstream may say that they should not even be called Muslims or Christians, and yet the motivation of these terrorists appears to be religious. They attribute their actions to their faith.

The American specialist in ritual violence, Dawn Perlmutter, begins her detailed study of religious crime in the United States by commenting: 'Throughout history and across cultures sacred violence has been sanctioned, condoned and deemed necessary for religious principles.' The difference today, she continues, does not lie in the attitude to violence, or in its being condoned by religious groups, but in the technology which gives them such power. 'Some religions not only justify violence but specific acts of bloodshed are often ritually required for proper worship' (2004: 2). Aref Al–Khattar points out that expressions such as 'thug' and 'assassin' have religious origins (2003: ch. 4).

Although fanaticism sometimes seems to spring up in an individual without being nurtured by a conservative group, most contemporary religious fanatics do claim to be the spearhead of larger movements within their tradition. Religious leaders must face the question about what it is in Islam or Christianity or Judaism which makes such distortion possible. Even pointing out that such extremism only emerges under very severe political or cultural pressure, the fact remains that it is in the name of religious faith that these people kill. Aref Al-Khattar invited Jewish, Christian and Muslim leaders to role-play the justifications which might be offered by a terrorist of their own faith. He concludes:

> among the participants from the three religions in this study there is a tendency to not recognize any violence as terrorism in the name of their own religion when it comes to defining religiously based terrorism, most subjects from each religion tried to exclude their religion from this kind of violence, to refuse to accept the idea that there is terrorism in their religion. (2003: 44)

Al Khattar remarks that the religious leaders in his study, although denying terrorism, accept justified violence in the name of their religions in certain carefully defined cases.

Characteristics of fanaticism

Fanaticism has an affective aspect and a cognitive aspect. The link between these is a value. The fanatic places an intense evaluation upon a certain belief. Josef Rudin distinguished fanaticism of intensity and fanaticism as a problem of value-attitude. He speaks of 'radical purism', introducing the concept with the remark that 'man's [sic] need to represent something absolute seems ineradicable'. If this urge for absoluteness is repressed and the desire for certitude renounced, one can for a while live in uncertainty and can tolerate a world full of many diverse opinions, but for some people this becomes untenable. Unconscious irrational impulses can then become dominant and the person 'falls victim to extremes' (1969: 6–7).

Intensity is related to the values, and absolute values naturally evoke high degrees of passionate intensity, but a point is reached where intensity begins to overwhelm the values. When that point is reached, the person becomes preoccupied with the intensity itself. The capacity to select means and ends corresponding to the value diminishes. We should distinguish acting *with* passion and acting *from* passion. To act from passion is to be driven by instinctive desire; to act with passion is to assimilate feeling and action into the whole of one's life. To act with passion is to become an integrated person; to act from passion is to become fanatical.

There is another kind of fanaticism, in which the intensity flows not from the emotions but from the will. These 'fanatics of will' are particularly dangerous. In their preoccupation with the ultimate objective they seek, all short-term or intermediate consequences are neglected, and all other objectives are swallowed up. But did not Jesus say to Mary: 'One thing is needful' (Luke 10: 42)? Yes indeed, but that one thing is attainable through all things. The rage of will is often fed by the value of commitment, and this reminds us that fanaticism of the highest and most dangerous kind is essentially spiritual. In fanatical commitment, commitment itself becomes the supreme value, or amongst the range of values which any religion presents one is selected above all others.

This leads us to consider the relationship between fanaticism and competition. The anthropological theory of Réné Girard (2001) distinguishes biological desire, which is instinctive or driven by the id, from mimetic desire, which is social and driven by the ego. This second kind of desire is aggravated in a society of intense symbolic consumption. Identity and self-esteem are attached to various symbolic representations, which are competitively desired to the point where violence breaks out between competitors. Only when the violence is turned toward a scapegoat who absorbs it will this fury be appeased. It is certainly no coincidence that fanatical intensity has been heightened during the present period of globalized competition. Competitive relations between religions have become more intense, partly because of world domination and partly because of the inescapable character of local religious pluralism. The mere possibility of otherness is now foisted upon one, and fanaticism seeks to create distance from the other and then opposition. The fanaticism of modern religious terror is other-directed, in the sense that it is oppositional in character. The threat, whether perceived or real, comes not only from the competition provided by the other religion, but from the overwhelming power of the secular state, and is further aggravated by restrictions or even persecution imposed by the state (Kepel, 1994).

The next characteristic of this kind of religious fanaticism is that it is non-hermeneutical or even anti-hermeneutical. Virtually the whole of contemporary thoughtful theology is hermeneutical, in the sense that mediation is recognized between the reader and the text and between the text and the world which produced it. Because the fanatical imagination rejects mediation, the fanatic cannot escape the impression that the sacred text bears down upon him in all of its literal power. The fanatic is then defenceless against instinctive urges from within and cultural pressures from without, which, unknown to him, constrain him toward a particular interpretation of the text, an interpretation of which the fanatic is oblivious, in the sense that it is not recognized as an interpretation but stands out as the obvious and only truth. The fanatic believes that the meaning of the text is absolute. In the absence of the mediating factors, the text becomes a fetish. The text is isolated from its context within the original society, or in the transmitting culture, or in the context of immediate reception. The fanaticized text even loses its context within the sacred document of which it is a part. Since the part, whether a particular saying, a verse or a group of passages, is set apart from all the rest, it glows with all the concentrated power of the whole. It is as if the general intensity which should be stirred up by obedience to the sacred text, an obedience which is to some extent generalized by the sheer variety and multiplicity of the sacred tradition, is focused by a single burning lens. Stripped of their hermeneutical context, the biblical sayings or the Qur'ānic verses stand out as if they were facts. They have a fact-like simplicity and clarity. The rationality of the obedient will cannot escape the clear demand of the fetishized text. A frightening example of the irresponsibility of this kind of text fanaticism is provided by the true story told by Thomas Thompson (1975).

The inability to establish a distinction between fact and myth or between reality and ideal, between the sacred canopy and daily life, further fanaticizes the obedient believer, causing him to seek for the immediate implementation of the overarching ideals of the faith (Armstrong, 2000). This helps us to understand the significance of apocalyptic in many fanatical forms of faith. The end is overshadowing them: Jesus may return at any moment; the occluded imam may appear, or may present his will through his scholarly representatives. The climax of history, the wars of Armageddon, will soon break out. The fanatic lives in a foreshortened time. The effect of this is to reverse the locus of authority from the transcendent to the human. Although in theory God is the lord of history, the fanatical imagination immerses the transcendent goal of history in the immediate, to the point where it becomes a human responsibility to move the levers upon which the cosmic culmination turns. So fanatical Christians for whom the apocalyptic promise is unmediated, and who read that 'Before the end shall come, the gospel must be preached in all the world' (Mark 13: 10), conclude that in order to hasten the end they should get on with proclaiming the gospel in every tongue. This leads to the peculiar fanaticism of organizations such as the Wycliffe Bible translators, who at least used to believe that the mere fact of translating the Bible into previously unscripted languages would fulfil the requirement and hasten the second coming of Christ (Stoll, 1982).

For the fanatical believer, there is no faith development either of the tradition or personally. This may be expressed in some forms of Christian fundamentalism through a denial of biological evolution or, more significantly, through denying the development of doctrine. Sometimes such denial is more a matter of sheer ignorance, and it is not an accident that, although some leaders of fanatical groups are persons of considerable but often narrow scholarship, the majority of their followers are people with little education. This inability to understand development leads to a sense of disconnectedness from the past and a consequent alienation, which finds consolation in obedience to an autocratic leader, the security of a closed future or guaranteed immediate access to a golden past. This alienation or helplessness gives us an insight into the relationship between the fanatical mind and power. The violence of the fanatic is always intended to attract maximum media attention, to be sensational, to strike at the symbols of the hated power, to give the feeling that one's actions and beliefs are of some significance in the world. We could consider conversion as a ritual for imparting power, and the historical experience of Christianity and Islam offer a contrast in relation to power. Christian faith was born in weakness and has been corrupted through power; Islam was born in victory but is now having to endure the presence of a dominating power.

The fanatical mind has a compulsion for consistency. There can be no wrinkles in the tablecloth of pure belief. Such consistency may be mistaken for faith itself, and inconsistency is repellent to the fanatical mind because it would lead to doubt. For the fanatic, faith is the very opposite of doubt. Instead of stimulating faith, doubt would destroy fanatical faith. Thus, there can be little or no self-criticism and the ideas of other people are of interest only insofar as they confirm those of the believer. This rejection of the possibilities of creative doubt leads to a certain rigidity in the thought patterns of the fanatic. We can speak of the ideological fanatic – the person who does not develop close personal ties, and for whom the abstract ideals of truth and justice are supreme over compassionate understanding. The ideological fanatic is ruled entirely by the belief-system. It is a kind of idolatry of belief itself (Babic, 2002). God is replaced by belief in God. It is the belief, rather than the living God, which comes to exercise command over the life of the fanatic. These beliefs, disconnected from their object and disassociated from the rest of the personality, acquire the character of a fetish. The outsider or observer may suspect a political or economic interest, but the fanatical believer may be unaware of this. In such cases we may regard fanaticism as a form of false consciousness, and the believer to be suffering from self-deception. It is failure to appreciate these dynamics that leads many commentators to claim that the 'real motive' of the terrorist is not usually religion. In cases like these, this observation, although perhaps correct, is unhelpful unless one distinguishes between real and conscious motivation.

An anthropological perspective

We may also consider the problem of the fanatical religious personality from the perspective of the anthropology of religion. Greatly increased understanding of the significance for human development of the hundreds of thousands of years of hunter/gatherer society, together with recent advances in genetic biology and in brain research, have led to the theory that religion may first have appeared in the context of tribal splitting. A hunter/gatherer group probably consisted of no more than about 40 to 50 people. As the population increased, the gathering of or hunting for food would require longer and longer periods of absence from the rest of the group, and this would become increasingly dangerous. It is thought that when the group had reached a population of about 100 to 120 the immediate natural environment could no longer support it. It would be necessary for the group to divide. Perhaps a third or one-half of the members would leave, either peacefully or after an outbreak of violence, and would move off to settle a new area. The breakaway movement would perhaps be led by a charismatic prophet, a shaman, a visionary – someone who was able to lead and inspire his followers (such leaders would usually be male) with a new hope, a command received by inspiration.

In this period of primal religion, however, there was no such thing as conversion. Religious affiliation took tribal or kinship forms, rather than being ideological. It was not until the appearance of the great world religions, during the axial period (c. 1200 BCE to 700 CE), that doctrine, sacred text, uniformity and consistency led to the possibility of conversion from one system to another, enhanced by the promise of personal transformation in a religion of salvation.

In the light of such theories, we can interpret the modern religious fanatic as someone in whom the instinct for tribal survival has been combined with the ideological demands of religious competition, creating a powerful mixture of genetic predisposition and a software program offered by the salvific religions.

Educating fanaticism

It is extremely difficult to change the fanatical mind through education. Several cases of fanatical personality disorder are described by Robert Lindner (1999), but they all deal with people who wanted healing, or who had been referred for psychoanalytic treatment by the law courts or by a hospital. As remarked above, the kind of religious fanatic discussed in the present article seldom seeks healing, since he regards society as being sick, not himself. Moreover, we are concerned with education, not psychotherapy. Nevertheless, it may be possible through the adoption of certain educational policies to take the sting out of fanaticism, and it is certainly very easy to inflame the fanatic if policies of a different kind are followed. The whole history of fanatical religion proves that it flourishes under persecution and is encouraged by repression (Kepel, 2002). Since such individuals or groups often have paranoiac tendencies and believe that society is conspiring to destroy them, repression only confirms their interpretation and leads to fanatical resistance. This creates a dilemma for governments, who have the responsibility of defending their citizens against violent fanaticism. Wise leadership will seek for pre-emptive policies which will ameliorate injustice, even if it is only apparent, and will endeavour to reduce the competitive character of society. It is almost universally agreed that the intrusion of the state into the religious area can proceed peacefully only through compromise. If there is an exaggerated insistence upon secularity, to the point where religious groups are excluded, or feel they are excluded, from the practice of their religious faith, there will be resistance. On the other hand, if religious groups are permitted to engage in provocative proselytizing there may be resentment from secular citizens. Bearing in mind the fact that modern religious fanaticism has emerged at least partly as a reaction to the growing secularization and commercial globalization of society, it would be wise for states to be as gentle and tolerant as possible.

Although the preceding considerations may be very relevant to the administration of educational systems, the role of education itself is less clear. The most realistic view is that religious education can make it less likely that religious young people and adults will become fanatical, and that the residual spirituality of secularized people will be more resistant to political and social parties who seek to stir up traditional folk religiosity (Appleby, 2000: 168–75)

In preparing such a religious education, we must proceed with caution. The religious fanatic is a religious person, not an irreligious person. Fanaticism is a narrowing and an intensification of certain aspects of religion: aspects which in themselves, or taken in the context of the faith as a whole, may be true and valuable. We will not succeed in the pre-emptive religious education of fanaticism unless we show respect for the conservation of the traditions of faith. For example, it might be thought that since fanaticism is intolerant, we can inhibit its appearance by teaching for tolerance; since fanaticism tends to be literalistic, we could pre-empt it by teaching about symbolism. In our anxiety to avoid fanaticism we may finish up with nothing but disillusionment and secular scepticism. Returning to the dilemma with which this essay began, in seeking to avoid Jesus fanatics we do not wish to create fans of Christianity. We want to help people (including ourselves) to be thoughtful and socially responsible in their religious living, if they are religious, and not to be prejudiced or patronizing toward religion if they are not religious themselves. Religious education is not a religion, but it seeks to promote an understanding of religion which is both critical and respectful.

The following suggestions will be grouped under four headings: administrative, curriculum, pedagogy and personal.

Administrative considerations
Education against fanaticism is probably most effective if religious education is offered in a state system of education. There is, I believe, a growing agreement about this, as is indicated by the United Nations Conference on teaching against intolerance and racism (Madrid, 2001) and the policies of the Council of Europe (Parliamentary Assembly of the Council of Europe, 2005). Although sponsoring their own programmes of state-funded religious education, governments must also permit and encourage private religious schools. Parents are less likely to demand private religious schooling if they have confidence in the religious education offered by state schools. But if state education should become noticeably humanist and if state funding for religious education is denied, sectarian private religion will be provided with the best conditions for its flourishing.

State-provided religious education should be taught by professional teachers trained sympathetically in broadly based secular institutions or in religious colleges inspected by and partly funded by the state. Legislation should require education to be morally and spiritually responsible, and should require a broadly based religious education right across the compulsory years of schooling, without appearing to give unfair advantage to any one religion. Governments must seek, through reasonable policies, to attract the cooperation of religions in the community, but ultimately dissent must be permitted.

Curriculum
A curriculum which hopes to inhibit emerging fanaticism and to create responsible citizenship should be conceived in terms of the inner-religious, the inter-religious and the intra-religious. In its inner-religious aspect, the curriculum should develop children's understanding of the history of any faith within which they have been brought up, or one or two of the major religions of their society. This history should help young people to see that the faith tradition has been understood differently by the faithful down the centuries. It should emphasize the diversity within each major tradition and should focus upon the creative personalities of the

tradition, selecting those who are admired but who were inspired by different aspects of the faith. The principles of self-transcendence within each faith tradition should be brought to the attention of pupils, whether these are actual in the teaching or only implicit. For example, in Hinduism we have the idea that the canon of sacred scripture is still open, and that the divine may be revealed afresh in every human crisis. Within the Christian tradition, we have the idea that it is the role of the Holy Spirit to lead the Church into further truth, which implies that the truth is not yet fully possessed. In Islam, the idea of the greatness of God suggests that any interpretation of the sacred text is subject to the greatness of God, and the concept of the divine unity suggests that the Qur'ān must be read in its entirety, the mercy and compassion of God never being overshadowed by the severity and the judgements of God. In all religion, belief in the transcendent always implies only partial apprehension by the believer of the truth, and therefore the religious life is a quest for truth and not a confident possession of the entire truth (Hull, 2006). Abraham was prepared to sacrifice his son, surely an act of fanatical devotion; but God, who is always greater, and always the educator of humanity, had something else in mind.

The inter-religious aspect of curriculum development means that religious education should be conceived of as dialogue, and that topics and themes which at least some religions have in common should help pupils to see that while sometimes a religion will have clear boundaries, at other times the border is quite porous. Elements drift between traditions, and religions influence each other. This is not inconsistent with belief in the unique character of each faith. Particular attention should be given to the teachings of the principal religions on peace, and the capacity of religions to produce peace militants should be emphasized (Appleby, 2000: 121–56).

The intra-religious aspect means that religion as a general phenomenon and the specific religions should be understood not only in their own terms (that is, devotionally or theologically), but through the perspectives of the social sciences, and of history, philosophy and the study of language. It is greatly to be deplored that in England and Wales such studies were not encouraged in the so-called model syllabuses of 1994, and a major concern of contemporary syllabus-makers should be to include studies in the anthropology and psychology of religion.

Pedagogy

The essential method for the teaching of religion so as to deepen respect without encouraging fanaticism is the question. Good religious education depends upon the development of the art of asking questions. This is well developed in the current emphasis on teaching thinking skills, which is a very significant movement (Baumfield et al., 2002), and should be encouraged both in state schools and in private religious schools and, indeed, in family religious upbringing. Most of the contemporary pedagogies of religion may be thought of as inhibiting fanaticism, whether we think of approaching religion through the life-world of the pupil (Heimbrock et al., 2001), the ethnography of family life (Jackson, 2004), the 'gift to the child' approach or through constructivism (Grimmitt, 2000) – all these pedagogical strategies suggest a hermeneutical approach to religious truth.

Personal

The teaching of religion makes considerable demands upon the personality, the belief structure and the spirituality of the teacher. It is not enough that the teacher should adhere to professional ethics. How can an adult teach children in such a way as to produce respect for religion and criticism of religion if that adult has not come to terms with the religious archetypes, and has not been able to develop a mature understanding of the ways in which religion has (or has not) interacted with his or her life?

Conclusion

Many problems remain, some empirical, others conceptual. It would be difficult, but not impossible, to verify the criteria for defining fanaticism through research methods such as case study, interview and documentary research. Would the life histories of fanatics reveal stages in the development of fanaticism? Are there discernible psychological differences between Jewish, Christian and Muslim fanatics? What is the place of religious experience in the subjectivity of the fanatic? Further conceptual clarification is also necessary. Is it the case, for example, that the religious fanatic has simply acquired a faulty theology? In that case, cognitive therapy might be appropriate. On the other hand, the fanatic usually regards himself as being highly orthodox, or he regards it as permissible to suspend orthodoxy temporarily in the defence of the faith. Is it possible to set out convincing criteria that would distinguish the fundamentalist from the fanatic? Is fanaticism consistent with sanity?

We have asked whether and in what ways education might have something to offer in a world where religious fanaticism has become increasingly common. We have seen that if this dangerous phenomenon is to be held in check, new attitudes toward religious faith must be incorporated into contemporary secular policies. In such a climate of respect, religious education whether private or public may make a contribution. After all, if education should fail, what then?

Acknowledgement

The author would like to express his thanks to the Allan and Nesta Ferguson Charitable Trust, whose generous support made the production of this article possible.

References

Al-Khattar, A. M. (2003). *Religion and Terrorism: An Interfaith Perspective*, Westport, CT, Praeger Publishers.

Almond, G. A., Sivan, E. and Appleby, R. S. (1995). 'Explaining fundamentalisms', in Martin E. Marty and R. Scott Appleby (eds), *Fundamentalisms Comprehended*, Chicago, IL, University of Chicago Press, pp. 425–44.

Appleby, R. S. (2000). *The Ambivalence of the Sacred: Religion, Violence and Reconciliation*, Oxford, Roman & Littlefield.

Armstrong, K. (2000). *The Battle for God*, New York, Alfred A. Knopf.

Babic, M. (2002). 'Violence is founded on idolatry', in Francis R. Jones (ed.), *Reconstruction and Deconstruction (Forum Bosnae*, 2: International Forum Bosnia Serievo), pp. 21–36.

Baumfield, V. et al. (2002). *Thinking through Religious Education*, Cambridge, Chris Kington Publishing.

Girard, R. (2001). *I Saw Satan Fall like Lightning*, New York, Orbis Books.

Grimmitt, M. (ed.) (2000). *Pedagogies of Religious Education: Case Studies in the Research and Development of Good Pedagogic Practice in RE*, Great Wakering, McCrimmons.

Hauerwas, S. (2000). 'The non-violent terrorist: in defense of Christian fanaticism', in Michael L. Budd and Robert W. Brimlaw (eds), *The*

Church as Counter-Culture, Albany, NY, New York State University Press, pp. 89–104.

Heimbrock, H-G., Scheilke, C. and Schreiner, P. (eds) (2001). *Towards Religious Competence: Diversity as a Challenge for Education in Europe*, Munster, LIT Verlag.

Hill, C. (1972). *The World Turned Upside Down: Radical Ideas during the English Revolution*, London, Maurice Temple Smith.

Hull, J. M. (2006). 'Religion, violence and religious education', in Marian de Souza, Gloria Durka, Kathleen Engebretson, Robert Jackson and Andrew McGrady (eds), *International Handbook of the Religious, Moral and Spiritual Dimensions in Education*, part one, Dordrecht, Springer, pp. 591–605.

Jackson, R. (2004). *Rethinking Religious Education and Plurality: Issues in Diversity and Pedagogy*, London, RoutledgeFalmer.

James, W. (1985). *The Varieties of Religious Experience*, London, Harvard University Press.

Juergensmeyer, M. (2000). *Terror in the Mind of God: The Global Rise of Religious Violence*, London, University of California Press.

Kepel, G. (1994). *The Revenge of God: The Resurgence of Islam, Christianity and Judaism in the Modern World*, University Park, PA, Pennsylvania State University Press.

Kepel, G. (2002). *Jiyihad: The Trail of Political Islam*, London, I. B. Tauris.

Küng, H. and Moltmann, J. (eds) (1992). *Fundamentalism as an Ecumenical Challenge*, London, SCM.

Lindner, R. (1999 [1954]). *The Fifty-Minute Hour: A Collection of True Psychoanalytic Tales*, New York, Other Press.

Madrid (2001). *International Consultative Conference on School Education in Relation with Freedom of Religion and Belief, Tolerance and Non-Discrimination* (Madrid, 23–5 November 2001), Office of the High Commissioner on Human Rights (OHCHR). http://www.unhchr.ch/html/menu2/7/b/main.htm

Marty, M. E. and Appleby, R. S. (eds) (1995). *Fundamentalisms Comprehended*, Chicago, IL, University of Chicago Press.

Parliamentary Assembly of the Council of Europe (2005). *Education and Religion*, Doc. 10673, Strasbourg, Council of Europe.

Perlmutter, D. (2004). *Investigating Religious Terrorism and Ritualistic Crimes*, London, CRC Press.

Rudin, J. (1969). *Fanaticism: A Psychological Analysis*, London, University of Notre Dame Press.

Smith, H. W. (1928). *Religious Fanaticism: Extracts from the Papers of Hannah Whitall Smith*, ed. Ray Strachey, London, Faber & Faber.

Smith, N. (ed.) (1983). *A Collection of Ranter Writings from the Seventeenth Century*, London, Junction Books.

Spero, M. H. (1996). *Psychotherapy of the Religious Patient*, London, Jason Aronson.
Stoll, D. (1982). *Fishers of Men or Founders of Empire? The Wycliffe Bible Translators in Latin America*, London, Zed.
Thompson, T. (1975). *Hell and High Water*, London, André Deutsch.

4
Hospitality and the voice of the Other: confronting the economy of violence through religious education

ANDREW WRIGHT

Introduction

In this essay, I examine approaches to religious education that are concerned to counter the intellectual, moral, spiritual and physical economies of violence, which all too frequently characterize the relationship between the various religious and secular belief-systems encountered in the global village. I question the validity of forms of religious education driven by a concern to establish an economy of sameness and solidarity, and argue instead in favour of an economy of alterity and difference as the most appropriate framework within which to present religion in the classroom. I conclude by suggesting that such a framework has the potential to open liberal societies to the possibility that non-liberal religious and secular traditions may possess alternative resources for the combating of violence.

Religion, violence and solidarity

The tradition of western liberalism has emerged as a major resource for the combating of violence: in 1972 the Council of Europe adopted Friedrich von Schiller's *Ode to Joy* – which encapsulates a liberal vision of human solidarity cutting across religious and cultural divisions in society – as its official anthem. John Locke's political philosophy constitutes a key source of this vision. He viewed disputes over conflicting religious beliefs and doctrines as a major source of violence, which threatened to plunge society into a state of anarchic depravity (Spellman, 1988). Consequently, he had no time for 'fiery zealots correcting . . . their friends and familiar acquaintance for the manifest sins they commit against the precepts of the Gospel' (Locke, 1993: 391). In his *Letter Concerning Toleration*, he appeals 'to the consciences of those that persecute, torment, destroy and kill other men upon pretence of religion', and claims that the heart of the Christian religion is charity and a 'faith which works, not by force, but by love' (ibid.: 390–1). Locke's latitudinarian suspicion of religious dogma, grounded in his concern to undermine superstition by testing revelation in the court of human reason, led him to distinguish between the primary ethical core of religion and its secondary 'theological' doctrines. The result was an understanding of Christianity congenial to the humanistic concerns of the Enlightenment:

> short on dogma, long on historical criticism and ethics . . . Locke praised what he called the 'admirable wariness' of his [Jesus's] carriage . . . there was plenty for the Christian to do, conforming his life to his master's law and the social good. You knew where you were with Locke: feet on the historical bedrock, eyes on the neighbour. (Drury, 1993: 205)

This distinction between the moral nucleus of religion and its largely dispensable theological trappings provided the foundations for Locke's liberal vision of the commonwealth of all nations. Asserting the twin principles of freedom of belief and tolerance of the beliefs of others, he called for the privatization of religious belief: by restricting religion to the private sphere and insisting that religious disputes do not come under the jurisdiction of the magistrate, he sought to neutralize a key source of violence in society. Once this principle is accepted, then religious believers of all persuasions are free both to believe whatever they like within the privacy of their own faith communities, and to work together with others in the public arena to establish the common good. Whilst private faith communities may elect to pursue the ultimate religious good of salvation or enlightenment, the public pursuit of the commonwealth of all was for Locke a far more limited affair. He viewed the public sphere as 'a society of men constituted only for the procuring, preserving, and advancing of their civil interests . . . life, liberty, health, and indolence of body . . . the possession of outward things, such as money, lands, houses, furniture and the like' (Locke, 1993: 393). Locke's strategy for upholding the common good was simply: take religion out of the equation.

Brian Barry's *Culture and Equality* offers a contemporary version of Locke's liberal vision (2001; cf. Wright, 2004a). This is a polemical work, aimed at those willing to defend 'the latest piece of foolishness, and sometimes bestiality, perpetrated somewhere in the world ... in the name of multiculturalism' (Barry, 2001: viii). Though Barry is happy to acknowledge the reality of cultural diversity, he attacks advocates of what he terms the 'politics of difference', whose attempts to institutionalize cultural diversity, he believes, threaten to undermine the stability of society. His argument is rooted in an egalitarian or 'difference-blind' liberalism, driven by a core commitment to equality and universal human rights. He makes frequent appeal to Thomas Hobbes and John Rawls, and draws sustenance from the French *Declaration of the Rights of Man*, the American *Declaration of Independence* and the United Nations' *Universal Declaration of Human Rights*. Though he differs from Locke in elevating the principles of equality and justice above those of tolerance and fraternity, he shares with him the belief that religion has no place in the public sphere.

This liberal tradition of privatizing religion and bracketing out conflicting religious truth claims in order to further the common good has had a significant impact on religious education, particularly in the United Kingdom, where the subject has been used instrumentally as a means of helping to cement a fragmented society (Swann Report, 1985: 496). Through the cultivation of empathy, tolerance and a sense of human solidarity, it is anticipated that pupils will learn to recognize the human face behind religious and cultural difference. To take one influential example: John Hull has coined the term 'religionism' to describe 'an adherence to a particular religion which involves the identity of the adherent so as to support tribalistic or nationalistic solidarity' (1998: 55). Religionist attitudes are rooted in an economy of rejection and exclusion: 'We are better than they are. We are orthodox; they are infidel. We are believers; they are unbelievers. We are right; they are wrong.' Such tribalism identifies the Other as 'the pagan, the heathen, the alien, the stranger, the invader, the one who threatens us and our way of life'. Hull contends that, though religion is in principal universal in outlook, 'it seems to be difficult for religions to evolve without taking on religionist tendencies'. As the theology of a religion develops, so 'religionist elements may be built into the very structure, to the point where the deconstruction will be resisted in the name of the integrity of the religious tradition itself'. Hull's proposed solution to this challenge is to introduce anti-religionist training in the classroom. The mere cultivation of tolerance does not go far enough: what is needed 'is the deconstruction of the religious consciousness and its theological structure so as to reveal religionist features, isolate them, and overcome them by the genuinely religious features of the spiritual tradition'.

Despite the superficial attractiveness of this response to the problem of religious violence, my contention is that it actually has the potential to increase inter-religious strife. This is because it tends to impose an understanding of religion that is largely unacceptable to the vast majority of religious adherents, and as such functions as a tool of cultural colonization. Three examples will illustrate this point. First, many religions reject the notion that faith can be limited to the private sphere: the notion of the Islamic state, for example, has always been an important tenet of Muslim identity. Secondly, the assumption of an ethical core of religion and the ensuing relegation of theological doctrines to the level of disposable accretions is unsustainable: thus, for example, the Christian ethic is *dependent* on Christian theology. It is the servant God who calls Christians to the service of humanity, not a morality of service that leads to the projection of a particular understanding of God. Thirdly, the vast majority of religious traditions make exclusive truth claims that are essential to their self-understanding, but which do not necessarily lead to tribalism and religionism. Thus Buddhists are in the main tolerant and irenic, but hold fast to an exclusive theology that rejects the notions that God was incarnate in Jesus Christ, or that the Holy Qur'ān reveals the will of Allah. Hence, the suggestion that religions must relocate themselves in the private sphere and treat their theological beliefs as subservient to a universal liberal ethic of freedom and tolerance actually constitutes an act of intellectual violence perpetrated against them. This is especially clear in Hull's suggestion, noted above, that religious education should actively seek to deconstruct the religious consciousness and its theological structures.

The inability of 'difference-blind' liberalism to recognize and appreciate the distinctiveness of particular religious traditions leads directly to the imperialistic imposition of a normative liberal metanarrative. We do well here to heed Edward Said's warning about the dangers of Orientalism, in which the Other is categorized in terms imposed by the dominant discourse of western liberalism (Said, 1978, 1993). If, as Said argues, all 'knowledge is tinged and impressed with, violate by, the gross political fact', then it appears that the religious Other is being both misrepresented and disempowered (Said, 1978: 11). 'By enclosing alternative narratives within the hegemony of its own moral discourse liberalism asserts paternalistic control over the Other, projecting its own understanding as to what constitutes Otherness and how Others should behave and think' (Wright, 2004b: 43). Despite its best intentions, the liberal policy of religious privatization actually constitutes a direct threat to normative religious traditions, one all too easily equated with the aggressive foreign policies of some western democratic states. Such paternalism, however well intentioned, assumes a position of superiority over non-liberal religious traditions. Whenever such assumptions drive public policy, this becomes a direct threat to the integrity and identity of religious adherents. Violence begets violence; intellectual violence begets physical violence. There appears to be little in the liberal tradition capable of actually *resolving* the problem of violence: at best, it can only hope to police the problem over the short term.

Levinas and the voice of the Other

Having argued that liberal religious education's strategy for countering violence itself constitutes an act of violence, our discussion now turns to a consideration of the philosophy of Emmanuel Levinas. I will suggest that he opens up a route towards the solidarity of humanity via an honest acceptance of the inherent differences between religious traditions, rather than through a fabricated account of the underlying unity of religion. Levinas has made a major contribution to attempts by postmodern philosophers to reinstate the categories of alterity, difference and otherness (1969, 1998; cf. Ford, 1999; Peperzak, 1993). His approach is rooted in twin sets of binary opposites, which posit fundamental distinctions between the Same (*le Même*) and the Other (*l'Autre*), and between Totality (*la Totalité*) and Infinity (*'Infinité*).

Levinas identifies the categories of Sameness and Totality with the legacy of the Enlightenment, suggesting that the modern desire to avoid the threat of chaos and anarchy resulted in a drive to transform difference into identity, thereby giving birth to a totalitarian regime of sameness that undermines any possibility of a genuine encounter with the Other. The justification of this strategy of assimilating the totality of things within a narrowly conceived world-view is rooted in a high view of the power of reason and of the human race as master of its own destiny. Since the Other is encountered as foreign and alien, as offering a direct threat to human security and well-being, modernity responds by denying the alterity of the Other and seeking to colonize it within its own dominant economy of sameness and identity. By emphasizing common bonds underpinning diverse traditions, modernity seeks to neutralize difference. Yet this can be achieved only through an authoritarianism that ultimately totalizes, dominates, manipulates and controls the Other. As Oliver Davies points out, the ontology of sameness 'eradicates the otherness of things in order to establish its own supremacy of knowing: it reduces otherness to the transparency of sameness, and in the social realm institutes a totalizing order of violence and control' (2001: 130). Where modernity seeks to enclose the world in a narrowly conceived totality, Levinas is concerned to open up an infinite range of alternative possibilities.

In *Totality and Infinity*, Levinas sets out to deconstruct those strands of the western philosophical tradition that seek to reduce difference to sameness. He contends that, despite the totalitarian assumptions of modernity, we cannot avoid the 'irreducible otherness' of the world we find ourselves thrown into: our experiences of death, time and God constitute realities that are beyond human control. Similarly, we cannot avoid encounters with those whose world-views are different from our own, and whom we cannot hope to control without resorting to violence. When we encounter the 'Other' we find ourselves faced with a reality that stands over against our familiar life-world, and as a result confronts us as a mystery that challenges our self-understanding. Like it or not, we are not masters of all that we encounter, and the desire to impose prematurely a level of mutual understanding and solidarity runs the risk of undermining the integrity of the Other, through an imperialistic act of colonization.

It follows from this that Levinas rejects the equation of goodness with human solidarity rooted in a common value-system. Instead, he insists that goodness is ultimately dependent on the cultivation of my ability to gaze into the face of the Other and recognize the gulf between us as 'sacred space', into which I trespass at my own peril. Authentic morality lies not in the overcoming of difference, but rather in a celebratory vision of difference: 'The experience of morality does not proceed from this vision – it *consummates* this vision' (Levinas, 1969: 23). The Other is not simply a useful part of my world, a tool for confirming and reinforcing my sense of identity, but a radical Other that challenges my self-understanding and opens up an infinite range of new possibilities. As Peperzak notes, another person

> comes to the fore *as other* if and only if his or her 'appearance' breaks, pierces, destroys the horizon of my egocentric monism, that is, when the other's invasion of my world destroys the empire in which all phenomena are, from the outset, a priori, condemned to function as moments of my universe. (1993: 19–20)

Since the Other is irreducible to the sameness of my treasured world-view, my experience of alterity and difference brings about a disruption that challenges me to look beyond myself towards a wealth of new horizons.

The Other has a moral claim on me, calling me to embrace the stranger precisely as stranger, and to approach that which stands over against me with a sense of infinite care and ultimate responsibility. As Marion notes, if I gaze into the face of the Other and see nothing more than the pale reflection of my own face, then I make an idol out of my self-understanding and undermine the integrity of the Other-as-Other (1995). If, on the other hand, I learn to gaze into the face of the Other and see the face of a stranger, then a host of moral possibilities are opened up that were previously unavailable to me. Morality, that is to say, is dependent on our ability to distinguish between mirrors and icons: 'Instead of the invisible mirror, which sent the human gaze back to itself alone and censured the invisible, the icon opens in a face that gazes at our gazes in order to summon them to its depth' (Marion, 1995: 19; cf. Wright, 2004b: 102). Thus, the simple act of goodness portrayed in Jesus's parable of the Good Samaritan is not dependent on the overcoming of differences between Jew and Samaritan, or on the prior bracketing out of these differences: rather, the force of the parable lies in the fact that goodness prevails precisely *in the face of* the ongoing confrontation between conflicting traditions.

In such a relationship of difference mere tolerance is not enough, since tolerance is no more than a resigned acceptance of the need to endure difference, and such endurance constitutes little more than a benign means of policing and controlling alterity. Our desires, argues Levinas, are not authentic if they are driven by a craving for safety and security; rather, genuine desire 'is the desire for the absolutely other ... the disinterestedness of goodness' (Levinas, 1969: 34–5). Similarly, authentic freedom is not freedom-from-relationship but freedom-for-relationship: 'freedom denotes the mode of remaining the same in the midst of the other' (ibid.: 45). Genuine morality resides in my responsibility towards the Other-as-Other: 'For the presence before a face, my orientation toward the Other, can lose the avidity proper to the gaze only by turning into generosity, incapable of approaching the other with empty hands' (ibid.: 50).

Hospitality as a response to the economy of violence

The central contention of this essay is that an economy of alterity, rather than an economy of sameness, will best serve the pedagogical task of utilizing religious education as a tool for combating violence. Historically, the economy of sameness has tended to operate by imposing the 'truth' of a single dominant culture on all others. Despite appearances, the liberal attempt to bypass such hegemony by bracketing out all truth claims, and appealing instead to the underlying brotherhood and sisterhood of humankind, turns out to be little more than the imposition of the liberal tradition itself as an alternative dominant culture. A group whose fundamental beliefs are identified, acknowledged and, wherever possible, respected by the rest of society is likely to feel less threatened, and hence less inclined to violence, than a group whose fundamental beliefs are subjected to censure, whether through an aggressive form of cultural imperialism, or through a benign, but no less all-encompassing, cultural paternalism. It will never be possible to establish the peace of Jerusalem through the final 'victory' of any single religious tradition, or through an idealistic bracketing out of deeply held religious commitments. Rather, it will depend on an open and honest acknowledgement of irreconcilable religious difference, and on the rediscovery of those traits within specific religious traditions that demand of their followers compassion, hospitality and love of the stranger (Bretherton, 2006).

This, broadly speaking, is the position adopted by a loosely knit group of defenders of what Barry antagonistically terms a multicultural 'politics of difference' (Galston, 1991, 2002; Kymlicka, 1995, 2001; Parekh, 2000; Taylor, 1992, 1993; Young, 1990, 2000). Rejecting Barry's egalitarian reading of liberalism rooted in the rights of the autonomous individual, defenders of this 'politics of difference' draw instead on a relational understanding of personal identity: we are the people we are, not merely by virtue of our distinctive individualities, but, more fundamentally, through the way we relate to others-in-community (Wright, 1996). Identity, that is to say, is always culturally embedded: consequently, differences between traditions cannot – contra Barry – be reduced to the level of insignificant and incidental cultural accretions. Cultural identity is deeply rooted: it is not merely a consequence of minor *quantitative* differences between traditions, but rather the result of fundamental *qualitative* differences that flow from contrasting and conflicting world-views. It follows from this that it is not the abstract notions of justice and equality, but, rather, the concrete reality of culturally embedded identity that is fundamental for the well-being and flourishing of individuals-in-community. Barry's exclusive concern for *individual* human rights is blind to the imposition of a western moral discourse, whose roots lie in a world-view grounded in the secular Enlightenment, in a manner that seriously undermines and threatens minority groups. It is against this background that Kymlicka has developed a theory of *collective* rights that sets out to support minority communities in their struggle to maintain their distinctive identities in the face of an often inhospitable liberal polity (1995). Where Barry's egalitarian liberalism seeks to play down the significance of cultural identity via an economy of sameness, Kymlicka's concern for minority rights seeks to open up the moral significance of cultural difference, and as such to acknowledge and, where possible, value those minority cultures and non-western world-views that exist in tension with the dominant liberal legacy of the Enlightenment. Cultural diversity constitutes a fundamental value in itself, and members of minority communities ought, whenever possible, to be free to live their lives in accordance with their deepest beliefs. Given the all-pervasive dominance of western liberalism, such freedom needs careful nurturing and proactive support: it is not enough simply to adopt a stance of neutrality with respect to alternative beliefs, values, lifestyles and world-views. This is because the modern liberal state constitutes a specific value-system grounded in a discrete world-view derived directly from the Enlightenment, and as such its vision of 'neutrality' is nothing more than a commitment to a political economy rooted in a particular set of assumptions and civic expectations.

Without denying the force of this argument, I would like to introduce a significant qualification at this point. Elsewhere I have distinguished between 'hard' and 'soft' forms of liberalism: the former constitutes a closed and non-negotiable world-view, the latter an open 'interim ethic' designed to enable contrasting and conflicting traditions to live and learn together in a spirit of goodwill (Wright, 2001). Where 'hard' versions of liberalism tend to view cultural pluralism as a relatively insignificant affair, 'soft' forms of liberalism seek to take pluralism seriously by stressing the deeply rooted nature of cultural difference. One of the effects of the ascendancy of hard forms of liberalism is a tendency to colonize non-liberal communities by forcing them to conform to liberal norms and expectations. There is a double irony at work here. First, the adoption of a strategy of neo-colonialism, albeit by default, seriously compromises the core liberal values of freedom and tolerance. Second, such a strategy can only encourage segregation, since whenever minority groups perceive their cultural identities to be under threat their instinctive response is frequently to adopt sectarian strategies in an effort to secure and protect them. My suggestion is that the recovery of a 'soft' form of liberalism opens up the possibility of a polity grounded in the acceptance of alterity rather than the struggle for sameness.

This reading of liberalism is not without significance for religious education. By adopting the strategy of bracketing out the distinctive theological truth claims embraced by minority religious traditions, and seeking instead to establish toleration based on common values, hard forms of liberal religious education run the risk of seriously misrepresenting the self-understanding of adherents of the world's religious traditions. First, this is because their search for salvation and enlightenment transcends the narrow commitment of liberalism to the virtues of freedom, justice and the pursuit of happiness. Secondly, it is because they affirm exclusive public truth claims that cannot be 'bracketed out' without recourse to acts of cultural violence. An alternative strategy, advocated here, is that of a 'soft' religious education that seeks to highlight difference and hence respect the distinctiveness of minority traditions. This alternative approach, I suggest, has much to learn from the concept of 'hospitality', and an examination of moral responsibilities of both 'host' and 'guest'.

Davies draws attention to Levinas's understanding of the self's 'at homeness': 'The supreme sphere of this "at homeness" is domesticity itself, which is comprised of "nourishment", "habitation" and the intimacy of familial relations. In Jewish terms this is the realm of well-being, contentment, plenitude or shalom' (Davies, 2001: 132). Whenever a stranger enters into the sphere of our own 'at homeness', we must assume the responsibilities of the host by responding appropriately to the intrusion of the Other into our previously secure and comfortably domesticated environment.

> It is into the comfort of this realm that the Other enters – as widow, orphan and stranger – facing the self and summoning the self to an entirely new and infinite relationship of unmediated desire, in which the interiority of the self, which is the self's own self-positing and resistance, is emptied into pure externality. (ibid.)

To rephrase this, in perhaps more familiar language, Davies is suggesting two things. First, that the host, in welcoming guests into his or her home, has a primary responsibility to extend them hospitality by caring for them as strangers who have entered an alien situation in which they are naturally ill at ease. Second, that in the act of extending hospitality the host must be prepared to take the risk of opening himself or herself up to any claims the guests may make.

My suggestion is that the religious education classroom constitutes a home, and that the teacher as host bears the responsibility of welcoming students, together with the various religious and secular traditions they represent, into an alien environment as strangers and guests. As hosts, religious education teachers will seek to construct and work within a specific home environment, whether this be a classroom within the western tradition of secular liberalism or a classroom grounded in the faith of a specific religious community. The ensuing host–guest relationship makes moral claims on both parties. On the one hand, teacher-hosts are entitled to a level of respect from their student-guests, who can legitimately be expected to demonstrate behaviour appropriate to that of a guest entering the alien environment of someone else's home. On the other hand, teacher-hosts have a primary duty of respect to their student guests: they must be sensitive and open to their culture, beliefs, values, lifestyles and world-views. It follows that religious educators who host the religious and secular traditions they teach are duty-bound to avoid enforcing an arbitrary solidarity that denies the alterity of their guests, and instead must strive to understand their guests in and through their particularity and individual identities. Of course, if the hospitality offered is of a sufficiently good quality, a frequent visitor to somebody else's home may in time come to regard it as a home-from-home. In such cases it is likely that the positive outcome of the offer of hospitality is a result, on the one hand, of the host being willing to allow the guest to 'be' himself or herself, and on the other of the guest coming to respect the customs and values of the home into which they have been invited. The crucial point here is that host and guest establish mutual respect and understanding by openly acknowledging any fundamental differences that might exist between them. This notion of hospitality is poles apart from a vision of religious education in which a false economy of sameness prematurely sets aside such differences. There can be no genuine hospitality if the guest must conform to the values and expectations of the host, especially if the ears of the host are deaf to the voice of the guest.

Opening up paths to salvation

I have suggested that religious education can best contribute to the cessation of violence in society, not by ignoring religious differences by imposing a false economy of sameness, but by openly and respectfully acknowledging the deeply rooted differences that exist in society. It would be tempting to end the argument at this stage; however, it seems to me that the notion of a guest–host relationship opens up an even more fundamental set of possibilities for the role of religious education in contributing to the cessation of violence.

We noted earlier Locke's liberal vision of a harmonious society in which human beings are free to flourish. For Locke, human flourishing is rooted in the avoidance of misery and the maximization of happiness: 'A sound mind in a sound body is a short but full description of a happy state in this world' (1989: 83; I have modernized Locke's punctuation and capitalization). This notion of the freedom to pursue personal happiness is a relatively consistent feature of the liberal tradition. Indeed, the core focus of this present essay, namely the role that religious education might play in challenging economies of violence, is a direct reflection of the liberal agenda. Liberalism seeks human flourishing through the cultivation of peace, justice and happiness within the immanent world of time and space, and considers education as a significant path to this end: it recognizes a strong link between violence and ignorance, and hence a close connection between education and the cessation of violence. As Locke puts it: 'I think I may say, that of all the men we meet with, nine parts of ten are what they are, good or evil, useful or not, by their education' (ibid.).

This path to human flourishing, happiness and peaceful coexistence reflects the optimistic view of the Enlightenment that human beings are capable of engineering their own salvation. It is now no longer clear that this optimistic understanding of human nature and the efficacy of education is fully justified. The horrors of Auschwitz, Dresden, Hiroshima and similar atrocities directly challenge any positive evaluation of the moral legacy of the Enlightenment. Indeed, there is a school of postmodern thought that offers the opinion that the Enlightenment's search for secure knowledge leads, not to a new moral order, but rather to the totalitarian excesses of the twentieth century. Knowledge, according to this school of thought, is inseparable from power, and power breeds violence. The solution offered to this dilemma is the deconstruction of all forms of knowledge and the celebration of a thoroughgoing relativism, in which the rejection of knowledge leads to the undermining of power, and hence to a non-violent utopian future. The problem with this particular version of postmodernity is that it actually makes a claim to knowledge about the nature and origin of violence, and as such is itself immersed in a particular economy of power (Wright, 2004b). Applied in the religious education classroom, such a solution to the issues raised by the decline of modernity leads directly to the deconstruction of all religious traditions, in an act of intellectual violence that is imperialistic in the extreme, and as such entirely unacceptable.

We can no longer take for granted the assumption that the liberal tradition, whether in its modern or postmodern guise, offers a coherent and viable solution to the moral and spiritual dilemmas facing humankind. Consequently, it would appear to be a sensible option to look beyond liberalism towards other world-views, be they secular or religious, which may possibly offer alternative paths to salvation and enlightenment. As Tom Wright points out, world-views provide narratives and stories through which human beings make sense of reality by offering answers to the basic questions that determine human existence: Who are we? Where are we? What is wrong? What is the solution? Through their cultural symbols and shared praxis, world-views offer their adherents ways of being in the world that seek to resolve the problems of suffering and violence and enable human flourishing.

> The choice of life-aim – to make money, to raise a family, to pursue a vocation, to change society or the world in a particular way, to live in harmony with the created order, to develop one's own inner world, to be loyal to received traditions – reflects the worldview held; and so do the intentions and motivations with which the overall aim goes to work. (Wright, 1992: 124)

How might all of this be related to religious education? I would like to suggest that the strategy of encouraging a regime of sameness by bracketing out religious truth claims and encouraging a blanket tolerance actually commits religious education to an acceptance of a liberal world-view, and consequently limits access to potential solutions to the problem of violence to those offered by liberalism itself. In contrast, a religious education framed within the notion of hospitality opens up the possibility of attending to radically different narratives that offer alternative, and in many cases drastically dissimilar, ways of responding to the reality of violence. In theological terms, religious traditions offer paths to salvation or enlightenment that contrast sharply with those offered by secular humanism. If religious education is serious in attempting to listen and respond to the voices of religious 'Others', then it should be willing to listen to the solutions they have to offer to the general problem of human flourishing, and the specific problem of violence. Such a religious education will not simply seek to address the problem of violence from within the world-view of secular liberalism, but will seek to supplement the liberal narrative with the substantive possibilities offered by alternative traditions. In the long term, that is to say, the solution to the problem of violence may lie, not in the refinement of the liberal tradition, but in resources offered by the world's religions themselves. Thus, religious education, ultimately, will contribute to the cessation of violence, not instrumentally, as a tool designed to make a reality of the liberal utopian dream, but substantively, as a means of opening up the possibility of alternative paths to salvation, enlightenment, and the cessation of violence and suffering.

Conclusion

This essay has sought to defend four key theses: (a) that the contribution of religious education to the cessation of violence predicated on an economy of sameness, in which the specific truth claims of discrete religious traditions are bracketed out, itself constitutes an act of intellectual violence; (b) that the philosophy of Levinas opens up the possibility of a religious education predicated on an economy of difference, in which mutual understanding and the cessation of violence is rooted in the recognition of the Other-as-Other; (c) that the host–guest relationship constitutes a useful heuristic framework, through which a pedagogy of difference, capable of cultivating non-violence through an open acknowledgement of irreconcilable difference, may be developed; (d) that such a pedagogy promises to open up responses to the problem of violence from beyond the limited horizons of the current liberal hegemony.

References

Barry, B. (2001). *Culture and Equality: An Egalitarian Critique of Multiculturalism*, Cambridge, Polity Press.

Bretherton, L. (2006). *Hospitality as Holiness: Christian Witness amid Moral Diversity*, Aldershot, Ashgate.

Davies, O. (2001). *A Theology of Compassion: Metaphysics of Difference and the Renewal of Tradition*, Grand Rapids, MI, Eerdmans.

Drury, J. (1993). 'On the love of our neighbours', *Theology*, 96, 205–8.

Ford, D. (1999). *Self and Salvation: Being Transformed*, Cambridge, Cambridge University Press.

Galston, W. A. (1991). *Liberal Purposes: Goods, Virtues, and Diversity in the Liberal State*, Cambridge, Cambridge University Press.
Galston, W. A. (2002). *Liberal Pluralism: The Implications of Value Pluralism for Political Theory and Practice*, Cambridge, Cambridge University Press.
Hull, J. M. (1998). *Utopian Whispers: Moral, Religious and Spiritual Values in Schools*, Norwich, Religious and Moral Education Press.
Kymlicka, W. (1995). *Multicultural Citizenship: A Liberal Theory of Minority Rights*, Oxford, Oxford University Press.
Kymlicka, W. (2001). *Politics in the Vernacular: Nationalism, Multiculturalism, and Citizenship*, Oxford, Oxford University Press.
Levinas, E. (1969). *Totality and Infinity: An Essay in Interiority*, Pittsburgh, PA, Duquesne University Press.
Levinas, E. (1998). *Otherwise than Being, or Beyond Essence*, Pittsburgh, PA, Duquesne University Press.
Locke, J. (1989). *Some Thoughts Concerning Education*, Oxford, Clarendon.
Locke, J. (1993). *Political Writings*, Harmondsworth, Penguin Books.
Marion, J.-L. (1995). *God Without Being: Hors-Texte*, Chicago, IL, University of Chicago Press.
Parekh, B. (2000). *Rethinking Multiculturalism: Cultural Diversity and Political Theory*, Basingstoke, Palgrave Macmillan.
Peperzak, A. (1993). *To the Other: An Introduction to the Philosophy of Emmanuel Levinas*, West Lafayette, IN, Purdue University Press.
Said, E. (1978). *Orientalism*, London, Routledge & Kegan Paul.
Said, E. (1993). *Culture and Imperialism*, London, Chatto & Windus.
Spellman, W. M. (1988). *John Locke and the Problem of Depravity*, Oxford, Clarendon.
Swann Report (1985). *Education for All: The Report of the Committee of Inquiry into the Education of Children from Ethnic Minority Groups*, London, HMSO.
Taylor, C. (1992). *Multiculturalism and 'The Politics of Recognition'*, Princeton, NJ, Princeton University Press.
Taylor, C. (1993). *Reconciling the Solitudes: Essays on Canadian Federalism and Nationalism*, Montreal, McGill-Queens University Press.
Wright, A. (1996). 'The child in relationship: towards a communal model of spirituality', in Ron Best (ed.), *Education, Spirituality and the Whole Child*, London, Cassell, pp. 139–49.
Wright, A. (2001). 'Religious education, religious literacy and democratic citizenship', in Leslie J. Francis, Jeff Astley and Mandy Robbins (eds), *The Fourth R for the Third Millennium: Education in Religion and Values for the Global Future*, Dublin, Lindisfarne, pp. 201–19.
Wright, A. (2004a). 'The politics of multiculturalism', *Studies in Philosophy and Education*, 23, 4, 299–311.

Wright, A. (2004b). *Religion, Education and Post-modernity*, London, RoutledgeFalmer.
Wright, N. T. (1992). *The New Testament and the People of God*, London, SPCK.
Young, I. (1990). *Justice and the Politics of Difference*, Princeton, NJ, Princeton University Press.
Young, I. (2000). *Inclusion and Democracy*, Oxford, Oxford University Press.

5
Power, force and violence

GABRIEL MORAN

John Dewey, agonizing over whether to support United States entry into the First World War, tried in several essays to distinguish force and violence, force and war (1967: 211–15, 244–51). Dewey never carried through consistently on his distinctions. His efforts were dismissed by commentators who pointed out that in international conflicts, 'force' and 'war' are used interchangeably. That criticism is true, but it is a statement of the problem, not a reason for dismissing the question. Until the language of power, force, violence and war is reformed, discussion of war will always be between 'realists', who are certain that war is an inevitable fact of human life, and 'idealists', who think that the use of force is immoral.

What is needed is to change the use of the term 'force' in international discussions of conflict. Can the term 'force' be changed in meaning? Actually, the most common meaning of force is precisely the one that is needed. In practically all uses of the term outside discussions of war, force is distinguishable from violence. While violence is thought to be a dangerous possibility when force is introduced, the term is not equated with explosions of obscene amounts of violence that destroys every living being in its path. Why then, in international discussions, do people say 'force' when they mean 'war'? It seems to be a euphemism, but one that has the unfortunate result of closing off imagination about how force and forces could be used to avoid war. When the European Union, in February 2003, tried to dissuade the United States from war on Iraq, it stated: 'War is not inevitable. The use of force should be the last resort' (*New York Times*, 19 February 2003: 1A). Wouldn't they have spoken more logically, realistically and effectively if they had said: 'Force *is* inevitable. But war should be the last resort'?

Force is a pressure upon humans or nonhumans to get them to act in a desired way. For nearly everyone, the use of force is a daily occurrence, from forcing open a jar of pickles to forcing one's way through a crowd. As a one-directional action, force is always questionable. Especially in attempting to coerce human agreement to a certain way of acting, force is a restriction on the freedom of another. Although force may slide into violence, there is sometimes a need for the force of restraint on a human being who is incompetent or is criminally dangerous. Force may be needed to keep a child from running into the street, or force may have to be used to stop a would-be rapist. Less obvious uses of force are present in the business and political worlds, and even in religious and educational institutions. Force allows for innumerable degrees of exercise, from psychological intimidation to a swift blow in the mid-section.

Force is constantly used against the physical environment. Since there is no resistance by another's will, the moral issue is less ambiguous. Nonetheless, human beings have slowly been learning that they cannot be cavalier in the use of force against the environment. Force has to be carefully rationed because a human being can never grasp all the effects of any action in trying to make the world suit his or her desires.

Power

The misuse of the term 'force' in international conflicts is not likely to be corrected unless a deeper linguistic confusion in using 'power' is unearthed. 'Power' stands on one side of 'force', as 'violence' does on the other. Linguistically, force collapses into violence because power has already collapsed into force. Unless the term 'power' is used in ways that do not inevitably lead to force, then a nation's use of force becomes equated with war.

'Power', like so many important words, has two almost opposite meanings. When people who call themselves 'realists' talk about power, they have one very clear meaning of power in mind. Power means the exercise of force: power in this context is the means to coerce and dominate. One of the most discussed essays on international affairs in 2002 was Robert Kagan's 'Power and weakness'. Slightly expanded, it was published as a book with the title *Of Paradise and Power* (2003). There is no question in Kagan's mind that power is the opposite of weakness, and that the United States represents power while Europe represents weakness. The reference to paradise in the book's title might suggest something positive about Europe but, for Kagan, Europe's living in a paradise is a delusion made possible by United States (military) power. Kagan would probably acknowledge other kinds of power than military power, but his standard use of the term is to equate power and military power. Therefore, a country that does not spend a sizeable part of its budget on military power is 'weak'.

Liberal commentators in the United States were sceptical of Kagan's crude stereotypes. But a book which they did praise was Joseph Nye's *The Paradox of American Power: Why the World's Only Superpower Cannot Go It Alone* (2002). Nye distinguished between 'hard power' and 'soft power'. This distinction was widely hailed as a breakthrough in thinking about United States power. Many people were therefore surprised when Nye supported the United States' war on Iraq. Where did soft power go? The answer, I think, is that a distinction between hard and soft is only a minor issue of degrees in the exercise of one kind of power. Nye never gets to the real paradox of power. His hard and soft powers still refer to coercing people in a one-way exercise of force. If manipulation with soft power does not get us what we want, there is hard power (bombs) as a back-up.

The real paradox of power is that power can be almost the exact opposite of force. In addition to meaning active coercion, power can also mean passive receptiveness. In fact, this latter meaning is the root from which all power springs. Power belongs to the same linguistic family as possible, potential, passive. In classical and medieval philosophy, power is the lowest and weakest form of being – mere possibility that has yet to be realized or actualized. Power is capacity for action but needs to be brought to act.

When one comes to the human as the paradoxical union of matter and spirit, what was weakness can be turned into strength. The fact that humans, in contrast to other animals, are mostly unformed at birth can be turned to advantage. Humans are born with capacity, the power that is receptiveness. They are not born with wings but they can invent an airplane. Among the other animals, they are on the weak side in 'brute strength', but the human strength of intelligence gives them an advantage far beyond the other animals.

The paradox of power is that power begins as weakness or passivity, an undesirable condition in the material world. But humans have a passiveness or receptiveness that is their strength. They are able to exercise control of their surroundings by ideas and language. True, elements of force are mixed in with the human efforts to control. When threatened, humans may mistakenly equate their power with force. For defending themselves against hostile animals or dangerous weather, force may be an appropriate defence. But with other human beings, human power resides in listening and responding. Between humans, force is a sign that human power has failed.

When human beings enter into mutual exchanges, then the power of each is enhanced. Human life becomes richer the more that receptivity to others is exercised. Of course, not all human encounters are mutually affirming. Some people, for whatever cause, never grasp the paradox of human power. For them, the world has a top and a bottom: they are willing to do whatever is necessary to get on top. Other people who are on the receiving end of this kind of force are tempted to act the same in return. Worse, they are pressed to accept this picture of the world with a top and a bottom. One of the worst aspects of being a slave is that it can make you desire to be a slave-owner.

The most appropriate human response to a force that has turned violent is to act asymmetrically. That is, human power resides in not returning violence for violence. Whatever is done, it must be action to break a cycle of violence so that a degree of mutuality can be restored. Doing good to one's enemies is not a form of weakness but of human strength. What is sometimes called 'passive resistance' can be misunderstood as doing nothing. But 'passive resistance' is an action, the most intensely human action. The Sermon on the Mount is often cited as an advocacy of doing nothing in the face of evil. But showing love to one's enemies and deliberately refusing to offer violence for violence requires courage, determination and an understanding of power.

In 'realist' literature, the Sermon on the Mount is often praised as an ideal that individuals should try to live by. But to protect these good and innocent people the government has to be amoral: it cannot be naive and idealistic in a world of predators. The assumption is that the only thing that counts in international affairs is 'self-interest' (Smith, 1986). However, the question for a nation is the same as for the individual: What kind of self are you becoming? That is, what are your interests? The nation state has a proclivity to feel threatened and therefore to use the crudest forms of force. One nation cannot change this long history, but it is possible that the world's nation states might establish a system that allows for nations to have other 'interests' than that of being more militarily powerful than their neighbours.

The United Nations is the present fragile structure for international cooperation. The right wing in the United States contemptuously dismisses the United Nations as a debating society, but that is precisely what it should be. As a forum for discussion, it needs the help of other international or transnational bodies to facilitate numerous forms of national exchanges, such as business, athletic or religious dealings. It also needs a legal and judicial structure to be a restraint on the misuses of force that continue to be part of human experience.

Terrible conflicts are not likely to disappear soon, but it is time to start speaking a language of power, force, violence and war that will reduce human violence and unlock human power. A country that equates power to military power is on the way to self-destruction. The alternative is to use the human power of mutual pacts that provide as much security as human beings are likely to have in this world.

Terror

I think a good litmus test for understanding the limits of this 'security' is the way in which terror and terrorism are spoken about. When power and force are misunderstood today, an obsession with fighting 'terrorism' is almost bound to follow. The perennial tactic of fighting violence with violence has evolved into a special format for today's world. The phrase 'war on terrorism' has become ubiquitous in the United States. But what must be said is that there isn't any war on terrorism. The phrase is nonsensical, which is not to say that it isn't a useful tool for some parties. My thesis is that there cannot be a war on terrorism because war *is* terrorism. War is the most obvious, most widespread and most deliberate use of terror. The reason why this simple fact is not acknowledged is because of the peculiar way in which 'terrorism' has been defined.

Caleb Carr's book (2003), *The Lessons of Terror*, was criticized for blurring the distinction between war and terrorism. It allowed Carr to cite numerous examples from military history as examples of terrorism. I think blurring the difference made sense and made for a more interesting book. However, I think Carr gets it badly wrong by claiming that 'terrorism is war'. That leads him to advocate that (their) terrorism should be met with (our) war. The real lesson of terror is not that terrorism is (a form of) war but that war is (a form of) terrorism. And the way to respond to (their) terrorism is to examine (our) terrorism and find a non-symmetrical response that might reduce the terror of violence on both sides.

'Terror' has a very clear meaning in the English language. People have little difficulty in understanding the feeling of terror or identifying something as a cause of terror. Terror is an emotional reaction to a situation in which one fears for one's safety or for one's life. The threat may be shadowy or even illusory, but mental anguish is central to how severe is the fear of physical harm.

A 'terrorist', then, would be someone who uses terror as a means to an end. Someone using terror is a terrorist at that moment, although the act does not necessarily constitute one's identity. There are few people whose identity is to be a terrorist. Many people at times in their life have been involved in terrifying a group or an individual. This is especially true if one recognizes that many kinds of organizations use tactics of terror.

The cause of the confusion and blindness regarding terror and terrorist comes from the use of the word 'terrorism'. Like most words ending in -ism, it is an abstraction that any powerful group can define as they like. In this case, the powerful group can be a nation state which has simply decided that a nation state cannot engage in terrorism. Only individuals and sub-national groups are designated as terrorist organizations.

The most influential definition of terrorism was issued by the US State Department in 1998. The beginning of the statement reads: 'The term "terrorism" means premeditated, politically motivated violence perpetrated against noncombatant targets by sub-national groups or clandestine agents, usually intended to influence an audience' (Gordon and Lopez, 2000: 103). This statement limits terrorism to non-state actors. The exclusion of the state from terrorism delimits the methods employed by terrorists to those available to non-state actors. Tanks and war planes are not used by terrorists: when tanks and war planes are used, then by definition that is not terrorism.

The second clause of the State Department's definition is: 'The term "terrorist group" means any group practicing, or any group that has significant subgroups that practice, international terrorism.' By distinguishing between a group that practises terrorism and a group that has 'significant subgroups' that practise terrorism, the State Department makes room for the idea of state-sponsored terrorism, without granting that states are actually perpetrators of terrorism.

The manner in which the State Department defines terrorism determines the data incorporated into its 'terrorism databank'. The CIA conceives terrorism to be the illegitimate use of force by non-state actors, supported by 'rogue nations', such as Syria and Iran. But whatever is done by the United States or Israel is outside the State Department's definition of terror. In this context, war is not terrorism. The firebombing of sixty-seven Japanese cities in 1945 or the bombing of Belgrade to convince the Serbian government to change its ways cannot be called terrorism, despite the extraordinary terror caused to millions of people.

The definition of terror should exclude the actor. If there was a focus on the nature of the act, it would be harder to persevere in the common practice of referring to terrorism practised by the state as 'maintaining order', 'ensuring security' or 'upholding democracy'. The meaning of terrorism that I have proposed resists seeing terrorism as induced by a disposition that compels the actor toward violence.

If one thinks of international terror as the unleashing of violence to reach a political end, there can be little doubt that most of the world sees the United States as the chief terrorist organization. The United States, with more military might than most of the rest of the world combined, uses its firepower to achieve what it decides are good ends. The US military insists that it does not 'target' civilians, and military planners no doubt try to avoid the civilian population. But if one looks at the act and the results of military operations, especially aerial bombing, the effect is terrifying for anyone in the vicinity. All wars spread terror, but a war from the sky multiplies the terror tenfold.

The torture of prisoners is a part of the terror of war. Not all soldiers practise torture, but training to kill the enemy is hardly good preparation for taking care of the imprisoned enemy. The Geneva Conventions are a noble attempt to resist the full logic of war. They are a continuance of Christian theology's rules for going to war and rules for conducting a war. But the twentieth century should have made obvious the illogicality of declaring that some aspects of war are illegal.

The United States has killed thousands of Iraqis. Scandalously, the US government openly admits it has no interest in counting the number of Iraqis that have been killed. In the United States this slaughter seems to have been accepted with a shrug: So what do you expect in a war? And yet the pictures of a few dozen Iraqis being tortured and humiliated set off a worldwide furore. The pictures are able to focus attention on the inhumanity of the whole operation.

Shouldn't the next step be to have a fifth Geneva Convention that war is illegal? If torture and assassination are illegal, how can war be legal? It is true that so long as international authority is not sufficiently developed, there would remain conflicts. But a nation that unleashed a war on another nation should be considered a terrorist state. The international community would have the power to authorize a degree of force to resist violence, but not to wage war.

The United States, in disregard of international opinion, has launched a tirade of violence, with no end in sight. In 2001, the United States met terror with terror. The metaphor of war was introduced immediately. It resonated with all sorts of other metaphorical wars – on poverty, drugs, illiteracy, pollution. The metaphor is nearly always hideously inaccurate (although 'cold war' captured some of the real conflict that involved proxy armies). The problems require education and political skill. Declaring a 'war on terrorism' was absurd. Where is the battlefield on which this war was to be fought? It turns out to be everywhere. 'Terrorism', a doctrine about practices of terror, is in any country that one chooses to name.

We now know that the executive branch of the US government decided from the start on one country against which to wage an actual war. A 'war on terrorism' was the gateway to a war on Iraq. It was not a war *with* Iraq, which would suggest two nation states being at war. It was a war launched on a country that supposedly embodied terrorism. The 'war on terrorism' as a nonsensical phrase did not prevent it from being a linguistic preparation for a war on Iraq. One can hope that the unexpected difficulties of this venture will call a halt to preparations for knocking over other countries that are defined as hotbeds of terrorism. But the evidence is not clear that any lesson has been learned or that a 'war on terrorism' might not continue without end.

References

Carr, C. (2003). *The Lessons of Terror*, New York, Random House.
Dewey, J. (1967). 'Force and coercion' and 'Force, violence and law', in *Middle Works*, ed. Jo Ann Boydston, Carbondale, IL, Southern Illinois University Press, pp. 244–51, 211–15.
Gordon, N. and Lopez, G. (2000). 'Terrorism in the Arab–Israeli conflict', in Andrew Valls (ed.), *Ethics in International Affairs*, Lanham, MD, Rowan & Littlefield, pp. 99–113.
Kagan, R. (2003). *Of Paradise and Power*, New York, Knopf.
Nye, J. (2002). *The Paradox of American Power: Why the World's Only Superpower Cannot Go It Alone*, New York, Oxford University Press.
Smith, M. (1986). *Realist Thought from Weber to Kissinger*, Baton Rouge, LA, Louisiana State University Press.

6
Developing an ethos of anti-violence: the role of Christianity in Africa

EUNICE KARANJA KAMAARA

The world is in crisis. In spite of the scientific and technological advances of the modern world, human life is under serious threat from disease, poverty, terrorism, war, the indiscriminate use of knowledge and corruption, among other things. All these threats are related to violence in one way or another. The people of this age desperately need to change their thinking and to do so in all aspects of their lives, in order to counter violence and its resultant effects.

In Africa, violence resulting from socio-political, economic and religious issues characterizes the continent: domestic violence, civil wars, ethnic conflicts, religious wars, among others, continue to threaten human life. Most of the countries of the continent, such as the Democratic Republic of Congo (DRC), Liberia, Sierra Leone, Sudan, Somalia and Uganda have active conflicts, while other countries, such as Kenya, have latent conflicts that threaten to turn active at any time. At the family level, violence continues to manifest itself at alarming levels, especially against women and children.

Efforts by governmental and non-governmental agents, for example United Nations agencies, have applied various strategies to seek to control violence in Africa without much success. Scores of Africans continue to lose their lives and hundreds are rendered homeless every day, while thousands lead unhealthy lives. From a concern for this, the present writer proposes the development of an ethos of anti-violence. The basic assumption is that, if the contemporary fundamental values of African peoples change, an effective and sustainable strategy against violence may be adopted. For theological, moral and utilitarian reasons, it is possible to convince people that violence is against people's self-interest as individuals and as groups. Moreover, since traditional values were generally in favour of anti-violence, these may be appealed to for the development of an anti-violence ethos for Africa today.

Without wishing to ignore the role of other religions in Africa, this essay focuses on the role of Christianity in the development of the proposed ethos. Drawing illustrations from the Kenyan case, where Christianity has been politically functional as well as dysfunctional, the effectiveness of religion will be presented. More specifically, the essay will cite the proactive engagement and tremendous success of Christianity in civic education against violence for peaceful political transition in 2002. Further, the role of religion in the development of an anti-violence ethos all over the world, and more specifically in Africa, will be analysed.

Some forms of violence in Africa

Among the major forms of violence in Africa are ethnic conflicts. These characterize the whole region, in the sense that even where active conflicts have not been experienced, latent conflicts prevail that threaten to become active at any time. Ethnic conflicts are definitely undesirable, particularly because they threaten human life in a direct way: many people lose their lives, others are maimed, and a lot of property is destroyed. Moreover, many people lose their lives as an indirect consequence of ethnic conflict. For example, many die from the unhealthy conditions prevalent in refugee camps. Further, ethnic conflicts retard development, leading to poverty and poverty-related problems.

Prior to the advent of colonialism in Africa, ethnicity as a doctrine of exclusion was rarely applied. Essentially, ethnic groups lived in isolation, with little association between them. It is true that contacts between ethnic groups were not unknown: for example, barter trade was practised because of the need to obtain essential commodities. A community that had a lot of salt, for instance, would exchange this for beads. However, this form of trade was governed more by cooperation than competition, so that exploitation did not feature. Some historians and anthropologists claim that 'ethnic wars' existed among traditional African societies. But these were not quite as we understand ethnic conflicts today. In Kenya, for example, the Maasai occasionally raided cattle from the Kikuyu. But such raids do not qualify as 'ethnic conflicts' because they were not driven by hatred for the other tribe. Moreover, the raids rarely involved the destruction of lives and property. For nearly all communities, the killing of fellow humans, regardless of their ethnic identity, was considered taboo, as was the destruction of property.

It may therefore be argued that, although ethnic consciousness was there in traditional African societies, as a 'process by which a community sees itself as distinct – with a group identity and common interests' (Hansen, 1984, cited in Ogot, 1996: 189), it was advanced by colonialism. New definitions and exercise of power, and the individual ownership of property introduced by colonists, have continued to ignite ethnic conflicts throughout the continent. In Rwanda and Burundi, for example, the past colonial distribution of land presents a significant explanation for ethnic conflicts, which have existed in the country since independence. The infamous Rwanda genocide of 1994 resulted from a politicization of ethnicity, whereby people's cultural differences were used to exclude them in favour of the interests of a few. The Hutu were portrayed as the indigenous people of Rwanda, while the Tutsi were excluded.

In Kenya, the ethnic conflicts of 1992 and 1997 also illustrate the politicization of ethnicity for the benefits of the few. These clashes, which rocked mainly the Rift Valley Province, were instigated by the introduction of multi-party politics in a country where a few powerful individuals were against sharing power. Throughout Africa, ethnic conflicts are generally the product of the interests of individuals or particular segments of society at the expense of others.

The other major form of violence in Africa is gender violence. This is especially manifested in the family, but it is not limited to it. On the basis of their sex, women are discriminated against in terms of access to, control over and ownership of resources and processes. Moreover, certain attributes and roles are attributed to women, leading to unequal gender relations.

To understand gender in modern African societies, it is essential to understand how gender relations, roles and attributes have changed over the years. Within traditional African economies, women were equipped to manage their environment despite the social limitations placed on them. There were checks and balances to ensure that they were protected from abuses within patriarchal power structures. Within a traditional economy that was based on the principles of communality and reciprocity, individual ownership of property was unheard of, and women had satisfactory access to and control of resources. Moreover, gender roles were clearly designated within a systematic form of division of labour, based on age and sex. For example, while women were expected to grow certain crops on the family land, men were expected to provide women with the soil types suitable for these crops. Similarly, even though public positions in political life were the preserve of men, according to the systematic division of labour, women could question what they did not like and propose changes, at both the family and the societal levels. Further, when beyond reproductive age, women could be admitted into governing councils, such as the Council of Elders found among the Kikuyu of central Kenya. Thus, women were not powerless.

With the colonization of African states and the introduction of new economic systems with no clear system of division of labour, gender roles began to change. Unfortunately, women ended up taking many of the roles that were previously male gender roles, without dropping any of their traditional ones. For example, with the introduction of a money economy and the imposition of taxes, the need for money was generated. This forced men to leave their homes to work in settler farms and in other forms of waged employment. Thus, women began operating as the functional heads of families.

At the same time, the privatization of land eroded women's autonomy in decision-making, particularly with regard to what crops were to be grown and for what purposes. The lands were registered in men's names, thus giving them ultimate control and ownership. Cash crops were introduced. Since men owned the land, the proceeds from these crops went to men who, because of urbanization and labour migration, were not the ones working on the farms. The result is that women ended up as labourers on farms without enjoying the benefits of their labour. Access and control of property was completely taken away from women.

The introduction of formal education and formal employment has served to worsen the situation further. Women were initially kept away from education and from wage employment. This automatically gave men the power to make financial decisions for their families. With time, women have entered formal education and formal employment, but this has not changed the situation much. Men continue to dominate in decisions about how the family income is used, so that although there is substantial pooling of resources in situations where both husband and wife are in formal employment, the man is the actual financial controller in most cases.

It is against this background that gender programmes were popularized in Africa in the 1980s. Initially, the programmes were exclusively concerned with women's development (Women in Development approach – WID) but later opened up to include men (Gender and Development approach – GAD). However, the shift from WID to GAD has not quite taken root, as most gender programmes are women's programmes, in the sense that the focus is on women's empowerment in all aspects. This may be justified, given that the women have been disadvantaged over the years. However, the result is that women sometimes receive empowerment at the expense of men, and, eventually, at their own expense. From an African understanding of human rights, or from any other understanding for that matter, this is definitely not acceptable. There are no competitive efforts in the struggle for justice, since no individual or group's human right is derived from another person or group's lack of it.

Economically, women have received support to join the formal labour market or to develop entrepreneurship. This has helped women to take up breadwinning, a traditional male gender role. Breadwinning is therefore no longer a preserve of males. As they take up these roles, women also take up the attributes associated with them, such as dominance in decision-making. Of course, some men resist such moves, and the result is tension and violence.

With economic empowerment, women continue to take up more and more of the traditional gender roles, but without dropping any of their former roles. This is essentially because there are no social support systems and no gender programmes or policies encouraging *men* to take up traditionally *female* gender roles. This leaves men without responsibilities at the family level: a dangerous situation for any human being to find herself/himself in. The findings of a study carried out by M. Silberschmidt in Kisii, Kenya, indicate that, with the empowerment of women, the men are increasingly losing social value and self-esteem and are essentially feeling irrelevant (Silberschmidt, 1999). To compensate for this loss, some men become careless, irresponsible and aggressive. Once more this leads to antagonism and violence.

In essence, gender development programmes have not improved the situation of women in Africa. Economically, the situation may have improved, but not socially and culturally. Gender violence is on the rise in both intensity and frequency, with serious repercussions.

Like ethnicity, gender is a social construct. Gender conflicts, like ethnic conflicts, result from individual or group pursuits of interests at the expense of other individuals or groups. Gender violence results from a situation where men's interests and needs are met at the expense of women's interests and needs, and vice versa. Unlike ethnic violence, gender violence occurs in various forms. It may be expressed in sexual violence, whereby men's sexual needs are met at the expense of women's sexual needs, or it may be in physical violence, whereby violence is administered 'to maintain women in a dependent and submissive state' (ECA-WIDNET, 1997: 15). Gender violence is also manifested in situations where women's needs for economic and social empowerment are met at the expense of men's needs.

Having discussed the two major forms of violence in Africa, we may analyse them further to see what are the root causes of violence.

Root causes of violence

A diagnosis of a disease is the first step towards treating it. Similarly, a prerequisite for addressing an undesired social phenomenon is a critical appreciation of its root causes. Any attempt to address a phenomenon without this appreciation is as bad as treating a disease without diagnosis, because at its worst it may have fatal consequences. This explains the necessity of exploring the root causes of violence.

The *Decade To Overcome Violence: Churches Seeking Reconciliation and Peace 2001–2010*, (DOV), an instrument of the World Council of Churches, has recognized 'the roots of violence in the way power is understood, exercised, feared, and glorified by the perpetrators, victims and even spectators of violence'.[1] I could not agree more. A critical analysis of the various forms of violence prevailing in Africa, as discussed in the preceding section, concurs with the

DOV. Basically, it is wrong attitudes to and abuse of power that leads to violence.

As illustrated in the discussion above, violence in Africa is very much determined by our interpretation of power, as well as by the use and abuse of power. Traditional African societies had no concept of power: in many African languages there is no word for power. The concept of justice (*haki*) is what may be interpreted as power in traditional societies in Africa. Justice was what empowered people to make decisions and it was the ultimate end of all decisions. Those on whose docket administration of justice lay were the ones who were considered to be 'powerful'. In being equated to justice, power was not something that an individual could use for his own interests at the expense of another or of others. It was something to be exercised for the benefit of all. In this context, power was to be shared so that nobody had a monopoly of power. Power was not something that could be possessed or held, but was an instrument through which just decisions could be made and resources distributed according to one's needs, rather than one's desires or position in society. Among the Kikuyu, for example, land was distributed according to one's ability to work on it. It was not individually owned but held only as inheritance from past generations, and at the same time held in trust for future generations. This explains why violence was rare.

In our contemporary world, however, power is interpreted to mean a political resource that one can hold or even possess, and through it access public resources, be they social or economic. Hence, the powerful are often rich and socially prestigious. Through power, an individual person or group of people can access political, economic and social resources to almost limitless levels. In the process of competition for this power, violence erupts, as the powerless resist exploitation while the powerful seek to maintain the status quo. The literal translation of this understanding of power in traditional African societies is strength (*nguvu*). The use of strength at the expense of justice was meticulously guarded against and controlled. For example, many proverbs and tales ridicule and condemn strength when it is used at the expense of justice.

According to Bethwell A. Ogot, ethnic conflicts are an expression of underlying social and political conflicts between classes, population segments or interest groups within the wider society (Ogot, 1996: 1–6). Ogot is correct. The cases of ethnic conflicts in Rwanda and Kenya, cited above, illustrate this. It was in a bid to prevent the Tutsi from sharing the national resources that the Hutu sought to exclude them. Resistance by the Tutsi against exploitation, on the one hand, and resistance by the Hutu to letting go their perceived powerful positions, on the other, are what led to the great historical tragedy of Rwanda in 1994 (Aguilar, 1998).

In Kenya, ethnic conflicts have been explained in two interrelated ways. First and foremost, they have been interpreted as situations where a small part of the elite and the politically powerful used ethnic resources to protect their positions of economic and political power, when they were threatened by multi-party politics. In a sense, therefore, the conflicts may not even be regarded as ethnic. Ethnic groups were simply being used against other ethnic groups for the political and economic survival of the powerful. It is because a few powerful individuals understood power as something that one uses to access his or her interests that they used it to get ethnic groups to fight one another. Secondly, the conflicts may be viewed as the culmination of many years of exploitation of groups of people by a powerful ethnic group, namely the Kikuyu. With a Kikuyu president taking the reins of leadership soon after independence, this community, driven by need, expanded to move and own property in areas that were indigenously not theirs. Basically, they acquired land, a major resource in Africa, from other groups through the famous land-buying companies initiated by the first president of Kenya. The communities who had sold off their land in ignorance of their future need for it were easily 'politicized': the powerful appealed to ethnic consciousness, buttressed by economic exploitation, to evict from the Rift Valley those who were defined as 'non-indigenous peoples'. The formerly exploited ethnic groups, particularly the Kalenjin, were now empowered by the fact that the then president of Kenya was one of their own.

From these two interrelated perspectives, power is understood as something that individuals or individual groups own to their advantage, even at the expense of other individuals or groups. Ethnic conflicts continue in Kenya, though in latent forms. The so-called 'Kikuyu Mafia' and other powerful leaders continue to define power as something which they own and can use to manipulate resources, including human resources, in their favour. Although the situation is much more complex than this, to a significant extent competition for power in Kenya today is driven by a specific definition of, and specific attitudes towards, power. The fact that political parties are essentially ethnic-based, and that each ethnic group is struggling to access power in order to use it to access resources for individual persons and ethnic groups, explains to a large extent the squabbles that characterize the current ruling coalition party, the National Rainbow Coalition (NARC).

With regard to gender, it may be observed readily that power is associated with men and not with women. Because of their ownership of power, men then access resources for individual interests and use. Women are defined as property to be owned and used to the advantage of men, even when it is at their expense. Sociocultural definitions of masculinity and femininity expect men to dominate and women to submit. In their attempts to dominate, men resort to all forms of violence. As has already been mentioned, physical violence, manifested in wife-battering and sexual abuse, is practised to keep women in submissive positions.

In spite of decades of gender and development programmes in Africa, gender justice has remained elusive, and gender violence is, paradoxically, on the increase. This is because definitions and attitudes of power introduced by colonialism have not changed. Power remains something which enables the owner, an individual person or group, to access resources without regard for justice. Men as individuals and as a group continue to hold on to gender power, often at the expense of women. Gender programmes have served to enlighten women on the injustices they suffer. But the strategy to reverse these injustices cannot achieve results because women are struggling for the same power that men have, in order to use it as men have used it: that is, to dominate as men have done. Men are resisting this in the strongest ways possible, especially through violence, because they do not want to be dominated. Having themselves dominated for so long, they know what dominance is all about. It is in the context of this process of competition for power that gender violence has escalated to alarming levels.

With this diagnosis of the causes of violence it is possible to determine the way forward in terms of developing an ethos of anti-violence in Africa. Christian education may be regarded as the tool through which this ethos may be developed. To this topic we now turn.

The power of religious education: the case of Christian education in Kenya

Religion is a basic human need, rooted in human nature. It is as old as humanity, though the term 'religion' has been variously conceived, and therefore misconceived. Only through religion can the purpose of human existence and the goal of life be found. Religion is concerned primarily with the redemption of evils. Bharathi (1989: 240) accurately observes that the different religions of the world are an attempt to overcome evils. Religion is not merely talking about God. It is a way of life in relationship with God (in theistic religions), with fellow humans and with the rest of creation.

The functional theory postulates that society is made up of complex institutions, which cease to exist when they have no functions (O'Dea and O'Dea, 1993). Religion continues unabated, in spite of earlier predictions that it would die. This implies that religion remains functional. Among the major functions of religion is to maintain the following: social order, harmony, peace and justice. This is done by facilitating desired changes or controlling unnecessary changes. The violence that characterizes the African continent is undesirable, and religion is called upon to facilitate the desired change away from it.

While this essay focuses on the positive role of religion, and more specifically of Christian education in society, it is important to observe that religion is not always functional. At times it may be dysfunctional, facilitating an undesired change or impeding a desired change. As observed by O'Dea and O'Dea (1993: 3):

> in sacralization of the norms and values of society, a religion can make norms of behaviour, which evolved in certain circumstances and which lose their appropriateness under changed conditions, appear to have eternal significance. In this way it can impede a more functionally appropriate adaptation of society to changing conditions.

In the context of this essay, for example, religion has been used to endorse patriarchy and the attendant discrimination against women. At its worst, religion has even been a direct source of conflict and violence, as exemplified by the situation in Northern Ireland and Nigeria, where religious conflicts continue to manifest themselves.

I begin by illustrating the effectiveness of Christian education in Africa. Christian education involves inculcating in individuals the values displayed by our Lord Jesus Christ in his life and teachings. The goal is to develop Christ-like characters in human persons as they engage in their daily lives. Such values as humility, peace, love and concern for others are encouraged. The basic assumption of Christian education is that this is the only way through which humanity can lead fulfilling lives here and now, and eventually achieve redemption. It is essential to remember that education is both verbal and non-verbal. That is to say that a Christian educator teaches in both words and deeds. One may want to know whether Christian education has had a sufficient impact on Africa for us to bank on it in the future. A critical analysis of the history of Africa indicates that Christian education has been instrumental in the socio-political and economic lives of Africans throughout the years.[2] For want of space, we may illustrate this by briefly surveying the role of Christian education in political development in Kenya since independence.

First, it may be observed that people who had received Christian education through the mission schools heralded Kenya's struggle for independence from colonial rule. This education had introduced to them the idea of liberation as God's will for them. Indeed, this was the driving force behind their sacrifices. We may argue, therefore, that Christian education was of great significance to Kenya's liberation from colonial rule. Soon after independence, Christians – like all other Kenyans – felt that the control of government by indigenous leaders would naturally be democratic. They were carried away by the euphoria of self-governance. Hence, the citizenry, guided by the Church, waited patiently to reap the fruits of independence. This dormant moment of the Church, insofar as providing Christian education to guide people's thinking and acting in life is concerned, saw democracy trampled without any opposition. The first president adopted the colonial model of power to dominate. Corruption and the gross abuse of human rights, with other evils, manifested themselves in all spheres of life.

The year 1978 marks a great political landmark in Kenya. The first president of the republic, Mzee Jomo Kenyatta, died and the immediate former president of Kenya, Daniel Toroitich arap Moi, took over. The country enjoyed a peaceful transition. The new government continued with the wrong attitude to power, and therefore corruption and gross violations of human rights persisted. Shortly after Moi took over as the new president, many people began to express their dissatisfaction with the abuses of power in the distribution of national resources. Unfortunately for Moi, the global economic crisis of the 1980s, with the resultant introduction of policies like cost-sharing in public services, worsened the people's dissatisfaction. By the late 1980s, civil rebellion could be felt all over the country. This culminated in the introduction of multi-party politics in 1992.

The Church in Kenya played a major role in the events leading to this change in governance. However, Christian education was still lacking. Hence, in spite of the introduction of multi-party politics, undemocratic rule was to continue in Kenya for another ten years. Kenyans competed for power as ethnic blocks, understanding power as something to be used against others, rather than something to be shared. Political parties were therefore created along ethnic lines. Each ethnic group competed against the others for power to control and dominate. Worse, the Church, rather than educating the masses on the need for unity and sharing, became party to ethnic competition. Certain denominations aligned themselves with certain ethnic groups and parties. In so doing, the Church failed in its educational and liberating mission. It was no surprise therefore that, in spite of the introduction of multi-party politics, the then ruling party, KANU, used its powerful position to ensure that it remained in power.

Writing about the challenges to the Church all over the world wherever ethnic strife threatens human rights, a 1994 report on the ecumenical consultation 'Ethnicity and Nationalism' observes: 'Church leaders are often caught between their own understanding and knowledge of the gospel of reconciliation and ethnic ties and obligations. They must be encouraged to stand for the gospel, which is above ethnic ties and to work for peace in their communities' (Consultation, 1994). This could not be more accurate for Kenya over the 1992 and 1997 general elections and ethnic violence. Ethnic tension, hatred and conflict in Kenya were closely identified with religious and denominational interests. Of course there is a deeper theological issue because historical processes in Africa, which I will not dwell on here, make people more loyal to their ethnic identity than to their Christian identity.

With the defeat of the opposition for the second time in 1997, Christianity led the way to national maturity. Various religions and Christian denominations put aside their historical and doctrinal differences to work together for democracy. They formed the Ufungamano Initiative for democratic reform. This initiative may be credited with the religious education that united the opposition leaders and the people of Kenya unanimously to vote out a dictatorial government, something that was not possible earlier because of ethnic fragmentation. Religious education, in the form of civic education, appealed for a unity of purpose and a sharing of vision and mission. The Ecumenical Civic Education Programme (ECEP), for example, in conjunction with the National Council of Churches in Kenya and the Catholic Justice and Peace Commission, produced a lot of educational materials, through which they enlightened people on the need for unity and their role in ensuring democratic governance. Press releases and notices were jointly published and issued in local daily papers by Muslims, Hindus and Christians, among other groups. Such religious education and unity had never before been witnessed in Kenya.

This was the power behind the unanimous declaration for change by Kenyans through the ballot box on 27 December 2002. KANU, which had ruled Kenya for thirty-nine years, was unanimously voted out in favour of NARC, a coalition of over fifteen parties that were previously conceived as ethnic blocks. The contribution of Christian education to the current political dispensation in Kenya cannot be overemphasized. Unfortunately, sharing of power is re-emerging as an issue that is threatening to break the coalition. More than ever before, the Church is challenged to educate people about the proper understanding of power, as something to be used in service to others and to be shared.

The power of love and the role of Christian education in developing an anti-violence ethos in Africa

The relationship between the interpretation, use and abuse of power, on the one hand, and violence, on the other, has been discussed. Love for domineering power is the root cause of violence in Africa. This section analyses the Christian understanding of power and indicates the role of Christian education in developing the desired ethos of anti-violence in Africa.

'Ethos' is a term borrowed from the Greek language, meaning 'conduct' or 'customs'. It refers to the summative behaviour or characteristic spirit of a people in life situations. A. J. De Jong defines ethos as 'the sum total of all values, traditions, attitudes which together functions in a unique balance and proportions of that particular institution' (1990: 155). An anti-violence ethos that is derived from Christian education therefore means a character that seeks to be Christ-like: to treat other human beings with love, respect and dignity. Such a character does not violate another's rights but, on the contrary, safeguards them. The result of such a character in a community is peace, social order, harmony and justice. In the context of the prevailing abuse of power and the resultant violence in Africa, a peaceful, orderly and just community is the vision of Christian education.

Throughout the Bible, the contemporary understanding of power is contradicted. Power is presented not as mastery, but as service. A good leader is presented as one who uses power not to amass wealth and resources for himself or herself but to serve the welfare of others. While we conceive of and equate power with strength, wealth, honour and dominance, the Bible conceives power as servitude and equates it to weakness and humility. Our contemporary understanding of power makes us compete for it and, sooner or later, 'it gets into our heads',[3] corrupting us absolutely. It would seem that, in their pursuit of power, humans seek to be God. The end result is violence.

The biblical model of power is presented best in the life and teachings of Jesus Christ. Jesus, as the Son of God, had all the power to choose to remain as God omnipotent. But he chose to become mere man, that through this state he could serve humanity and reconcile it to himself. Having become man, Jesus lived a life of service. Rather than being served, he sought to serve. In a very explicit way, Jesus contrasted the worldly and corrupt understanding of leadership with authentic leadership:

> You know that the men who are considered rulers of the heathen have power over them, and the leaders have complete authority. This, however, is not the way it is among you. If one of you wants to be great, he must be the servant of the rest; and if one of you wants to be first, he must be the slave of all. For even the Son of Man did not come to be served; he came to serve and to give his life to redeem many. (Mark 10: 42–5)

In essence, Christ calls his disciples, and indeed his followers, to love in order to serve. Just as he loved the world so much that he gave his life for it, Christians are called to love and serve one another, especially as leaders. Love is presented as a powerful manifestation of power, so that to be powerful *is* to love; it is to serve.

The most powerful symbol of Christianity is the cross. It uniquely symbolizes the love of God for humanity and the power of this love. Yet the image of Christ hanging on the cross is an image of shame, weakness, humiliation, sorrow, pain and defeat. It marks the height of Jesus's suffering in service. Paradoxically, this is the moment that heralds the exaltation and glorification of Christ. As presented on the cross, real power is felt in weakness, humility and suffering. A famous Christian theologian, Jürgen Moltmann, accurately observes: 'Man seeks God in the will for political power and world domination. If he sees and believes God in Christ who was powerless and crucified, he is set free from this desire to have power and domination over others' (1974: 69). Indeed, Christ is the perfect role model for humanity, especially with relation to the meaning and use of power.

In referring to the cross as the most powerful symbol of Christianity, I do not wish to encourage any romanticization of the violence it represents. I look beyond the suffering to the mission of Christ from the beginning of all things, to his eternal glorification as a totality. Isolation of the crucifixion from the events before and after it has led to its misuse to endorse suffering as part of life. I am aware that some feminist theologians have identified the cross as a reinforcement of the subjugation of women.[4]

While I totally agree that the theology of the cross has been abused to endorse gender violence and other forms of violence through history, I do not agree with Ivone Gebara that to cling to the cross as the major symbol of Christianity is tantamount to affirming suffering and male martyrdom as the only way to draw attention to gender injustice, especially against women. It is not. On the contrary, the cross negates injustice to affirm liberation and salvation. Except for the cross, we have nowhere else to cling.

In the context of this essay, identifying the cross as a symbol of power is accurate because the suffering of Jesus could have been avoided, but it was not avoided because of the good it was to achieve. Given the imperfect world in which we live, the cross encourages us that good will triumph over evil, but not without our struggle. Hence, the power of the cross is seen in the fact that he who had the power not to suffer, because he was ultimately powerful, chose to suffer in order to liberate humanity. As long as we understand power as we do in our contemporary world, it will remain a cause of suffering, no matter how well intentioned is its exercise. However, love absorbs power to become selfless service. As Philip Yancey has eloquently put it, on the cross Jesus presented the reality of an omnipotent God, whose love for humankind was so great that he was willing to relinquish power for the sake of their salvation (Yancey, 2004). Christ assumed and experienced humanity in its worst manifestation of violence because of the power of love, as opposed to the love of power.

It is important to emphasize that the cross does not symbolize the toleration of evil or exploitation. Indeed, it indicates an ultimate resistance of and struggle against evil. A critical analysis of the attitudes of Christ indicates that he took great issue with selfish ambitions (Matthew 20: 20–8) and confronted all forms of exploitation (Matt. 23: 1–39). The attitude of Christ was rooted in a concern for others, so that for him to be powerful was to be of service to others, by liberating them from all forces of evil and leading them to redemption. As far as the struggle against gender violence is concerned, it is worth noting that Jesus may actually be a role model for individual African men seeking to liberate themselves from traditional male gender stereotypes that define men as unemotional. Jesus expressed emotion during his life, at times literally weeping tears out of love (weeping for Jerusalem and for Lazarus). Jesus's life therefore indicates that it is possible for powerful men to love, and even to express this emotionally, without losing their masculinity.

It is this understanding of power which Christian education in Africa has to teach people. This teaching should be not just in word but also in deed. Christian educators have conformed to the contemporary misconception of power: they need to be liberated from this if they are to lead others. As the old adage goes, actions speak louder than words.

One could argue that this biblical model of power is too ideal to be taught and practised here and now. But it is not. As we observed earlier, this understanding of power was prevalent in traditional African societies. Oral tradition indicates that a leader was a servant of the people, in the sense that his riches were shared with all, including strangers. Among the Kikuyu, for example, travellers were not required to carry food for the journey, because whenever they felt hungry they could get into any rich farm, pick some of the crops, cook them and eat. As long as he or she did not take any away, what a person ate was regarded as theirs. Another practice, still found in Africa today, though rare, is where people who have not had a good crop in their farms are allowed to go and pick scraps from a rich man's farm. To ensure there are enough scraps, a rich person is expected to ignore some of the crop when harvesting.

Further, this understanding of power is not limited to traditional societies. Such historical figures as Mother Teresa, Mahatma Gandhi and Martin Luther King illustrated the practicality of this model of leadership. These literally served their people, not in spite of but because of the power of love that they wielded. Through their service, they demonstrated Christian education in action to liberate humanity from evil. The effectiveness of their method of education and their influence continue to be felt many years after they passed on.

A contemporary scholar, Robert K. Greenleaf, coined the term 'servant-leadership' to explain the biblical understanding of power, and applied this to the secular institutions and organizations in North America (1977). For Greenleaf, the great leader is first experienced as a servant to others, a fact that is central to his or her greatness. The centrality of servanthood to Christ's life and teachings, not in spite of but because of his power, is indisputable.

To develop an ethos of anti-violence in Africa, Christian education has to work towards changing people's attitudes to power. This involves emphasizing the Christian interpretation of power as love, to replace the contemporary love for power. To love is to be powerful, and to be powerful is to be non-violent. Gandhi taught about non-violence as the greatest human virtue, equating it with love. As paraphrased by Bharathi:

> non-violence is not cowardice. In fact, to Gandhi, non-violence is a supreme virtue of the brave. Exercise of non-violence requires much more bravery than anything else that he could think of and cowardice is inconsistent with non-violence. Non-violence indicates ability to strike, powerfully and virtuously restrained. (1989: 18)

The tragedy for Africa is that our leaders claim to be Christian. They love power, yet they have little understanding of the power of love. Until and unless Christian education instils in people the biblical understanding of power, all strategies to overcome violence will remain largely ineffective. This involves two things.

(i) First and foremost, Christian education has to be directed to the Christian leaders themselves, so as to engage them in a process of changing their leadership methods towards the model of Christ. As mentioned already, Christian leaders have exercised their ecclesial power in a destructive way: to manipulate political leaders and the led, to subjugate men and women, to accumulate material riches and social prestige, and to monopolize the gospel of our Lord Jesus Christ. Church leaders have to change their ways; otherwise Christian education will continue to fall on deaf ears. The Church has to change itself before it can seek to change others. It is only through example that the Church can reach out to political leaders, and to all other leaders, to emulate them and control violence in the continent.

(ii) The second strategy involves the development of meaningful civic education programmes that touch on the root causes of violence. This could be in the form of both written and oral resources, through all kinds of media, such as Christian education training and seminars, radio and television broadcasts, pamphlets, posters and booklets. The successful use of these resources by the Church in Kenya prior to the 2002 general elections indicates their effectiveness. Without consistent and persistent messages to change people's conception of and attitudes to power, Christian education will suppress the 'virus' causing violence, only for it to re-emerge later with even greater viciousness.

Beyond this, Christian education has to appeal to people's rationality and spirituality to understand that an ethos of anti-violence is in their own interests. According to Julia Annas, self-interest is compatible with other-concern, because self-interest demands moral agents to think about the interests of others (Annas, 1992). Annas is correct. Equated to love, non-violence enables justice to take root. As illustrated in specific cases of violence throughout time and space, violence begets violence. This implies that the one who uses power to violate others cannot be secure, because at some point the violated, however weak they may appear, will seek redress. The cycle of violence that characterizes our contemporary world has to be broken. This requires a community with an ethos of anti-violence to resist violence in a sacrificial way, as Christ did. It is this community that Christian education is hereby challenged to establish.

In appealing to sacrifice, the present writer may be thought of as endorsing exploitation. But this is not the case. All that the writer is affirming is that violence will never be a solution to violence. While it is ethical to struggle against injustice, a fact that has so often been neglected in ethics is that the use of force does not become ethically permissible because it has an ethical aim; in addition, it must be applied with a completely ethical disposition (Annas, 1992). Further, as Albert Schweitzer observes:

> The important thing is not that only non-violence should be employed, but that all worldly purposive actions should be undertaken with the greatest possible avoidance of violence, and that ethical considerations should so dominate ourselves as to influence also the hearts of our opponents. (Bharathi, 1989: 13)

This implies that the role of Christian education is not just to establish the spirit of anti-violence, but also to ensure that this spirit touches the hearts of those who are abusing power, in order to embrace a new understanding of power as a tool for service to others.

Notes

[1] Cited in *Aide-Mémoire* from a theological consultation on 'Interrogating and Redefining Power', held in Cret Berard, Pidoux, Switzerland, 10–13 December 2003; February 2004 draft.

[2] For a more comprehensive analysis of this, see Eunice Karanja Kamaara, 'The role of the Christian church in socio-economic and political development in Kenya', *Journal of Third World Studies* (2000), xvii, 165–76.

[3] In Kenya, this phrase is popularly associated with the ninth vice-president of Kenya, the late Kijana Wamalwa, who is significantly credited with fostering opposition unity prior to the historic 2002 general elections in Kenya. Kenyans remember him fondly for using the phrase to warn Kenyan politicians against the abuse of power.

[4] See, for example, Gebara (2002).

References

Aguilar, M. I. (1998). *The Rwanda Genocide and the Call to Deepen Christianity in Africa*, Eldoret, AMECEA Gaba Publications.

Annas, J. (1992). 'The good life and the good lives of others', in E. F. Paul, F. D. Miller and J. Paul (eds), *The Good Life and the Human Good*, Cambridge, Cambridge University Press, pp. 133–48.

Bharathi, K. S. (1989). *Socio-Religious Thoughts of Mahatma Gandhi*, Nagpur, Dattsons.

Consultation (1994). Report on 'Ethnicity and Nationalism', consultation hosted by the Ecumenical Institute for the Study and Dialogue in Colombo and the National Christian Council of Sri Lanka, November 1994; *Ecumenical Review*, 47, 2, 1995, 225–31.

De Jong, A. J. (1990). *Reclaiming a Mission: New Direction for the Church-Related College*, Grand Rapids, MI, Eerdmans.

ECA-WIDNET (1997). *Violence Against Women: Trainers' Manual*, Nairobi, Paulines Publications.

Gebara, I. (2002). *Out of the Depths: Women's Experiences of Evil and Salvation*, trans. Anne Patrick Ware, Minneapolis, MN, Fortress Press.

Greenleaf, R. K. (1977). *Servant Leadership: A Journey to the Nature of Legitimate Power and Greatness*, New York, Paulist Press.

Hansen, H. B. (1984), *Mission, Church and State in Colonial Setting in Uganda 1890–1925*, Nairobi, Heinemann.

Moltmann, J. (1974). *The Crucified God: The Cross of Christ as the Foundation and Criticism of Christian Theology*, New York, Harper & Row.

O'Dea, T. F. and O'Dea, J. A. (1993). *The Sociology of the African Family*, Princeton, NJ, Prentice-Hall.

Ogot, B. A. (ed.) (1996). *Ethnicity, Nationalism and Democracy in Africa*, Maseno, Institute of Research and Post-graduate Studies.

Silberschmidt, M. (1999). *Women Forget that Men are Masters: Gender Antagonism and Socio-economic Change in Kisii District, Kenya*, Stockholm, Nordiska Afrikainstitutet.

Sinaga, D. (2004). 'Biblical and theological reflection on power and the right use of power', paper presented to the Consultation of Younger Theologians from the South, held in Chiang Mai, Thailand, 23–8 February 2004.

Yancey, P. (2004). *The Jesus I Never Knew*, Nairobi, Evangel Publishing House.

7
Education for peace: a multidimensional approach

KARL ERNST NIPKOW

Historical contexts, sources of research, methodology

This chapter is bound to specific contexts. It is located in an international context of research and a national biographical context of personal experience. Born in 1928, during his youth the author suffered from indoctrination shaped by the spirit of Hitler nationalism, abhorrent racism and crude militancy. On the level of research, this essay draws first on the author's own studies, dealing with the anthropological question concerning how destructive aggression that leads to violence and war can be explained at all (there is also civilized and even creative aggression) – and not only by social factors in specific situations.

My sources for obtaining general insights in this area are historical in a wide sense, reaching back to the early stages of human development. One focus is the anthropology of the Bible, in particular the Hebrew Bible (Old Testament), which is brimming with experiences about friend and foe, good and evil, suffering from injustice and longing for peace. The related focus is on the anthropology inherent in modern evolutionary psychology and ethics. Together, biblical tradition and evolutionary research disclose the most realistic view of human nature (Nipkow, 2003). My second source is represented by ongoing historical studies on peace theology, peace philosophy and peace education in changing political contexts from the time of Erasmus of Rotterdam to the present (Nipkow, 2007). In sum, my methodology interrelates hermeneutical methods and empirical data, descriptive analysis and normative reflection.

Theoretical approaches and normative horizons

In Germany, a theory of peace education worthy of that name is only in its infancy. As far as the explanation of aggression, violence and war is concerned, my own theoretical approach follows a four-dimensioned framework, with one dimension from the field of the political sciences (the democracy–peace hypothesis), another from social psychology, a third following psychoanalysis, and, last but not least, hypotheses from evolutionary theory.

In practice-related disciplines, such as education and politics, no theory can make do without normative reflection. In my case this will be based on the consciousness of a post-national and post-colonial age. The normative conclusions result from educational, philosophical and theological criteria, according to my model of 'critical dialectical convergence' between education and theology, which was developed in religious education in the early 1970s (Nipkow, 1975: I, 173–7). Educational theory has to assess theological and philosophical theory, and vice versa: theology and philosophy have to examine educational stances. As Paolo Freire and others affirm, education can never be neutral, either in fact or in intention. The issue of war and peace as a challenge to educational action implies the taking of sides. With regard to a peace education which includes religion-based conflicts, the disciplines of religious studies can deliver important facts, descriptions and explanations of their own, but the methodological principle of 'bracketing' forbids religious and educational valuing. The approach of critical convergence, mentioned above, differs at this point. By the mutual critical relationship of theology and educational theory-building, with an accompanying philosophical ethical reflection, I hope that such a normative framework will avoid both an obsolete dogmatic theological dominance, on the one hand, and a one-sided ideological educational bias, on the other.

Voices of peace educators: the marginalized and the condemned in German history

It is a sad and discouraging project to trace this topic in German history (Nipkow, 2007). You will find many more sources focused on preparation for war than for peace. The few philosophers, theologians and educators who raised their voices in favour of peace were either harshly criticized by their contemporaries, as was the case with John Amos Comenius (1592–1670), the last Moravian bishop, condemned mostly by Lutherans, and the Catholic educationist Friedrich Wilhelm Foerster (1869–1966), accused by the whole German elite of being *Vaterlandsverräter*, 'fatherland-traitor', and forced to emigrate. Other advocates of a peace policy for education were marginalized (as was the case with Sebastian Franck, 1499–1543), persecuted by both Lutheran theologians and political authorities, or had their educational training programmes at universities and seminaries silenced (in the case of Jean Paul, 1763–1825, because of his scurrilously romantic style).

Preparation of youth for warfare as normal: a critical democratic public as a counterpoise

In Germany, the conviction that wars are necessary was inculcated as normal, especially after 1890 under Kaiser Wilhelm II. It was a view transmitted to each of the following generations through formal educational programmes and, more effectively, by informal or structural socialization, as a sort of 'hidden curriculum'. What is considered normal does not become a topic of public discussion. Processes of socialization take place without any open discourse. Or, to put it in more positive terms, in the hypotheses of the political sciences it is the enlightened citizens who must organize open and honest discussions on peace and war.

The German philosopher Immanuel Kant (1724–1804) was among the first to do this. In his essay, 'Perpetual Peace' (1795), he demanded republican constitutions instead of monarchies, to provide for and stimulate such a critical 'public' discussion. However, if peace is to endure, it also needs peace-supporting institutions. Therefore, Kant argued for the establishment of peace by means of a league of nations or confederations of states. About 150 years before him, J. A. Comenius had made the same recommendation, arguing for an international alliance of statesmen: 'A Dicastery of Peace' (Comenius, 1995). Today such transnational institutions (for example, the United Nations) have been established, but they do not provide a secure guarantee of worldwide peace, since any superpower can undermine the power of international agreements. In the political sciences, however, a 'democracy–peace hypothesis' is defended, according to which democracies will not wage war against one another. This is a sign of hope, but it does not prevent them from undertaking wars or strikes against non-democratic nations. Whatever progress the future may bring in political reality and in its study, one fact is obvious: education for peace is a crucial part of education for lived democracy and critical citizenship.

Using history and religion in schools for nationalism and racism: education for peace as cognitive resistance to dualistic either/or patterns

In the past, the chief subjects in schools that promoted a spirit of war or peaceful attitudes, feelings and concepts were history and religion. A study of history in German grammar schools in the nineteenth century (Weymar, 1961) shows how, in the context of the Liberation Wars against Napoleon I, there developed a belief in a spiritual (idealistic) national mission, based on a sharp contrast between the wonderful German 'culture' and the rotten Roman 'civilization' (thus J. G. Fichte). This contrast was founded in God's will, for God was supposed to have chosen the German people as the only 'true' and 'pure' people, stock and race. (The broadest success of this ideology was in schools, as the historian F. Kohlrausch claimed.) The religious and metaphysical starting-point of this philosophy, with its ruthless dualistic either/or thought-patterns, seemed to legitimate even an education for hate (see the very popular poet E. M. Arndt). In the second half of the century, a 'Prussian war-pedagogy' (Weymar, 1961: 151–5) reached its peak, with the glorification of acts of fighting and dying on the battlefield.

In Europe, the cult of heroes in history and the misuse of a theology of God's will were widespread phenomena. The core of the argumentation and propaganda rested on cognitive simplifications. Even today, the fundamentalist wings of Christianity, Judaism and Islam foster a dualistic religious thinking, which is absorbed very easily by very many people, both young and old. Here we touch the second aspect of theory, that is, explanations from the background of social psychology. Lionel Tiger's 'ease of learning hypothesis' refers to cognitions and emotions that do not afford much reflection. People are satisfied with simple political and religious messages. Most effective of all are 'images', as

R. D. Deutsch (1998) has found in the context of research on the 'indoctrinability' of people by 'ideologies' as a factor in preparing for warfare. 'Meaning is extracted selectively from only a small portion of what we already know and expect.' Thus, people 'concoct an image with an emotional bottom line: positive or negative' (ibid.: 302). Education for peace has to resist such cognitive simplifications, along with their simplifying images (stereotypes) of foreigners, strangers and enemies, and the exploitation of human indoctrinability by agitation and propaganda.

Alibis for hidden and open aggression in European bourgeois societies

From a psychoanalytical theoretical perspective, which is our third theoretical approach, the German–American historian Peter Gay (1993) has investigated the mentality of the nineteenth-century bourgeois classes in England, France and Germany (and, to a minor degree, their parallels in the USA), under the heading *The Cultivation of Hatred*. He identified three main forms of legitimizing aggression. Gay starts with the way conflicts were explained and justified by the new theory of a necessary struggle for survival. This was applied to crude economic competition (Manchester liberalism), the denigration and despising of the other side during the waves of colonial expansion, and hate-fuelled racist differences. It was Herbert Spencer who propagated this thesis, in his *Social Statistics* of 1850 – earlier than Darwin in his *Origin of Species* of 1859 – arguing that in contemporary society, as evidenced by the social statistics, and over the long term (in evolution) the weak and sick will not survive. As this is how the world goes, they deserve to be neglected, and even eliminated if necessary. The future of mankind lies instead with the 'survival of the fittest', as the laws of nature clearly demonstrate.

The second alibi is deeply rooted in the human feeling that certain 'others', mainly 'strangers', do not belong to and fit with our own group. Thus the Jews do not fit with the Christians, the French with the Germans, the indigenous Negroes with the Europeans in the new colonies.

The third powerful factor related to war and peace, again a psychological one, is reflected in the masculine ideals expressed in typical cults of masculinity. It is easy to reconstruct the first and the third factor of Gay's factors in the data given above about anti-peace education in Germany.

In-group amity and out-group enmity and the two codes of morals: evolutionary explanations and educational answers

Gay speaks of the 'others' in psychoanalytical categories, as those who function in one's own imaginations and actions as a screen of 'projection'. That is to say, they serve: (a) deep-rooted needs to maintain one's own individual and collective identity; (b) to protect the self from self-accusations concerning its own ugly moral traits; and (c) simply as outlets for aggression. I shall complement this explanation by hypotheses from evolutionary psychology, the fourth of my theoretical approaches.

Everywhere in the demarcations between 'us' and the 'others', two codes of morals may be observed, which lead to a hypocritical self-image of individuals, nations and cultures. On the one hand, 'in-group amity' can be explained by the learning, transmitted from generation to generation of warm affiliative feelings of bonding within one's family, clan and tribe. On the other hand, 'out-group enmity' can be explained by the complementary need to learn how to protect oneself and one's group by demarcations and militant defences (or pre-emptive strikes) against others. In this second perspective, the well-known instruments that fulfil these functions are 'nationalism' or 'patriotism', the latter in those multi-ethnic states, like the USA, in which no common descent can provide the social oil of coherence and the common energies to fight the enemy (Shaw and Wong, 1989). The two inherent elementary factors leading to hostile disjunction refer to (a) social relationships (friend or foes), and (b) material dimensions (possessions and territory, our own or another's). Both are crucial for survival, and are expressed in two questions:

- *Who* belongs to me or us, and against *whom* do we have to protect ourselves?
- *What* do we have to defend or to expand?

'It is not simply *that* we classify that is so important, but (1) *what* we classify and (2) *how* we act on our classifications through cognition and related emotions' (Shaw and Wong, 1989: 81–2). The educational response that is needed in order to stop warfare and promote reconciliation and peace is also twofold: it consists of clarification of cognitions (for example, prejudices) and reflection on feelings (such as resentment, antipathy, hate). An accompanying educational task is to introduce the young, and adults through adult education, into a critique of ideologies. One example may suffice. Double moral standards are highlighted by the British philosopher, John L. Mackie (1982: 282), when he states, with some uneasiness, that 'it is perfectly possible for people to combine the finest moral sensitivity in relation to their fellows with extreme inhumanity towards ... human beings whom they see in some way alien to themselves and their associates'.

Transforming masculine ideologies

As old as the in-group/out-group contrast that nourishes both anxiety and projective reactions against it (refusing others and exaggerating our own strength) is the gender difference. We can leave aside the detailed biological factors and start with the fact that competition among males in winning females lies at the very beginnings of our species and has a long pre-human history. Interestingly, we meet the same double-sided result of evolution as was detailed above, with love and care on the one hand and rivalry and hostility on the other. The situation appears mostly among competing men, but also in relation to women who do not follow the men's masculine wishes – or, worse, betray them. The data on homicide in the investigation conducted by Martin Daly and Margo Wilson (1988) in metropolitan areas in the USA and Canada are conclusive (see also Vogel, 2000, and his data on infanticide amongst humans, 115–17; and Nipkow, 2003: 140–1).

A premature moralizing judgement on the pride of men and their desire to be strong and masculine would miss the point. We cannot deny the facts as such, nor will protesting help. The first educational challenge is how to civilize these negative, destructive expressions by transforming them. There are many ways of diverting masculine aggressiveness to harmless competition (women are not without aggressive emotions, but these appear in other forms and for different reasons). Sport has been the most popular vehicle of peaceful relations since the days of ancient Greece. As long as nations meet in playgrounds they will not kill one another. Hunting is another civilizing outlet, although today it has become very controversial. Historically, it was considered to be fun and at the same time a useful training for war – a typical ancient privilege of the aristocrats. But there are other ways.

The German reform educator Kurt Hahn (1886–1974), a Jew who was arrested by the Nazi regime in 1933, was saved by the British Prime Minister Ramsay MacDonald and soon forced to emigrate to England, where he had earlier studied at Oxford. He is well known as the founder of the famous boarding schools of Salem in Baden-Württemberg in Germany and Gordonstoun in Scotland. He also initiated the Outward Bound Schools (*Kurzschulen*), which he carefully sited either at the seaside or in the mountains, so that adolescents could learn and practise rescuing people in need. This, he argued, would divert the negative elements of their militant instincts and transform their characters. In his view, education should transmit an equivalent of war, encouraging conquests without the humiliation of the conquered. Unlike William James, Hahn was convinced that it is not war, but the passion of rescue, that reveals the soul in its highest dynamic. Moreover, he complained of the association of war with the erosion of compassion, coldness of heart and the 'death of the soul' (quoting the Archbishop of Canterbury, William Temple). The passion of rescuing others in dangerous situations may make friends and bridge divides on a totally different moral ground.

Hahn once said, with regard to the struggle between Jews and Arabs, and in the context of an application for a future king of an Arab country to enter Gordonstoun School, where some Jews also attended: 'If the Arab and one of these Jews were to go out sailing on our schooner ... perhaps in a northeasterly gale, and if they were to become thoroughly seasick together, I would have done something for international education' (www.wilderdom/Hahn.htm). ('International education' was at this time an early name for peace education.) The Boy Scout movement knows similar practices, but before 1914 it also served pre-military purposes.

A second aspect of masculinity invites our critical assessment of those cults by which masculine ideals are exploited for religious, political and military purposes. In 1879 Thomas Hughes, one of the most fascinating advocates of manliness, published a book with the title *The Manliness of Christ*. It is the general mentality of a society that generates changing religious and political ideals. Again, education for peace links with religious and political 'awareness-making' processes, which Paolo Freire called processes of 'conscientization'.

The dangerous exploitation of family-related feelings by 'family semantics' and the basic role of value education

People can be convinced in freedom and persuaded in dependence. In the last case, if its true purposes are intentionally concealed, education becomes indoctrination (for a broader discussion of indoctrination, see Nipkow, 2006). The evolutionary key to how this works is as follows. The genetic dispositions stemming from the affiliative bonds within the family are used to develop collective bonding. In the evolution of vertebrate social behaviour, the development of nurturant individualized broodcare seems to have constituted 'a turning point' (Eibl-Eibesfeldt, 1998: 25). As we have seen, human behaviour patterns are characterized by two strong features: aggressive demarcation against others and affiliative interaction in one's own groups – in short, hate and love. From the earliest stages of phylogenesis (and likewise in ontogenesis, that is, in individual development), caring and loving dispositions play a basic role: 'familial dispositions are the basis of humankind's prosociality' (ibid.: 21). In this interaction, in particular in interaction with the mother, the infant experiences the two modes of giving and receiving. The individualized mother–child bonds are also very strong because they are nourished by affective expressions. Caressing, embracing, kissing, and baby talk in a voice raised by one octave are deeply embedded in maternal behaviour (ibid.: 25–6). The learning results of the very long natural and cultural history of humankind have left traces in the individuals which, even today, can and will be used for the purposes of developing social attitudes of a wider range, for coherence in the tribe and the nation, and also for membership of a non-homogeneous religious society that assembles people from different ethnic and national backgrounds. In short, peaceful social relations in the world can be shaped according to the ideal of peace in a family.

This expansion develops if the emotional language of the family, the so-called family semantic, is used. The names 'father' and 'mother', 'children', 'brother' and 'sister', together with the term 'family', are emotionally welcomed by almost everyone. The language of kinship bonding, on the one hand, and the innate predispositions for becoming bound and mutually obliged, on the other hand, meet and match the first, as it were, by 'keying in' to the genetically and biographically given 'locks' or channelled 'traces'. Political and religious institutions know more or less consciously about this interrelation and apply it by speaking of God's 'children', the church as a 'mother' or as a 'family' (*familia dei*), and the pope as the 'holy father'; church members will address each other as 'sisters' and 'brothers'. The same happens in the political sphere. Thus we find this in a 'Chant of Soldiers' from French history:

> Fair France bids her children arise,
> soldiers around us are arming,
> on, on, 'tis our 'mother' who cries!
> (Quoted in Shaw and Wong, 1989: 91)

The expanding circle forming a larger peaceful community does indeed work effectively through processes of psychological identification, which build up a fictive lineage system of common descent. What, however, if this process stops at the level of a specific ethnic, national or religious unification? It will then necessarily exclude those who are not quasi-genetically adopted.

This way to a peaceful community, therefore, can (not must) become dangerous by supporting exclusion as the other side of inclusion. By accepting one sort of ally, others are left outside the closed circle – making them not akin, not 'belonging' to. Thus, the otherness of the non-fitting others is not only a result of nature (for example, the colour of their hair and skin), it is also socially produced, with the consequence that the demarcation can nourish the seeds of resentment and thoughts of retaliation. The alternative can only be an inclusive ethic, and a culture and education that is oriented towards the common values of equality, solidarity and human dignity.

Equality, solidarity, justice: rationality-bound and life-related inclusion

A recent empirical study on West African values (Fuoss-Bühler, 2006) shows that in their history Africans have developed both a form of democracy and an ethic of inclusiveness of their own. They do not need to be given a western moral value-system in order to develop peaceful altruistic attitudes that include strangers, reduce anxieties, mitigate aggression and foster a larger peaceful community. Indeed, it is not wise to import western criteria, for colonialism has left emotional and moral barriers.

As a first point, the indigenous concept of community is different in Africa: its focus is not the isolated individual, but the enlarged family, kinship and village. Everyone shares his own goods with the others as his or her 'brothers' and 'sisters'. This traditional 'democracy' is a participatory basic democracy. Even if a chosen, authorized person finally makes the decisions, a very long 'palaver' in an open-air assembly – with the symmetrical right of each member to raise his or her own voice – will precede the common actions or the modification of common rules. An individualistic approach is as alienating here as is the western image of society. The African traditional approach is not that of an aggregation of individuals under abstract 'rights' and 'contracts', as the European tradition of a *contrat sociale* has constructed it (see, for example, Thomas Hobbes, J.-J. Rousseau).

It is important, therefore, for education for peace to break through the boundaries of western thought patterns. The underlying topic of our book is education for peace in many contexts and dimensions. Conflicts, including wars, can result from both outer and inner struggles, from clashes between nations, cultures and religions. In the case of the last two elements, we enter the field of the tasks of inter-cultural and inter-religious understanding and reconciliation. From such inter-cultural studies as those of Simone Fuoss-Bühler (2006), it follows that the first task is to learn about cultural differences as such. If, on both sides, people fail in this learning, the chances of mutual understanding are weakened from the very beginning.

Peace is defined as the overcoming of hostile barriers between human beings. The western perspective on this process is deeply influenced by the belief in a Kantian universal rationalism, which is supposed to unite all human beings by the power of the same universal human reason (*Vernunft*). It is, however, just this general reason that necessarily glosses over the specific, historically grown values and religious beliefs (see Nipkow, 2007: ch. 7).

Kant's rejection of the traditions of Judaism and Islam is well known. Criticizing any moral observance based on religious 'prescriptions' and 'rituals', as not being 'true' morality, he envisages religion as being one and the same concept for all: a purified religion, as he would say; a plundered religion, as believers themselves might respond. Religion is reduced by Kant to a rational core that he calls *Vernunftglaube* ('reasonable faith') or *reine Religion* ('pure' religion).

In a much more aggressive way, the Kantian philosopher Jakob Friedrich Fries (1773–1843) became a passionate advocate of anti-Semitism. He not only denied Jews civil rights (as did many others), but demanded restrictions on their right to marriage and a halt to immigration; because of their failure to assimilate to Christian bourgeois standards, he insisted that they wear a sign on their clothing, and, as the last abhorrent device, he called for the execution of 'Pharaoh's law' (Exodus 1: 22: 'Every boy that is born to the Hebrews you shall throw into the Nile') (Lötzsch, 2005: 179–80).

Insofar as this western way of a rationality-bound inclusion is still defended, which is the case in rationalist approaches to inter-religious education, it is already questionable and problematic for those in Europe and the Americas, as it is in Africa. West Africans understand themselves to exist in a cosmos that comprises all generations. They also expand the notion of peace: for them, peace embraces young and old; the living, the dead and the unborn; the ancestors and the future generations; and all living beings, humans as well as animals. This model of inclusion has some traits in common with the approach to peace of the German writer mentioned above, Jean Paul (Friedrich Richter), whose peace education consists of an 'education for love' and rests upon the 'sanctification of life' (Jean Paul, 1807: §§ 116, 120). We can speak here of a life-related inclusion. West Africans and Jean Paul would understand each other, since they both go back to a similar universal experience, instead of a universal cognitive 'transcendental philosophical' construction.

In the context of life, real suffering and real help count. Peace grows as far as scarce goods are shared in solidarity. Suffering is overcome by compassion. The primary level is (1) that of the common 'goods' for survival, which is followed (2) by a ranking of 'values' that corresponds to those goods, with sharing and justice at the top. The overarching basic value is (3) human dignity. In order to protect goods and values, 'rules' and 'norms' have to be installed, with 'human rights' as the most abstract frame of normative reference.

Looking into one another's eyes: sharing life and face-to-face contacts

'Life' is a keyword for education for peace, in its several perspectives. There is a logical transition from the end of the last section, with its concern for the 'sanctification of life', to this section: from the love of life as the core of peace, to learning about one another in situations of real life. Our presentation has led from the political hypothesis that democracies will not wage war against one another and the preparation for critical citizenship in a critical society, through the critique of nationalist and masculine ideologies and learning to resist dualistic thinking (that is, either/or thought patterns) – a dangerous route, which is mostly accompanied by exploiting the predispositions for bonding by persuasion and indoctrination, to philosophical discussion of leading values and differing patterns of inclusion. These patterns have to do with our reason and with our heart. How can we support an education for peace that reaches the heart? We must do so, because the cognitive and the emotional domains of learning are closely interrelated.

In this context, physical nearness or distance plays a crucial educational role. Conflict separates people and creates a distance; whereas physical nearness can reunite enemies. The faces of our enemies are the corporeal windows into their inner lives. Faces manifest anger and hate, kindness and readiness to forgive and reconcile.

At the very first, a baby realizes dimly his or her mother's face. There are numerous references in the Bible to God's face or countenance, in particular playing a role in blessing by indicating a most intimate relationship as a source of consolation and peace (Numbers 6: 24–6). Here, in our earliest infancy, is the beginning of learning processes that can build up peaceful attitudes by face-to-face contacts and encounters.

In so-called 'primitive' societies, eye-to-eye contact is sometimes regarded as the beginning of personal exchange and will stop further aggression. On the Molucca Islands, head-hunting could be exercised only from behind the back. If the face of the adversary had been seen, the act of killing would have been murder. In this case the two parties would have 'exchanged' something, be it only the mutual look at their faces (Barash, 1979: 156–7). If hostages have been captured, the negotiations and decisions that take place in order to free them are mostly prolonged so that the kidnappers might learn about their hostages as individual people by face-to-face contact. Physiognomy embodies a person's individuality in a striking uniqueness and vulnerability.

Research data from the field of social psychology on the affective preconditions of helping another child who was sad because her toys had been damaged clearly support the claim that face-to-face contact stimulates compassion and a resulting readiness to help. If a child could directly watch another suffering child's tears, these close 'emotional signals' were influential in evoking 'empathetic reactions' (Halisch, 1988: 96). Reports from the Vietnam War by the Italian reporter Oriana Fallaci, who accompanied a bomber crew, speak for themselves as witness to the rapid deadening of compassion that occurs if suffering takes place at a distance.

> The third time I had put up with the thing and was only eager not to miss the moment when Andy would uncouple the bomb ... The fourth, the fifth, the sixth time I had become accustomed to it. Now I could observe the spectacle from a certain distance, and this spectacle consisted of little figures who fled from their bunkers and sandbag barricades, waving their arms to free themselves from the flames, and one suffocated in the flames: I would lie if I were saying that I had felt guilt or mercy. (Quoted in Wickler, 1991: 154)

Face-to-face encounters are a risk. The language of gestures, facial movements and the appearance of the body trigger spontaneous negative behavioural reactions, often within seconds, as research on prejudices and 'inferential communication' shows (Frey, 1998). By looking at each other more intensively, sympathy and trust can grow. Mutual trust is another indispensable step on the way to peace in everyday interactions, religious life and politics. In the conflict in the Middle East, mediators are permanently sent to negotiate between the hostile camps. In several countries, pupils learn the role of mediators by special programmes.

Insofar as conflicts have to do with ethnic, national, cultural, racial, and religious differences, schools can provide opportunities for inter-cultural and inter-religious education. Pupils' exchange programmes, as organized by Youth for Understanding and other institutions, are only one example. Today, our own society is often already a multicultural one, which confronts us with unfamiliar challenges. The sad fact is that minorities are prone to forming 'parallel societies' in towns and cities if integration fails because of the defective policy of the majority. Thus, both sides avoid nearness, and betray the spirit of good neighbourliness. The difficulties in transforming the spirit of a society in the direction of good neighbourliness are well known. In these cases at least, governments are obliged to make the state school system become a place of peaceful exchange. A heterogeneous composition in the classroom, or a systematic cooperation between different religious classes, can encourage the growth of 'life-related inclusion'.

My own hopes in this direction, however, are mixed with scepticism, since many schools in Europe are not free of racism, hostility between ethnic groups, bullying and open violence. I return here to the beginning, where the emphasis was laid on societal and school structures, and the general climate in society and school. Education for peace in the classroom is only one factor, and, without a peace-promoting society as a whole, it is a factor that will meet with little success. What is the moral and spiritual vision of a nation? Educators have to insist on this question for the sake of peace for the next generations. Governments lack insight and wisdom if they stick anxiously to the dichotomy of a friend–foe pattern (see above) and busy themselves chiefly in providing means of military defence, without a policy for world peace on the basis of social justice. They will further nourish violence, including terrorism. A wise policy is directed to a life *for* all, the economic and social solidarity *with* all, and a common obligation of human dignity *of* all.

Taking the first step for cooperation: a surprising theory

In the discipline of evolutionary ethics, sociobiologists do not reflect on the role of morality and religion in philosophical categories. Rather, theirs is a very restricted approach that deals with the phenomenon of altruism in two forms: 'kin altruism' and 'reciprocal altruism' (terms introduced by R. L. Trivers). The first form of altruism covers the basic source of all affiliative powers in human life as they are experienced, learnt and applied in the family. It becomes this source where there is success in transferring these powers of care and love, bonding and solidarity to political or religious communities across a wider range (see the function of the 'family semantic'). In extreme situations, this 'strong' altruism implies self-sacrifice, for instance when a mother dies for her child. The second form of altruism has its basis in a rational calculation of advantages and disadvantages, profits and costs, and plays a role in economic theories of cooperation.

In *God, Human Nature and Education for Peace* (Nipkow, 2003), I discuss Robert Axelrod's seminal study (1984), *The Evolution of Cooperation*, which asks under which conditions cooperation will emerge in a world of egoists without a central authority, and which form of cooperation would best benefit both economic partners. Cooperation is an aspect of our topic, for if nations want to make profit by business then war is misplaced (with the exception of the interests of the military-economic constituency). Axelrod's methodology, using the Prisoner's Dilemma from game theory, has its weaknesses: it puts aside many vital factors, such as the crude interest in military power as the preferred option, when war is more attractive than trade. Despite these theoretical handicaps, however, Axelrod's outcomes deserve attention.

By way of a computer tournament with a two-stage arrangement, a simple theory of relationships, called 'Tit for Tat', appeared as the one with the relatively highest profit for both competing parties in an economic cooperative relationship. The three characteristic features of this procedure are:

- First, Tit for Tat always *starts in a friendly way with a cooperative step* as its first action. Because of this wise rule, Axelrod speaks of it as a 'nice strategy'. It invites people to cooperate and behave in the same reciprocal manner, thus keeping the peace.

(*Reciprocity* – as in the *Golden Rule* – is a widely underestimated means to maintain peace: it is the essential element in a rational education for peace.)

- Second, Axelrod's most effective theory is also *retaliatory*, in that Tit for Tat immediately answers a defection from the other side by adopting the same stategy (reciprocal reaction). Taking advantage of the kindness of the other is thus quickly frustrated. 'Tit for Tat benefits from its own nonexploitability' (Axelrod, 1984: 53).

(It should not be overlooked, however, that this rule involves symmetrical steps, not an asymmetrical retaliation!)

- Third, the Tit for Tat strategy is also *forgiving*. If the other party apologizes (speaking metaphorically) and comes back to continue cooperating on equal terms, Tit for Tat will also continue with his or her own cooperation.

My presentation of this theory played a considerable role in the discussion following my paper at the twelfth conference of the International Seminar on Religious Education and Values in Kiryat Anawim near Jerusalem in July 2000, which took place some weeks before the new intifada broke out. The controversial point was whether in that region war could and should be the option, instead of cooperation. There was no controversy about the negative consequences of an asymmetrical military retaliation, however, for this violates the elementary feeling of reciprocity.

Paradoxical interventions against aggression and a value revolution: the Jesus Movement

The words 'inviting', 'retaliatory' and 'forgiving' come as a surprise in economic language. However, when we turn to the question of how Jesus of Nazareth and his followers (the so-called 'Jesus Movement': Theissen, 2004) behaved, we meet exactly the same three items. On the one hand, Jesus and his disciples invited people to listen to the gospel; on the other hand, filled with thoughts of revenge his followers cursed whole villages. At the very beginning of Christianity, the potential for aggression and the overcoming of it by non-aggressive strategies already lay side by side. Those who were sent out by Jesus to preach the Kingdom of God often became frustrated, and expressed their anger in violent fantasies – the images of which were drawn from tradition (Luke 3: 9, 19: 27; Matthew 8: 12, 13: 42, 25: 46). Of course, we have to differentiate between imagined aggression and real aggression: the first can help us avoid the second. In religious education today, teachers often invite children to portray conflict situations where aggression against the wicked is quite normal, which serve as the raw material for discussion.

For a theory of education for peace, two other elements are much more important however: (1) Jesus's violence-reducing strategies, and (2) his peace-oriented symbolic actions, which are both expressions of (3) a values revolution. The first element may be illustrated from Matthean texts:

> Blessed are the peacemakers; for they will be called children of God. (Matt. 5: 9)

> You have heard that it was said, 'An eye for an eye and a tooth for a tooth.' But I say to you, Do not resist an evildoer. But if anyone strikes you on the right cheek, turn the other also; and if anyone wants to sue you and take your coat, give your cloak as well; and if anyone forces you to go one mile, go also the second mile. (Matt. 5: 38–42)

> You have heard that it was said, 'You shall love your neighbour and hate your enemy.' But I say to you, Love your enemy and pray for those who persecute you . . . (Matt. 5: 43–5)

Among several forms of violence-reducing methods, the way of 'self-stigmatizing' in the examples quoted above has two coexisting, interrelated effects. The aggressor expects resistance because the normal reaction in human life and history is to beat back, but the retaliatory reaction does not happen – to the surprise of the aggressor, whose demands are voluntarily surpassed. Both forms of behaviour – to be able to do without counter-violence and to surpass the demands of the aggressor – can irritate the other very much. Viewed in terms of role behaviour, the person who is supposed to accept the role of a passive victim refuses this role by undermining it in an act of freedom. The weak becomes the strong in a new, unexpected way: his responses are examples of what has been called a 'paradox intervention' (see Theissen, 2004: 286).

In therapy, paradox interventions are well known and often applied: both Gandhi and Martin Luther King successfully used them in their political struggles. This behaviour pattern can be taught as an element within anti-violence strategies. Peace education should integrate and practise them, together with strategies of *Zivilcourage*. In political conflicts, 'non-violence' and *Zivilcourage* have become powerful instruments against bloody oppression. To a large extent, the breakdown of the socialist regime in the German Democratic Republic in 1989 was caused by peace demonstrations, later called 'candle demonstrations'.

Another non-aggressive step against violence is provided by symbolic actions. A famous symbolic action of Jesus was his politically symbolic entry into Jerusalem on a donkey, according to the prophetic announcement:

> Lo, your king comes to you,
> triumphant and victorious is he,
> humble and riding on a donkey,
> on a colt, the foal of a donkey.
>   (Zechariah 9: 9)

The Roman forces, by contrast, used to march in with full military pomp and weapons: the contrast was remembered.

The injunction about love of enemy and the symbolic actions were accompanied by an overall conversion of values. Jesus accepted among his followers and his twelve disciples men and women who had belonged to the class of those who were discriminated against and despised (for example, tax collectors, as in Mark 2: 14; Matt. 9: 9–13): he ate and drank with tax collectors and 'sinners' (see also Luke 7: 36–50). His acceptance of human beings was inclusive on the moral level, but hesitant on the ethnic level, for he felt himself sent by God primarily to his own people of Israel. (However, it was Jesus – before Paul – who transcended this boundary in specific situations: see Matt. 8: 5–13; Mark 7: 24–30.) He confronted the world with the message of forgiveness and practised it in loving inclusion (see above, the second model of inclusiveness).

Explicitly and convincingly, in words and deeds, Jesus withstood hate by love, and retaliation by reconciliation.

Conclusions

In Germany, the first broad approach in peace research and education for peace started at the end of the 1960s, with only a few pioneers before that time. Its beginnings were stimulated by the cold war between the western world and the eastern communist states and, additionally, by the dirty war in Vietnam. Mostly it was educationalists of the younger generation who were setting the agenda, and who characterized their approach as *kritische Friedenserziehung* ('critical peace education') (Wulf, 1973).

In religious education, some of us joined the new general debate from our own perspectives, looking back to the very origins of Christianity, to Jesus himself and his challenge of love for our enemies. We tried to take this demand seriously (Mokrosch, 1991). That was also new. In the past, war had been regarded as quite normal, justified from the standpoint of the Church as well as the state. Compared with past European history and its mentality, peace education is a very necessary and hopeful new beginning.

References

Axelrod, R. (1984). *The Evolution of Cooperation*, New York, Basic Books.
Barash, D. (1979). *The Whisperings Within*, New York, Harper & Row.
Comenius, J. A. (1995). *Panorthosia or Universal Reform*, trans. A. M. O. Dobbie, Sheffield, Sheffield Academic Press, chs 1–18, 27.
Daly, M. and Wilson, M. (1988). *Homicide*, New York, Aldine de Gruyter.
Darwin, C. (1859). *The Origin of Species*, London, John Murray.
Deutsch, R. D. (1998). 'Probing images of politicians and international affairs: creating pictures and stories of mind', in I. Eibl-Eibesfeldt and F. K. Salter (eds), *Indoctrinability, Ideology, and Warfare: Evolutionary Perspectives*, New York and Oxford, Berghan Books, pp. 301–21.
Eibl-Eibesfeldt, I. (1998). 'Us and others: the familial roots of ethnonationalism', in I. Eibl-Eibesfeldt and F. K. Salter (eds), *Indoctrinability, Ideology, and Warfare: Evolutionary Perspectives*, New York and Oxford, Berghan Books, pp. 21–53.
Frey, S. (1998). 'Prejudice and inferential communication: a new look at an old problem', in I. Eibl-Eibesfeldt and F. K. Salter (eds), *Indoctrinability, Ideology, and Warfare: Evolutionary Perspectives*, New York and Oxford, Berghan Books, pp. 189–217.
Fuoss-Bühler, S. (2006). *Werturteile in Westafrika. Eine texthermeneutische Interpretation des Umgangs mit Differenz*, Faculty of Social and Behavioural Sciences, University of Tübingen, Germany.
Gay, P. (1993). *The Cultivation of Hatred*, New York and London, W. W. Norton & Company.
Halisch, F. (1988). 'Empathy, Attribution und die Entwicklung des Hilfehandelns', in H.-W. Bierhoff and L. Montada (eds), *Altruism: Bedingungen der Hilfsbereitschaft*, Göttingen-Toronto-Zürich, Hogrefe, pp. 79–103.

Jean Paul (Friedrich Richter) (1807). 'Levana oder Erziehlehre', in *Sämtliche Werke*, Abt. I, Bd. 5, ed. Norbert Miller, München, Zweitausendeins, 1996.

Lötzsch, F. (2005). *Philosophie der Neuzeit im Spiegel des Judentums*, Münster, LIT Verlag.

Mackie, J. L. (1982). 'Cooperation, competition and moral philosophy', in A. Colman (ed.), *Cooperation and Competition in Humans and Animals*, Wokingham, Van Nostrand Reinhold.

Mokrosch, R. (1991). *Die Bergpredigt im Alltag: Anregungen und Materialien für die Sekundarstufe I/II*, Gütersloh, Gütersloher Verlaghaus.

Nipkow, K. E. (1975). *Grundfragen der Religionspädagogik* (4th edn, 1990), vol. 1, Gütersloh, Gütersloher Verlagshaus.

Nipkow, K. E. (2003). *God, Human Nature and Education for Peace: New Approaches to Moral and Religious Maturity*, Aldershot, Ashgate.

Nipkow, K. E. (2006). 'Christian education and the charge of indoctrination: a German perspective', in D. Bates, G. Durka and F. Schweitzer (eds), *Education, Religion and Society: Essays in Honour of John M. Hull*, London, Routledge, pp. 103–14.

Nipkow, K. E. (2007). *Der schwere Weg zum Frieden: Geschichte und Theorie der Friedenspädagogik von Erasmus bis zur Gegenwart*, Gütersloh, Gütersloher Verlagshaus.

Shaw, R. P. and Wong, Y. (1989). *Genetic Seed of Warfare: Evolution, Nationalism and Patriotism*, Boston, Unwin Hyman.

Theissen, G. (2004). *Die Jesusbewegung: Sozialgeschichte einer Revolution der Werte*, Gütersloh, Gütersloher Verlagshaus.

Vogel, C. (2000). *Anthropologische Spuren: Zur Natur des Menschen*, Stuttgart-Leipzig, Hirzel.

Weymar, E. (1961). *Das Selbstverständnis der Deutschen: Ein Bericht über den Geist des Geschichtsunterrichts der höheren Schulen im 19. Jahrhundert*, Stuttgart, Klett.

Wickler, W. (1991). *Die Biologie der Zehn Gebote: Warum die Natur für uns kein Vorbild ist*, München-Zürich, Piper.

Wulf, C. (ed.) (1973). *Kritische Friedenserziehung*, Frankfurt/M., Suhrkamp.

8
Does public religious education imply 'symbolic violence'? In search of a political theory of religious education

ELISABET HAAKEDAL

Introduction

Combining the phrases 'public religious education' and 'symbolic violence' courts negative associations, but I hope that it will also remind the reader of the principle of contextual understanding, a principle which is basic to this essay. The key concept in my title is symbolic violence, a concept that is central in the writings of the French sociologist Pierre Bourdieu. In the prelude to one of his later texts, he explains the concept as 'a gentle violence, imperceptible and invisible even to its victims, exerted for the most part through purely symbolic channels of communication and cognition (more precisely, misrecognition), recognition, or even feeling' (Bourdieu, 2001: 1–2). The language of this explanation is both value-laden and matter of fact, and thus in agreement with Bourdieu's reflexive epistemology (see below). One main source of the notion of symbolic violence is to be found in Bourdieu's early discussion of socialization and education (Bourdieu and Passeron, 1990) which is a field of particular scholarly and political controversy.

The word 'public' in my title delimits the essay's theme to those types of religious education in which the modern nation state has major interests and means of control. I particularly refer to the varieties of public religious education that are found in many European state school systems (Skeie, 2001). These varieties show different solutions to the historically rooted relationship between the democratic nation state and institutionalized religion. The former strong ties between European states and their established churches have now been broken or loosened as a result of pluralization. Political approaches to the cultural challenges of modern global migration vary from assimilation via integration to separation. State school systems have become central political instruments for handling cultural pluralism.

Publicly funded schools concerned mainly with the children of a local area may be called community schools. In pluralistic cultural contexts, such schools are generally expected to favour widely acknowledged values, such as tolerance and respect. Will religious education in such schools necessarily be symbolically violent in Bourdieu's sense? Must the pupils and the teachers (primarily women) who partake in public religious education be understood as unknowingly antagonistic agents, in the grip of the power structures and positions of a modern democracy? These basic questions are closely related to anthropological and epistemological themes and questions: language and highly developed communicative abilities are characteristics of the human species. Is language primarily an instrument of symbolic violence in a (subconscious) competition for power? Is communication basically competitive? If so, how should the element of symbolic competition be valued? Should it be encouraged or discouraged in the religious education of a community school praising tolerance and respect?

With issues and questions as those stated above, it is not satisfactory for religious education theory to consider religious education only as a (non-)subject or a (threatened) curriculum theme. In a recent study of the changing role of the religious education teacher in the Norwegian compulsory school, I have looked at religious education as an aspect of the whole school culture and its context (Haakedal, 2004). The approach in that study is primarily empirical, combining qualitative and quantitative methods, while researching regional and local school cultures and teacher practices. However, the study was motivated by an interest in theoretical and normative questions related to school values and a possibly hidden and symbolically violent curriculum. While exploring the connections between school culture and religious education practice in the classroom, I chose to draw on Bourdieu's general theory of practice and his field theory because these were extensive cultural and anthropological theories that take social conflict seriously. However, there seemed to be some implicit anthropological assumptions in Bourdieu's writings. By way of the Finnish theologian Tage Kurtén's linguistic analyses and moral philosophy I was able to focus and criticize these assumptions.

In this essay I shall briefly present some of Bourdieu's central concepts and systematic thinking. In doing so, I will draw on my study of religious education teachers. The presentation will be used as a stepping stone in order to emphasize some basic educational issues concerning anthropology and epistemology. Towards the end of the essay, I will discuss the concept of competition. In the translations of Bourdieu's texts which I have used, the concept of struggle dominates, while the concept of competition is used only a few times (Bourdieu and Wacquant, 1992: 98–107). I have already indicated a relationship between symbolic violence and the phenomenon of competition. I am thinking particularly of a type of linguistic competition connected with basic understanding and conceptualizing of human practice. With regard to method, my essay is analytical, using both sociological and philosophical arguments. In the discussion I will apply some of Kurtén's central concepts, among them the concepts of basic proposition, basic trust and life-view. The concept of trust especially carries some positive associations, which function as a counterbalance against the concept of symbolic violence. I will put forth an argument which acknowledges, with regard to the social function of community schools, the primacy of an anthropology based on moral philosophy. However, the discussion will also search for some kind of reconciliation between moral philosophy and an epistemology drawing on reflexive sociology. The purpose of the essay is to contribute to a political theory of public religious education.

Pierre Bourdieu's general theory of practice: a brief presentation

Contextuality and interrelatedness are two overarching characteristics in Bourdieu's research and academic thinking. At an early stage Bourdieu was a sociologist of education (Bourdieu and Passeron, 1990), arguing for the social and cultural reproductive function of the modern state school. Bourdieu soon extended his research to other social arenas, particularly those of cultural enterprise and preferences. His major empirical study is called *Distinction* (Bourdieu, 1984), meaning both 'difference' and 'superiority'. It should, for a better understanding of both, be read alongside his major theoretical work, *The Logic of Practice* (Bourdieu, 1990). The compilation of texts called *Masculine Domination* (Bourdieu, 2001) demonstrates how sex, gender and power are integrated themes in Bourdieu's research and theories.

The following statement belongs to the very basis of Bourdieu's thinking: 'Every power to exert symbolic violence, i.e. every power which manages to impose meanings and to impose them as legitimate by concealing the power relations which are the basis of its force, adds its own symbolic force to those power relations' (Bourdieu and Passeron, 1990: 4). The inner connection between the concepts of power, violence and force in this quotation calls attention to a basic tension in the social sciences, that is the evident theoretical diversity with regard to explanations of how individual actions are related to social structures. Different interpretations of teachers' relationship to school systems exemplify this tension very well. Bourdieu solves the tension by way of an implicit anthropology, arguing that at the basis of the human capacity of speech there is also a creative arbitrariness which involves the use of (symbolic) power.

A most important concept in Bourdieu's thought is 'habitus'. This signifies both the structural aspects (the embodied 'social baggage') and the agency aspects (the constructive individual prospects) of human contingencies. As a relational concept, habitus mediates between two other central concepts, 'field' and 'capital'. A field is the extension of homologous habituses. It may be defined as 'a network . . . of objective relations between positions' (Bourdieu and Wacquant, 1992: 97). Each field is held together by its capital, that is the goods and values that the members of the field aim at and – when scarce – compete for. A field is dominated by those in power who establish and maintain the principles for acquiring field capital.

Bourdieu distinguishes between three types of capital: economic, social and cultural capital. Economic capital refers to wealth and property measurable by way of money. Social capital relates to each person's supportive connections and networks. Cultural capital is primarily the ability to acquire and utilize valid knowledge and information at the right time and situation. Each type of capital includes an aspect of symbolic value connected to the ruling principles or impetuses of a field. Thus, different types of symbolic capital are at work in different fields. Bourdieu is particularly interested in the symbolic economy of the fields dominated by cultural capital. This is shown, for example, in his studies of the educational and academic institutions in France during the 1970s and 1980s (Bourdieu, 1988).

Bourdieu claims that people in general are socialized into their respective fields: they cannot just choose to become field members. Field membership is very much dependent on embodied, taken-for-granted practice. 'Doxa' is Bourdieu's conceptualization of this phenomenon, and a frequent metaphor for doxic practice is 'the feeling for the game' (Bourdieu, 1990). The educational system of a modern democracy is a major cultural field. Bourdieu's main explanation of the social and cultural reproductive function of public schooling is that ideas of meritocracy, equal opportunity and 'disinterested' knowledge are ingrained in the educational system's various subfields. He claims that the predominantly female habitus of teachers in the compulsory school is ambiguously doxic. Successful teachers show their occupational 'feeling for the game' very much by loyally and boldly transmitting a firm belief in the basic fairness of public education, thus securing their own middle-class social position. Since initial bourgeois socialization guarantees embodied cultural capital, children with this background will profit more from public education than will their classmates from the lower social strata (Bourdieu and Passeron, 1990).

The concepts of habitus, field, capital and doxa are all central to Bourdieu's general theory of practice, which is part and parcel of his overarching theory of interaction between the total space of objective social relationships and the total space of subjective tastes and preferences. Based on studies summarized in *Distinction*, he claims as a universal theory that the two main and interacting principles governing human practice are, on the one hand, the total amount of capital in one's possession and, on the other hand, the composition of this capital, that is its relative economic and cultural parts. These two principles enable Bourdieu to distinguish between hierarchical social strata and opposing fractions of each stratum. His social model also has a distinctive gender aspect. While men in general hold positions in fields dominated by economic capital, women as a rule occupy fields of cultural capital. Besides education, family and religion are examples of such predominantly cultural fields, all including strong aspects of symbolic economy.

Bourdieu's field theory seems to build on a linear understanding of differentiation. In the total space of social interaction, human aspiration (with its impetus for competition) means that new fields with a relative independence are constantly established, while older fields change or disappear. Contemporary organized religion is a field heavily based on a symbolic economy in which women especially invest (Bourdieu, 1998). Preparing food, decorating, running activities for children and youth, producing free magazines and pamphlets are examples of voluntary activities that secure praise from the leaders and status within the group. In the field of religion the struggle about the prevailing field principles turns on the question of legitimate religious power. Charismatic 'prophets' of nascent sects will challenge the 'priests' of the churches. The challenge of the expert contestants involves lay audiences. The more doxic the lay habituses are, the stronger the symbolic power of the leading experts. A 'classical', linear understanding of secularization seems to underpin Bourdieu's sociology of religion: thus, religious plurality will reduce doxa and encourage the deregulation and privatization of religion.

Although religion is a minor theme in Bourdieu's research, it is nevertheless an integrated aspect of his relational social model (Bourdieu, 1984). There is a clear parallel between his sociology of education and his sociology of religion: both education and religion are, to a large degree, based on symbolic and doxic field economies. When Bourdieu uses the term symbolic violence, he refers to the human tendency to base practices on what he claims are arbitrary dualistic perceptive (and linguistic) dichotomies. With male experts and female grassroots in the cultural fields, symbolic violence involves the intertwinement of the various types of capital (Bourdieu, 1990: 66–79; 2001: 5–53).

I find Bourdieu's theory of practice and his field theory generally persuasive and challenging. It is sensible, however, to bear in mind the contextuality of the theories. Compared with the Norwegian unitary state school system and its motto of 'one school for all', the French educational sector is much more competitive and seems to a much larger extent to be permeated by symbolic economy. It is also relevant that France has a fair number of private, religiously based schools, and that the state school system is based on a principle of secularity, excluding religious education as a separate subject.

In my study of the role of religious education teachers in the Norwegian compulsory school, I concluded that religious education at the lower levels of the educational system is hardly a separate subfield in Bourdieu's sense. The social arena of this education has been too insignificant for too long. Teachers with distinctive and rivalling expertise have not been queuing up to promote the subject. However, the study took place in the late 1990s, which was a crucial time in the history of Norwegian religious education. The 1997 school reform for the compulsory school meant a change from a confessional type of religious education, where the Lutheran clergy had a right of supervision, to a culturally based contextual type of religious education, where the various faith communities and life-view organizations in principle were equally positioned. During the preparation and the implementation of the reform, religious education frequently made it to the headlines of the national mass media – displaying distinctive rival expert positions. As the legal power of the Lutheran state Church was reduced at the same time as the power of the democratic state was emphasized, the reform may be interpreted according to linear secularization theory. On the other hand, the result of the reform may also be interpreted with reference to theories of cultural hegemony. In my study I generally agreed with Bourdieu's theory of cultural reproduction when I primarily interpreted the school teachers as municipal employees, influenced by the regional and local cultural contexts and practice. Rivalry over field expertise is obviously less discernible in the lower strata than in the upper strata of the total space of human interaction. However, because of the hot pluralistic public debate and the reduced influence of the state Church, I argued that after the 1997 reform there is a little more space for relatively distinguished and less doxic practices of religious education in the Norwegian compulsory school. In the contemporary pluralistic situation, the variety of (non-)religious habituses among the teachers will probably play a more significant role than before the reform.

After this presentation of the interrelatedness of the main concepts in Bourdieu's general theory of practice and its application to the Norwegian public school system and religious education teachers, I will examine some fundamental implications of Bourdieu's research and thinking.

A critical discussion of basic propositions: Bourdieu's implied anthropology and epistemology examined by way of research on life-views

In order to discuss Bourdieu's theory of practice in more depth and for the benefit of a political theory of public religious education, I will explain the concepts of basic proposition, trust and life-view, as used by Tage Kurtén at Åbo Academy in Finland. According to D. K. Naugle (2002: 73–82), Søren Kierkegaard coined the term 'life-view' as a Danish, and more existentialist, counterpart to the concept of 'world-view', which was much used by German philosophers in the nineteenth century. Both world-view and life-view refer to the assumption that the human mind tends to search for totality and wholeness.

The processes of differentiation, secularization and pluralization, especially with regard to public religious education, are important reasons for the development of research on individual life-views among theologians in Scandinavia (Skeie, 1999). Kurtén defines the concept of life-view as 'the verbal expressions of an (adult) individual's profound way of orienting himself in existence. A life-view therefore concerns beliefs, attitudes, values and ways of action related to this profound orientation' (1997: 110). I want to emphasize the existentialist flavour in the definition. By including 'ways of action', Kurtén deviates from traditions of life-view research more focused on its cognitive aspects, for example the tradition initiated by Anders Jeffner at the University of Uppsala (Kurtén, 1987). This particular matter, which may be called body-mindedness, is a point of similarity between the thinking and research of Kurtén and Bourdieu.

In an analysis of life-views among Finnish writers, Kurtén has recognized ways of expression that point to something self-evident, something fundamentally and culturally taken for granted. In order to signify such expressions of his informants, Kurtén applies the terms 'self-evident presuppositions' and 'basic convictions', referring to writings by the Welsh philosopher of religion D. Z. Phillips and to the later Wittgenstein's philosophy of language games (1997). By these references, Kurtén emphasizes the way context will always influence human life, both language and practice. Because of socialization, most people integrate certain basic assumptions and values. When we share a familiar context, we know its codes and values. There is no need to establish the 'rules of the game' each time we meet and interact. Listening to taken-for-granted elements in people's language, Kurtén has proposed and analysed a number of types of life-views to be found among Finnish writers (1995). Again I find a point of similarity: the self-evident in Kurtén's texts is a reminder of the phenomenon of doxa in Bourdieu's terminology.

Kurtén also links 'basic convictions' to the term 'basic trust', arguing both empirically and theoretically that there is a general feature of basic trust in all life-views. According to him, a taken-for-granted trust is basic in human life: basic trust precedes mistrust. Kurtén maintains this in a discussion with an opponent who claims that trust and mistrust function on the same level, both representing a particular life-view or paradigm, for example the contrast between 'religious' and 'scientific' thinking. If the opponent were correct, there would be no point in further communication and no possibility of understanding: there would only be a stated disagreement. Kurtén argues against this by way of language analysis. He points to the distinction between trust and reliance, the latter containing an element of rational consideration, which the former does not because it functions at the level of self-evidence (1997: 71–80).

In another text, Kurtén gives an example of a possibly meaningful communication between a religious and a more secular outlook on life. Analysing the concept of 'absolute values' in the context of work and consumption, he finds that 'the borderline between what we would call moral and religious language is not very clear', and that human life as an absolute value seems to unite the two types of life-views (1998a: 135, 141). With basic trust as an anthropological meta-level term, Kurtén has prepared the ground, so to speak, for comparing different types of life-views. Among the Finnish writers he found life-views based on five types of trust: trust in something transcendent, trust in the social community, trust in life and nature, trust in one's own self or ego, and finally a kind of 'nihilism' that expresses an attitude with hardly any traces of basic trust (1995).

I find that the conceptual distinctions made by Kurtén shed some light on the notions of doxic ambiguity and symbolic violence in Bourdieu's texts. Both authors emphasize the hidden, self-evident values and the way they function as an impetus for human interaction. On the whole, however, their anthropologies differ with regard to content and presentation.

In my study of religious education teachers, I have compared what I call the 'academic projects' of Tage Kurtén and Pierre Bourdieu in an attempt to span the huge distance between the (admittedly minor) subjective aspects of teacher role formation and the structural aspects of institutional school culture. The challenges involved in this attempt are related both to the academic fields of the two researchers and to their own explicit and implicit life-views. With their anthropologies in mind, I will now discuss Bourdieu's theory of practice, using the main concepts from Kurtén's studies of life-views.

As a sociologist, Bourdieu is an extremely ambitious theorist, challenging opponents to test his general theories empirically and statistically. He contests other sociological 'schools' of research. He claims that his theories are valid for academic organizations and practice in general, and, writing polemically, he makes the philosophical enterprise redundant. These standpoints are related to the epistemology included in Bourdieu's reflexive sociology. He maintains that a double reflexivity is necessary for constructing social research projects. Both researcher (subject) and informants (object) occupy positions in the total social space. Therefore self-reflexivity is as important as reflexivity with regard to the language and practice of the informants.

The main point about the self-reflexivity of a researcher is, according to Bourdieu, his or her relational position in a field of homologous, aspiring habituses. To stress individual biographical details will only further the relativity of multiple interpretations. Bourdieu's self-reflecting task has been to reveal empirically the struggle for power positions in what he calls the intellectual field. This is the dominated field, as opposed to the dominating field, within the upper, most independent strata of the total social space. The intellectual field is also a field where symbolic economy will manifest itself, for example through doxic adherence to arbitrary conceptual dichotomies (Bourdieu and Wacquant, 1992). Bourdieu claims that intellectual self-reflexivity within the subfield of sociology necessitates a break with doxic research terminology. A new, alternative terminology will succeed only to the extent that the 'prophets' of the field are able to win a response from sufficient field members (1987).

The consequence of this type of 'constructivist structural' epistemology is a permanent state of intellectual competition and strategic academic alliances. In an article about the relationship between the fields of sociology and history, Bourdieu gives an example which involves the study of religion:

> These are cases where that [that is, the use of 'native' concepts in scientific theorizing] can be scientifically and politically very dangerous: for example, in the sociology of religion, particularly the so-called universal religions, when religious ideas are used to discuss religion, the science of religion risks becoming scientific religion. (1999: 174)

It seems to me that Bourdieu here plays with words ('science of religion' and 'scientific religion'), and that, in this case, his notion of 'arbitrary conceptual dichotomies' may be turned against himself. The possibility of communication between scholars involved in different language games depends on a will to empathic listening as well as shrewd language analysis (see the discussion above between Kurtén and his opponent about the alleged contrast between 'religious' and 'scientific' thinking). In my study of Norwegian religious education teachers, I claim that Bourdieu maintains a linear secularization theory and a basic epistemological materialism (Haakedal, 2004: 80–90, 354). Below I will slightly modify this claim while referring to Bourdieu's metaphorical and ambiguous language. My aim is to encourage an epistemology and an anthropology underpinning a political theory of public religious education.

The constructivist aspect of Bourdieu's reflexive sociology does not mean that he holds a relativistic type of epistemology. He strongly believes in scientific truth and in the moral character of rational, scientific enterprise. Although he applies the epistemological distinction between subject and object, he still fights it, and thus exceeds the dichotomy between modern objectivism and postmodern subjectivism. Bourdieu's epistemology resembles critical theory in a broad sense, that is, any social theory that is at the same time explanatory, normative, practical and self-reflexive. For Bourdieu, science has the prerogative over the philosophy of science. His favourite methodological tool seems to be the statistical method of correspondence analyses (1984: 260–1). Altogether, this makes a dialogue between Bourdieu's theories and the theories of moral philosophy difficult.

In the following comment on the moral aspects of political practice Bourdieu most probably addresses his more humanistically oriented fellow sociologists.

> There is nothing discouraging, except perhaps for some 'do-gooders', in the fact that those whose task it is to criticize, unveil, and hold accountable ... will not be able to contribute to the creation of conditions for the institution of the rule of virtue unless the logic of their respective fields guarantees them the profits of the universal which are at the basis of their *libido virtutis*. (1998: 145)

The comment alludes mockingly to the field of (western) philosophy with its basic dichotomy of 'good' and 'evil'. But it also suggests that, in the symbolic economy of the overlapping intellectual and political field, there is an impetus at work that encourages the individual subject to claim universal (and rational) values. I would claim that this paradoxical relationship been cultural and economic capital is also attached to the field of western liberal education.

There is no explicit anthropology in Bourdieu's texts. His theory of practice explains human behaviour relationally. For Bourdieu to write about the human being per se would be a practical self-contradiction (Bourdieu and Wacquant, 1992). Implicitly, though, his texts reveal a picture of human enterprise which accentuates certain features above others. To Bourdieu, human beings are creatures of barter and competition, including an impetus to dominate. It may be that it is his preoccupation with the power found in the fields of the highest social strata that results in such a picture. Bourdieu did not follow up his early empirical research in the sociology of (compulsory) education. However, he has continually studied the historical conditions of the fields where reason and scientific knowledge are at stake, that is, the academic institutions. To Bourdieu, 'the scholastic fallacy ... consists in injecting *meta-* into discourses and practices', that is, in disregarding the economic and social roots of the phenomenon of reasoning.

> We must, by taking historicist reduction to its logical conclusion, seek the origins of reason not in a human 'faculty', that is, a *nature*, but in the very history of these peculiar microcosms in which agents struggle, in the name of the universal, for the legitimate monopoly over the universal. (1998: 130, 139)

Although I think Bourdieu deliberately plays down the role of philosophy, I agree with him that good reasoning takes economic and historical contexts into account. My study of Norwegian religious education teachers mainly supports Bourdieu's theory of a doxic ambiguity in the habitus of the general teacher. Most of the teachers in my study simply confirmed general values, such as tolerance, solidarity, empathy and justice, taking for granted the social democratic mainstream ideology (the harmonized Lutheran-Humanistic 'cultural heritage') of the Norwegian centralized compulsory school. In the practices of some teachers, however, there were signs of an awareness of difference and conflict. In these situations, teachers generally appealed to their pupils' conscience and empathy through a reference to common values. Only a few teachers were concerned about the further social effects of streamlined schooling (Haakedal, 2004: 215–39, 320–3, 380–403).

The very relationalism of Bourdieu's theory of practice creates a continuation and interdependence between the largest global institution and the smallest social group. Between the lines, he tells us that human beings are existentially vulnerable creatures struggling for social acknowledgement. Values are inevitably ingrained in human practice, and Bourdieu ends up with a type of result-oriented morality inspired by a universal wish for the greatest amount of freedom for the greatest number of people. Realistically, only people in the privileged upper strata are able to initiate substantial social change. Still, his '*realpolitik* of reason' is governed by a simple programme of 'working to universalize the conditions of access to universality' (Bourdieu, 1998: 137).

Bourdieu pictures human beings as relationally striving and competing creatures. Towards the end of one of his books, however, he seems to include another aspect of being human. In the dyadic loving relationship which is the elementary social unit, the principle of love, trust and perfect reciprocity may be found. Although Bourdieu in this context applies general terms like experiences of love or friendship, he also uses ambiguously metaphoric language ('the gift of self, and of one's body, a sacred object') that seems to limit the 'seemingly miraculous truce in which domination seems dominated' to durable and non-instrumental sexual relationships. One may ask whether Bourdieu allows for non-instrumental and non-competitive acts outside this type of loving partnership. What about stable triads of generous friends, or even larger bodies or institutions of symbolic economy? Bourdieu claims that the dyadic loving relationship may include a spontaneous and creative endearing language and thus it 'becomes endowed with the power to rival successfully all the consecrations that are ordinarily asked of the institutions and rites of "Society", the secular substitute for God' (2001: 109–12). This quotation is another indication of a linear theory of secularization: just as reason has reduced the power of 'God-language' (that is, the 'orthodoxy' of established religion), so in turn other 'orthodox' social institutions' euphemizing symbolic power may be challenged by heterodox language. I suggest that, to Bourdieu, this is a truthful, materialistic language. On the other hand, the quotation may also indicate that trusting and loving non-competitive relationships include aspects of symbolic economy which are not measurable or convertible, but are still experienced and yearned for. Here is probably one reason for Bourdieu's use of metaphors and linguistic ambiguity. By emphasizing the human communicative and creative capacity, he claims to balance a structural social realism with an ambitious universalistic constructivism, implying non-reducible moral human values.

In the introduction to this essay, I asked whether the pupils and the teachers partaking in public religious education must be understood as unknowingly antagonistic agents, and their practice must ultimately be seen as a hidden instrument for reproducing the prevailing power structures. Will compulsory religious education in a state institution of community schools necessarily be symbolically violent? Both before and after the 1997 Norwegian school reform, I observed episodes of religious education where the communication between teacher and pupil seemed characterized by mutual respect, humour and inquisitiveness. On the other hand, I also observed obviously authoritative and implicitly formative teachers on behalf of traditional Lutheranism. However, I think my questions can be answered empirically only to a small degree. The modern field of democratic education covers the social strata of a nation state from top to bottom. Obviously, there are several contextual forces at work with regard to the possibility for change in publicly funded education.

In my study of religious education teachers I have contrasted Kurtén's basically humanistic life-view with Bourdieu's seemingly naturalistic life-view (Haakedal, 2004: 64–107). In this essay I have also compared the concepts and arguments of the two scholars, but this time reached conclusions which may facilitate a dialogue between their positions. Bourdieu's insistence on a break between the ordinary language of common sense and a constructed scientific language is somehow modified by what may be called 'miraculous love-talk'. Human beings are not altogether creatures of barter and competition. The theory of struggling, competitive fields seems to be weaker in the lower than in the higher social strata. Even Bourdieu's deliberately ambiguous language (for example, the metaphor of 'miracle') may be interpreted as allowing for a type of reality which scientific reason is not able to include, but which may nevertheless be experienced as true. While Kurtén employs the concept of meta-language in his thinking, distinguishing it from the common-sense language, he still insists that empirical research is a necessary methodological first step in his contextual theology (1998b). In my next section, I will discuss the relevance of Bourdieu's theory of practice (including his anthropology) to public religious education. I will also draw on Kurtén's thinking. Of particular interest here are the moral aspects of the phenomenon of competition.

Religious education in community schools: competition and cooperative trust

Granted that communication and morality are distinctive features of the human species, the phenomenon of competition seems integrated in human interaction. A basic, anthropological understanding of competition involves a notion of (at least possible) conflicting interests between groups, rather than individuals. Individual aspects of competition are not excluded, though. Competition is more apparent among leaders and experts in the upper strata of the social space, but even at this level competing actors are generally dependent on social response. Thus, the moral aspect of competition becomes evident. Each individual is morally responsible. However, morality is at the same time a contextual phenomenon. The intuitive morality of embodied practice is thus acknowledged because it points to a potential for socially responsible change.

This type of reasoning has profited from Bourdieu's theory of human practice as a total social space and a dialectically corresponding space of distinctive tastes. The dialectics of the two constructed spaces involves various degrees of competition between social strata, and between different and interrelated principles of what is valuable and worthwhile. With regard to a political theory of public religious education, the gender aspect of Bourdieu's social model is probably more interesting than the power aspect, although the two are clearly related. Above I have suggested that Bourdieu is relying on a linear theory of differentiation, partly understanding religion as a relatively independent cultural field based on female symbolic economy, and partly implying the privatization of religion. In the first case, his understanding of religion has negative connotations, closely related to the doxic ambiguity of (mainly female) schoolteachers. In the second case, I have suggested a more functional understanding of religion, and an acknowledgment of the critical potential of 'heterodox' spirituality. Both these ways of understanding late modern religion are likely to take the perceptual and linguistic dichotomy of a public and a private sphere for granted, and thus underestimate the potential of women as social actors.

The British sociologist of religion Linda Woodhead uses a typology of religion that distinguishes between religions of difference, religions of humanity and spiritualities of life. She claims that classical, linear secularization theories have been gender blind. Discussing the second type of religion, she refers to empirical studies documenting a female religiosity which sustains the social capital of local communities (Woodhead, 2001). This is what I also found in my study of Norwegian religious education teachers. Agreeing in general with Bourdieu's theory of the educational institution's ingrained conservative function, I suggest that local community schools may still have the potential to contribute to an upbringing reflexively based on the idea and practice of trusting, non-instrumental relationships. Symbolic economy will be an important aspect of such community schools, but within a late modern, pluralistic society dominant doxic practice that may be challenged by competing, persevering educational practices.

Community schools are expected to favour widely acknowledged values, such as tolerance and respect. With a high degree of doxic practice, these values tend to become general phrases with little concrete meaning. Or, rather, teachers often lack a language to be able to distinguish, discuss and deal with situations where tolerance and respect are undermined. Although teachers may handle challenging situations by way of moral intuition, I see no reason why the anthropological notions discussed above – including concepts like communicative ability, morality and competition – may not become an integrated part of teachers' speech acts and professional language. Public religious education is certainly a stimulus for teacher education with regard to such competences.

In pluralistic societies, an important aspect of public religious education is plurality of content, not only with regard to religious traditions, but also with regard to acknowledging the diverse life-worlds of the pupils. The plurality and diversity of religious education makes it even more pressing to include a basically anthropological understanding of competition. According to a contextual, reflexive epistemology, there is an element of dialogical negotiation about meaning in all communication. Here I again bring in the concept of basic trust as understood by Tage Kurtén. The basic trust of various life-views facilitates dialogue because it points to the anthropological and contextual basis of all communication.

Public religious education in pluralistic societies is not necessarily doxic, because it does not have to be based on arbitrarily violent perceptual dichotomies. Arbitrariness is best fought by encouraging critical openness and stimulating dialogical meaning-making processes. Again, research with a gender aspect may help to explain how an anthropological concept of competition does not need to imply the powerful use of dichotomizing language. Although competition in everyday language involves the dualistic notion of winning and losing, the concept also implies connotations like interactive improvement and rivalry for the better. Tove Nicolaisen (2001), Heid Leganger-Krogstad (2003) and Heinz Streib (2001) are all contextual religious educationalists who have explored the ordinary language of everyday conversations, either between women of different religions or between children in religious education lessons. This type of dialogue is seen as different from the official dialogue of religious experts. When body language (role models, fashion, and so on) is included in human communication, it is easier to grasp the connections between morality, education and competition.

Linking a theory of public religious education to contextual epistemology and moral philosophy does not imply any kind of relativism. In the field of intellectuals, whose capital is predominantly cultural, members compete over the universality of their field interests. Such competition involves a moral understanding of truth. Truth is decided neither only by logical, rational theorizing, nor only by empirical testing. Truth is also about practice and action, including an existential, moral level as well as a mundane functional level. Thus, there is an interrelationship between universalistic claims and situational, contextual action.

Conclusion

In this essay, I have introduced Pierre Bourdieu's general theory of practice and, especially, explored its basic anthropological and epistemological assumptions. In doing so, I have made use of the concepts of basic trust and life-view as understood by Tage Kurtén. I have thus been able to discuss competition as a phenomenon ingrained in human existence. Bourdieu's 'academic project' – interpreted in the light of Kurtén's theory and research – is relevant for a political theory of public religious education, not least because it implicitly focuses on human competition. In my discussion of competition, I have found that a gender aspect is particularly important. With regard to religious education, female social practice may be reflexively competitive in a way which underlines the intrinsic importance of religion and life-views in symbolic economies. I have argued that public religious education need not be 'symbolically violent', in Bourdieu's doxic meaning. Especially, religious education teachers in pluralistic contexts may engage reflexively in competing for universal human virtues.

References

Bourdieu, P. (1984). *Distinction: A Social Critique of the Judgement of Taste*, London, Routledge & Kegan Paul.
Bourdieu, P. (1987). 'Legitimation and structured interests in Weber's sociology of religion', in S. Lash and S. Whimster (eds), *Max Weber: Rationality and Modernity*, London, Allen & Unwin, pp. 119–36.
Bourdieu, P. (1988). *Homo Academicus*, Cambridge, Polity Press.
Bourdieu, P. (1990). *The Logic of Practice*, Cambridge, Polity Press.
Bourdieu, P. (1998). *Practical Reason: On the Theory of Action*, Cambridge, Polity Press.
Bourdieu, P. (1999). 'On the relationship between sociology and history in Germany and France. Pierre Bourdieu interviewed by Lutz Raphael',

in F. Engelstad and R. Kalleberg (eds), *Social Time and Social Change: Perspectives on Sociology and History*, Oslo, Scandinavian University Press, pp. 157–86.

Bourdieu, P. (2001). *Masculine Domination*, Cambridge, Polity Press.

Bourdieu, P. and Passeron, J.-C. (1990). *Reproduction in Education, Society and Culture* (in French, 1970; in English, 1977; new introduction in the English 1990 edn), London, Sage.

Bourdieu, P., and Wacquant, L. J. D. (1992). *An Invitation to Reflexive Sociology*, Cambridge, Polity Press.

Haakedal, E. (2004). ' "Det er jo vanlig praksis hos de fleste her . . ." Religionslærerrolle, livstolkning og skolekulturell ritualisering – en religionspedagogisk studie av grunnskolelæreres handlingsrom på 1990-tallet', unpublished, Oslo, Det teologiske fakultet, Universitetet i Oslo.

Heimbrock, H.-G., Scheilke, C. T., and Schreiner, P. (eds) (2001). *Towards Religious Competence: Diversity as a Challenge for Education in Europe*, Münster, LIT Verlag.

Kurtén, T. (1987). *Grunder för en kontextuell teologi. Ett wittgensteinsk sätt att närma sig teologin i discussion med Anders Jeffner*, Åbo, Åbo Akademis Förlag.

Kurtén, T. (1995). *Tillit, verklighet och värde*, Nora, Nya Doxa.

Kurtén, T. (1997). *Bakom livshållningen. Studier i moderna livsåskådningar och deras begreppsliga förutsättningar*, Åbo, Åbo Akademi.

Kurtén, T. (1998a). 'Absolute values, work and consumption. Some conceptual remarks', in T. Kurtén, *Det handlande subjektet och det moraliska kravet. Studier kring etikens och trons roll i mänskligt handlande*, Åbo, Åbo Akademi, pp. 120–46.

Kurtén, T. (1998b). *Teologi i nutida sammanhang. Studier i kontextuell teologi, dess begreppslighet, metodologi och genomförande*, Åbo, Institutionen för systematisk teologi vid Åbo Akademi.

Leganger-Krogstad, H. (2003). 'Dialogue among young citizens in a pluralistic religious education classroom', in R. Jackson (ed.), *International Perspectives on Citizenship, Education and Religious Diversity*, London, RoutledgeFalmer, pp. 169–90.

Naugle, D. K. (2002). *Worldview: The History of a Concept*, Grand Rapids, MI, Eerdmans.

Nicolaisen, T. (2001). 'Dialog i KRL-faget', *Prismet. Pedagogisk tidsskrift*, 52, 2, 73–84.

Skeie, G. (1999). ' "Empirisk livsåskådningsforskning" og dens relevans for religionspedagogisk forskning', *Tidsskrift for kirke, religion og samfunn*, 12, 2, 149–68.

Skeie, G. (2001). 'Citizenship, identity politics and religious education', in H.-G. Heimbrock, C. T. Scheilke and P. Schreiner (eds), *Towards Religious Competence: Diversity as a Challenge for Education in Europe*, Münster, LIT Verlag, pp. 237–52.

Streib, H. (2001). 'Inter-religious negotiations. Case studies on students' perception of and dealing with religious diversity', in H.-G. Heimbrock, C. T. Scheilke and P. Schreiner (eds), *Towards Religious Competence: Diversity as a Challenge for Education in Europe*, Münster, LIT Verlag, pp. 129–49.

Woodhead, L. (2001). 'Feminism and the sociology of religion: From gender-blindness to gendered difference', in R. K. Fenn (ed.), *The Blackwell Companion to the Sociology of Religion*, Oxford, Blackwell, pp. 67–84.

9
Public and personal peace in life, religion and education: an exercise in ordinary theology

JEFF ASTLEY

In this chapter, I first introduce the conceptualization of 'ordinary theology' and discuss how it should be explored. I then report on a small-scale study of the understanding of the concept of peace by a group of ordinary theologians, and bring this into dialogue with some biblical, theological and psychological reflections on the categories of public and personal peace, before addressing the educational implications of this discussion.

Ordinary theology

I label the theological reflections of those Christians who have received no formal theological training, 'ordinary (Christian) theology'. The beliefs of such non-expert religious adherents are routinely ignored by academic theology, and I have argued that we ought to do more to remedy this ignorance (Astley, 2002; see also Thomson, 2006).

Theology is essentially the attempt to speak reflectively of the divine, or more generically of what we value enough to worship. The overwhelming majority of 'God-talkers' have not studied theology formally; but if they speak and think about the things of God with any seriousness at all, they are engaged in doing their own theology. Ordinary theology is in every way a *lay theology*. It takes us, as Edward Farley would urge, 'beyond the clerical paradigm' (see Farley, 1996). In doing so, we should note that ordinary theology recognizes its learning context much better than does academic theology (or 'theologically-educated theology'). Unlike the theology of the erudite, which strives to rise above context (and sometimes thinks that it has escaped all contexts) and to forget its more humble beginnings (from its mother's knee onwards), most people realize that their beliefs are personal, perhaps idiosyncratic, and bear upon their brow the marks of their formation. 'That's what *I* think, anyway', people say in research interviews. 'I came to see it that way when . . .'; 'As a parent, I suppose I'm bound to feel that . . .'; 'You see, I came from this background, so naturally I think . . .'. Ordinary theology is therefore manifestly a *contextual theology*. And because those who are innocent of theological training are more likely to show their workings than to display the completed calculations, they often reveal a theology-in-construction with an explicit and particular direction and concrete motivation.

Ordinary theology comprises what have been called 'subterranean theologies' (Martin, 1967: 74–6). Not only is such theology 'below the level of universally available, publicly articulated religious ideas'; it is also 'closer to the immediate experience and consciousness of ordinary people' than official theological formulations (Towler, n.d.: 5). Others have spoken of this as 'folk religion' or 'common religion', but I prefer to use a phrase that acknowledges that the phenomenon has a serious cognitive, and even critical, theological dimension (Astley, 2002: 88–95).

Ordinary theology is above all a *religious theology,* keeping closer to the religious impulses – the spirituality that drives people – than does much academic theology. As a style of theology, it is not so much a perspective *on* theology as a perspective *in* or *of* theology: it is more a 'kneeling theology' than either a 'sitting theology' or a 'holding-at-arm's-length theology', as others have characterized the distinction (but see below, p. 154). So my concern here is with theology as a self-involving expression of a person's deepest spirituality. A person's ordinary theology is an articulation of that which is creative and salvific for her or him, that which heals and restores and gives life – that is, their faith, spiritual wisdom and knowledge of God, and the deep value convictions on which they rest their lives and their deaths.

It is often best described as *onlook theology*. Donald Evans's 'onlooks' are not to be reduced to 'views' or 'opinions'; they are less intellectual than 'conceptions', but imply more commitment than do 'outlooks' or 'perspectives'. Onlooks take the form: 'I look on x as y'; 'I look on death as the mockery of human hopes'; 'I look on my work as a vocation' (or a necessary evil); 'I look on this mentally handicapped adult as a person and a child of God' (see Evans, 1963: 125). Onlooks express our feelings, our attitudes for and against something, our personal involvement with and our behavioural intentions towards it. In these ways, they bestow status. According to Vincent Brümmer (1981: 260), onlooks assert the *meaning* of something: in religions that assume a position of theological realism, they do this by relating that something to God.

Researching ordinary theology
Research into ordinary theology needs to be a multidisciplinary task, drawing on the theoretical and practical insights, and empirical methods and data, of a number of subject areas and disciplines. It certainly requires in-depth *empirical* study, using the appropriate tools of the social scientist – including in-depth interviews and participant observation. As a preliminary, pilot studies (as here) can explore the language of ordinary theology through discussion groups, questionnaires or dictionary studies.

But a full study of ordinary theology requires to be supplemented by *theological* work, for all theology must be subject to reflective theological and philosophical analysis. I believe that the ordinary theology of believers (and, indeed, the 'atheology' of non-believers) deserves the same careful analysis and critique as that which is routinely given to the reflections of professional theologians and scholarly critics of theology. Only by taking people's theology that seriously can we discover what ordinary people really believe and why, and begin to evaluate the strengths and weaknesses of the content and form of their believing and reflection. The fact that ordinary theology is usually not well formulated is not an adequate excuse for ignoring it. But it does mean that we need to be particularly sensitive in offering an account of the language and arguments that people use when they speak of God and religion, or of other things that they take very seriously. This descriptive work is essentially a task of conceptual analysis, as is much theological study. But a Christian theological study of ordinary theology must also include the *evaluation* of such beliefs, both from the standpoint and using the resources of Christian scripture, doctrine and ethics, as well as by employing the tools and criteria of the philosopher. In this way, the study of ordinary theology can claim the status of a real theological study, which in this case is directed towards the everyday believer.

Ordinary theology is itself more sympathetic to such evaluation, and less uncritical and naive, than many commentators are willing to acknowledge. Certainly, many ordinary believers are concerned about the plausibility and defensibility of their faith. And, despite all I have said elsewhere about the importance of formation and the *a*rational dynamics that sometimes ultimately undergird it (for example, Astley, 1994: ch. 5), some critical ('judging', 'assessing', 'evaluating') element is crucial, at least for most adults, if they are to own their faith. (Hence ordinary theology is not *wholly* practised in the posture of prayer.) Others have written of an inherently self-critical element within churches, where the evaluative norms are internal to the community, given in its beliefs and practices (Kelsey, 1992: 157; Frei, 1992: 2; see also Osmer, 1990: 226; Farley, 1996: 35).

So I am not advocating a 'merely descriptive' study of ordinary theology, which is in no sense analytical, corrective, reconstructive or *normative*. The task I commend here is not solely that of describing the beliefs of ordinary Christians, it also engages in theological judgements about their beliefs. Yet even description is not entirely untouched by theological evaluation. Don Browning argues that 'it would be a great mistake to believe that descriptive theology is simply a sociological task' (Browning, 1991: 47), because even in *describing* your theology I am implicitly engaged in an hermeneutical conversation between my theology and yours, at least to some extent. Hence 'listening is never perfectly neutral' (ibid.: 286), but is itself a theological act.

Such theological listening is well exemplified in the work of the radical Christian theologian, Don Cupitt, who holds that 'ordinary language is the best radical theologian, and significantly sharper than the professionals' (Cupitt, 1999a: Foreword; cf. 2005: 6, 16). His own research goes well beyond exploring the language of traditional religious believers, by engaging in a wide-ranging study of 'the philosophy of life and the religious and moral ideas that belong to us because they are built into our language'. He calls his method *ordinary-language theology* or *democratic theology*, and defines it as 'a descriptive study of the common religious philosophy' (Cupitt, 1999b: 102; 2000: Introduction; 2005: 15; cf. Woodhead, 2004).

Peace studies

Although Cupitt does not deal directly with peace language anywhere in his writings, one of his books provides an account of eschatological, prophetic and kingdom-type language (Cupitt, 2000). In the perceptive account he gives there of the dispersed, secular application of religious language, he draws attention to the phrase 'peace of mind' as it is used in a financial context, along with other related terms of the old theology, such as 'provident', 'assurance', 'mutual', 'interest' – even 'saving' (ibid.: 40; cf. Selby, 1997; Hull, 1999). This analysis fits Cupitt's own postmodern and post-realist theology, for which there is no other world or life than this one, and 'the way to religious happiness' is by what he calls *solar-living* – in the sense of 'ardently and unreservedly committing oneself to life in all its admitted contingency and transience' (Cupitt, 2000: 93, cf. 53). This is not so much a moral panacea as a spirituality (Cupitt, 2001a: 107), in which true peace of mind can come only from a radical acceptance of life as it truly is – and for Cupitt that is what, and all, 'God' means (Cupitt, 2001b: 26, cf. 50–2; 2003: 16–17).

If we adopt a similar method of theological listening to study more traditional believers, however, we should not expect to find ourselves faced by data that demand such a radical interpretation. My own reflections draw on a pilot study among adult 'ordinary theologians' in Britain – using questionnaires with open questions, focused interviews and discussion in small groups – to determine their understanding of how the English word 'peace' is used. Altogether, data were obtained from some twenty-nine individuals, all Christian churchgoers.

Public peace

This study suggests that current English usage falls into two fairly clearly demarcated categories, *public* and *personal*. Public peace is located in a society or nation, and is largely defined negatively, as the absence of war or other conflict. Although the spirituality and morality of the personal world is seen as affecting this (for example when people commit themselves to 'make peace, not war' – see the next section), the language of 'peace talks' and 'peace treaties' is remote from the personal involvement of most ordinary people. Closer to home, peace as an absence of civil disorder is expressed in a range of rather archaic phrases that we may still hear voiced in the theatre of English law: 'keeping (or breaking) the peace', 'Justice of the Peace' and 'the queen's peace' (that is, the general peace of the realm as secured by law).

Everyday speech has plenty of phrases that capture this public definition of peace as the absence of hostility. The way they are employed, however, suggests that many of them have been imported from the wider discourse of historical or contemporary politics. Some of the phrases listed below were often used in interviews and discussions as if they were quotations. They seem to have come to people through the mass media and were therefore voiced in the accents of newsreaders. (I have enclosed in inverted commas the language that particularly betrays such an origin.)

Here are the phrases from this study that seem to fall into the category of 'public peace':

- keep the peace
- fighting for peace
- peace talks/treaty
- peace time/a time of peace
- 'peace process'/negotiation/initiative
- a peaceful demonstration
- 'peace at any price/in our time'
- 'a fragile peace'
- the queen's peace
- the Peace Movement
- 'peace with honour'
- peacekeepers
- Justice of the Peace

Personal peace

There is, however, a more positive and concrete understanding of peace to be found in more personal discourse. Men and women speak of, yearn for, and sometimes claim to have experienced, a *personal peace*. They call it 'peace of mind' – remember Cupitt – or sometimes just 'a bit of peace'. At its core, this is a deep state of mind, spirit, heart or soul that is reflected in and may be evoked by a more outer experience of the 'peace and quiet' of a country walk away from the motorway, or of the family home restored to some semblance of serenity at the end of the school holidays.

To wish this peace for others, by means of Christmas card greetings, for example, lies close to bestowing a religious form of blessing, even when it is done by those who have no particular or explicit religious convictions.

One extension of this notion of personal peace is as a euphemism for death, and my respondents quoted a number of phrases from gravestones and obituary notices: 'at peace', 'rest in peace', 'died peacefully in his sleep'. Another usage frequently voiced in this study brings this personal peace closer to the negative connotations of public peace. I am thinking here of the widely acknowledged virtues of 'holding one's peace' (that is, keeping silent) and 'making peace'. Both of these are activities done for the sake of harmonious, tranquil relationships within the family, or among friends or colleagues.

I found that people spoke warmly and enthusiastically of this species of peace (personal peace). It seems that they locate it within the mind, or in that more personal space in which the individual and his or her relationships can best find sustenance. The most frequently repeated phrases were:

- really peaceful
- I'd just like some . . . / Oh, for a bit of . . . peace [and quiet]
- Peace, man (a slightly ironic 1960s reference!)
- holding one's peace
- wishing you peace
- 'peace at the last' (Newman)
- peace of mind
- peace, perfect peace (see the hymn by E. H. Bickersteth)
- shattered my peace (negatively, as an act that destroys this)
- making peace
- 'at peace'
- 'rest in peace'

Occasionally, quasi-religious phraseology was employed that reveals the link between everyday speech about peace and its biblical roots, in phrases such as:

- peace offering
- peace, heavenly peace
- no peace for the wicked (see Isaiah 48: 22)

Biblical and spiritual peace

While the fundamental sense of the Hebrew word 'shalom' is well-being, understood in terms of wholeness, health and stability (see Genesis 43: 27; Judges 19: 20; Jeremiah 16: 14), and eirene in Greek originally meant an absence of war, the biblical concept gradually broadened to refer to 'a harmony of wholeness, peace and justice' that is God's gift (Lebacqz, 1998: 167). It seems to be used in the Judaeo-Christian scriptures with two main denotations:

1. with reference to social situations within a 'peaceable kingdom' that is free from war or conflict, often as a result of personal and social reconciliation (for example Leviticus 26: 6; 1 Samuel 7: 14; 1 Kings 4: 24; Psalm 122; Matthew 5: 9; Luke 19: 42);
2. with reference to the personal conditions of reconciliation with God, and the personal experience of – or hope for – the grace, wisdom or salvation of God, which are often marked by a sense of tranquillity and security (for example Numbers 6: 26; Psalms 4: 8 and 85: 8; Proverbs 3: 17; Isaiah 57: 19; Wisdom of Solomon 3: 3; Philippians 4: 7).

Von Rad has argued, however, that there is no specific text in the Old Testament that denotes the spiritual attitude of inward peace. And it is true that most of the references in the Hebrew Bible are used of groups rather than individuals, and even when individuals are the recipients of shalom this is understood as a form of external well-being that is visible to others (Kittel, 1964, vol. II: 406).

In the New Testament, however, the situation would appear to be rather different. *Eirene* is essentially a salvific notion: here, peace is the normal state of the new creation and labels the salvation of the whole person. The 'God of peace' (Romans 15: 33) is known through the Christ who 'is our peace' (Ephesians 2: 14) and who proclaims, and is proclaimed in, the 'gospel of peace' (Eph. 6: 15). According to the Fourth Gospel, peace is Jesus's parting gift to his disciples: 'Peace I leave with you; my peace I give to you. I do not give to you as the world gives. Do not let your hearts be troubled, and do not let them be afraid' (John 14: 27). 'I have said this to you, so that in me you may have peace. In the world you face persecution. But take courage; I have conquered the world' (ibid. 16: 33).

It is hard to escape the view that such texts speak primarily of an 'inner' or 'subjective' peace, particularly as the ministry of Jesus evidently brought little outward peace, 'but a sword' (Matthew 10: 34). Nevertheless, scholars insist that this 'peace of soul' is a minority concern in the New Testament, while admitting that it is undoubtedly present there (Kittel, 1964, vol. II: 417). Such inner peace results from the disciples' recognition of Christ's victory over the world and over sin (see Romans 5: 1–2), and their acceptance of the good news of the graciousness of God in creation and redemption (see Matt. 6: 25–34; Luke 12: 32–4; Philippians 4: 6; Romans 8: 31–9). This gospel engenders a freedom from personal anxiety and foreboding, and even an intellectual repose ('joy and peace in believing', as in Rom. 15: 13). According to Augustine, it leads to a consummation or satisfaction of human desires, as we embrace our true *telos* or end: 'You made us for ['towards'] yourself and our hearts find no peace until they rest in you' (Augustine, *Confessions*, Book I, I; 1961: 21). It is this disposition of the psyche that is so significant in ordinary theology.

Such peace is not to be understood, however, as the negative Stoic tranquillity of a soul that is emptied of desires or has managed to control them. It is, rather, a positive recognition of the nature of our real and deepest desires, and an embracing of that which is our ultimate and enduring satisfaction. The will is therefore involved, in directing the self to its true resting place; the peace that is sometimes said to result from 'surrendering the will' is in fact the result of a positive reorientation of life. 'Acceptance' is not a negative thing.

Neither is this peace simply identical with or even dependent on conditions of 'peace and quiet', outer serenity and ease. It is something much more profound and paradoxical, a costlier form of peace.

> This is not peace as we see it. Jesus is a man profoundly not at home with his world and his contemporaries, and so in our terms a singularly unpeaceful person. And his isolation is not somehow smoothed over by a warming private conviction that all is well: his faith is a weightier and a darker thing than that. There is no peace for him on earth, in the present order. His life is directed towards the coming Kingdom –

which is an order of peace quite different from the 'quiet life' we may long for. Jesus's miracles are often seen as 'signs of the Kingdom', clues to the fact that it is at the door; and they are miracles of freeing from bondage, healing, feeding, and life-giving. They speak of a realm where the Father's will is done by the removal of what actively damages and limits human dignity. And the recurring image of the Kingdom's joy is the feast of the royal Messiah, the king's banquet thrown open to paupers, cripples, rogues and vagabonds.

There is peace at the banquet not because nothing is happening but because people are reconciled, accepted sufficiently to relate to each other in love, gift and enjoyment. They are at home with each other and their host; they are at peace and they are *making* peace. But the food at the messianic feast, the supply of nourishment which makes it possible, is the love and welcome of the host. And when we in the present crisis, the moving world of time, anticipate the feast, we do so by remembering just how that love took final shape for us. Our food is the crucifixion; a body broken. (Williams, 1983: 68–9)

Ordinary theologians, too, in yearning for personal peace, are often forced by their life's experience to recognize that its shape may be cruciform, and that it will never be wholly achieved *in via*. This element came out in a substantial minority of the pilot study interviews. It was recently vividly portrayed in a follow-up discussion to the 2005 BBC television documentary, *The Monastery*, in which five 'ordinary men' reflected on the forty days and nights they had spent in a Benedictine abbey. Those who referred to 'inner peace' or 'peace of mind' as one of the outcomes of their stay all agreed that this was a much more challenging and double-edged experience than mere 'ease' or 'comfort'.

Peace in the psychology of religion

In the general psychological literature the measure that seems closest to this notion of personal peace is the broader category of '*satisfaction* with life' – either with life as a whole, with a part of life or with one's self (Argyle, 1987: 5–8). This is said to be based in part on the experience of *joy* (ibid.: 146), but the basic emotion or 'mood' of joy perhaps takes us beyond satisfaction to connotations of delight, euphoria or even ecstasy (Solomon, 1983: 336). 'Delight is an indispensable component of Shalom', writes Nicholas Wolterstorff (2004: 99). (One is reminded here of Pascal's *Memorial*: 'Certainty. Certainty. Feeling. Joy. Peace.') *Contentment* may be even more central to our theme. This is a positive emotion:

'an affirmation of a state of affairs, an acceptance of oneself or some aspect of oneself. It is as if to say, "Now my world is as it ought to be" or "I am satisfied with myself"' (Solomon, 1983: 293). I recall a discussion with a colleague who had recently given up academic life to run a Christian retreat house. 'Are you happy?', I asked. 'Well, not always. But I have never before felt such contentment.'

Donald Evans has written of a set of fundamental attitude – virtues that he portrays as pervasive stances for living. These are both religious attitudes and moral virtues, and they undergird belief and practice in morality and religion. They include the attitude of *contemplation*, which Evans treats as a species of love and thus as part of the supreme goal of human life. It is the stance of a person who 'profoundly appreciates the reality and uniqueness of each particular in the universe, including himself' (1979: 7), and who is detached from self-preoccupation and narcissism (1993: 250–1). It is an attitude fostered by meditation, which is a discipline of the attention that can cleanse the vision and reduce distortion. It celebrates the sheer existence of people and things, and also promotes 'an awareness of a still centre within, which cannot be destroyed by anything that happens in body or mind or outside world'. This 'calm, peaceful, substantial center' is the core of my real self, Evans argues, yet part of a universal reality. Significantly, it is said to transcend competitive comparison with others (1979: 149–50). Introvertive meditation (see Stace, 1960: 61) of a dispassionate and somewhat austere kind, which involves the strenuous stripping away of our false, distrustful self, can help us arrive at this 'quiet haven of retreat', where our resources may be replenished. But Evans insists that this 'still point of the turning world' (quoting T. S. Eliot's *Burnt Norton*) is 'not an escape from everyday involvements', but rather a platform from which we can 'launch forth into a sea of troubles' – and therefore a true source of creative energy for the struggle that is real life.

Evans argues that contemplation is a culmination of all the other seven attitude-virtues, including the most basic of them all: the *trust* that incorporates elements of assurance, receptivity, fidelity, hope and passion. He writes that trust

> becomes a participation in a pervasive reality which pours out its creative abundance in both the outer world of people and things and the inner world of the still-centred self; and it becomes an unshakeable

assurance which arises at dawn after the dark night of the soul. (1979: 19–20, 152)

This account of basic trust draws heavily on the work of the neo-Freudian Erik Erikson (1977: 222–5), for whom the first and most significant psychic struggle is that between trust and mistrust during the infant's first year. Freud himself used the German term *Befriedigung* ('satisfaction') as descriptive of the child's relaxed relationship with his mother. This word, writes Heije Faber, 'has a deeper note – the echo of the word "peace"', itself originally a religious term. Thus, 'the heart of the relationship between mother and child is religious'. Faber finds in the poetry of Jan Luyken both an appropriate expression of the search for rest, trust and peace, and an account of *God* as 'the origin, the point where man is at home, the place of trust and peace' (Faber, 1976: 161–2).

Raymond Holley has also written of a spiritual strength that is the opposite of the arrogant imposition of one's self on to the world. He describes this as 'a quiet and humble steadiness', indicative of 'a peace which is confidence'. 'Such peace is not the pacificity of the non-combatant but the surety, joy and contentment of the person who knows that which is of ultimate value and which ultimately is, and who thereby recognizes the transient and ephemeral as the merely relative' (1978: 55). This, presumably, should be equated with 'that peace which the world cannot give' of the evening office of the *Book of Common Prayer* rather than with the 'peace at home' that John Cosin linked with the petition to 'keep far our foes' in his seventeenth-century translation of the 'Veni, Creator Spiritus' in the Anglican Ordinal.

Turning to more empirical studies, it is significant that Alister Hardy's 'natural history' of religious experience classified over a quarter of his responses (25.3%) as describing a 'sense of security, protection, peace'. This exceeds the number of responses classified as containing a 'sense of joy, happiness, well-being' (21.2%) or even a 'sense of presence' (20.2%). It is exceeded only by the descriptor 'initiative felt to lie within the self, but response from beyond; prayers answered' (32.3% of responses) (Hardy, 1979: 26, 52). Other empirical studies routinely point out that religious experience mostly results in positive psychological states that include a sense of peace (see Hyde, 1990: ch. 9). We may also note that Abraham Maslow's 'peak experience', the climax of a person's process of self-actualization, is said to result in more aware, focused and integrated persons who confess to feeling deeply at peace with themselves, others and their world (see Maslow, 1976: ch. 12); and that A. M. Greeley reported a positive relationship between such subjective perceptions of well-being and both peak and prayer experiences (Greeley, 1975). Others record a similar correlation with charismatic and healing experiences (see Wulff, 1995: 195).

From personal to public peace?

I accept that the connection between peace as a psychological or spiritual state ('personal peace') and peace as a condition of social and political life ('public peace') is not an inevitable one; but neither is it to be denied. Any account of spirituality runs the risk of focusing on the inner life to the neglect of the outside world and its challenges. Evans warns that meditation *can* become a sophisticated form of self-preoccupation – a 'merely self-conscious sensuality' or 'glorified narcissism' (1979: 150); and John Hull has frequently inveighed against a spirituality of passivity that is a mere escape from exposure to 'the dreaded belief system' (1985: 143).

But a holistic view of human beings should not unscrew the inside from the outside of the teapot in these ways, as spirituality and human activity arise, belong and are fulfilled together. This is particularly so, I would argue, with the notion of peace. Virtue ethics claims that the best account of the moral life and moral motivation begins with a description of our character dispositions and moral virtues, and leads on to their expression in overt human action. Thus the virtue of veracity disposes us to the activity of truth-telling, and that of fidelity to promise-keeping. But what is it that leads us towards *peacemaking*, so that we come to embrace what McDonald (1990: 49) calls 'the praxis of peace'?

I would argue that a peaceable nature is one that recognizes, desires and has largely found a personal or inner peace, contentment and self-acceptance. Here, the moral virtue is continuous with the spiritual attitude, and both are expressed in active involvement in peace creation in family and society. This psychological movement from the inner to the outer world is at least plausible; I believe that it is also normal. It is, perhaps, a rash claim that those who possess the most inner peace are the most *effective* peacemakers in the outer world. But this *is* taken for granted, I think, in ordinary theology's assumptions about the practical effectiveness of the homely virtues, and specifically in the claim (which came up occasionally in the pilot study) that peace in the heart issues in a peacefulness of temper and thus leads to observable, active peacemaking (see Ottley, 1917: 701). This is a hypothesis worthy of further empirical test.

But we should note yet again that personal peace is not identical with or intrinsically dependent on the comfortable absence of external disturbance. The insights of ordinary theology – if they are indeed insights – suggest that personal peace may be realized, at least in part, even in the midst of conflict, as something integral to a positive state or active virtue that can triumph over and redirect hostility. In this regard, a peaceful temper and the virtue of self-restraint (Matthew 5: 9; Galatians 5: 22–6; Romans 14: 19; Hebrews 12: 14; Ephesians 4: 31–2; Colossians 3: 12–15) should be viewed more positively than they often are, and respected as character strengths that tend to an active love that works for reconciliation and peacemaking. In our everyday experience, violence bred from ill temper is a negative, empty force. It returns creation to chaos and breaks down some of the hardest-won achievements of the human spirit.

Non-violence

One link between personal peace and public peace may be through the mediating state of *truthfulness*. Stanley Hauerwas is a doughty champion of public peace through non-violence, claiming that it is 'at the very heart of our understanding of God'. He also insists that there is 'an inherent relation between truthfulness and peacefulness because peace comes only as we are transformed by a truth that gives us the confidence to rely on nothing else than its witness. A "truth" that must use violence to secure its existence cannot be truth' (1983: xvii, 15).

> Violence used in the name of justice, or freedom, or equality is seldom simply a matter of justice – it is a matter of the power of some over others. Moreover, when violence is justified in principle as a necessary strategy for securing justice, it stills the imaginative search for nonviolent ways of resistance to injustice. For true justice never comes through violence, nor can it be based on violence. It can only be based on truth, which has no need to resort to violence to secure its own existence. (ibid.: 114–15)

'All warfare', writes Sun Tzu, 'is based on deception.' The English philosopher Michael McGhee comments:

> That is to say that *waging* war depends upon deception. But doesn't deception, doesn't lying, entail a *state* of war? Which is part of what is against lying. Truthfulness is then a product of peace, a condition in which one is not impelled to lie. And self-deception evinces a state of war within the psyche. (2000: 77–8)

May we argue, then, that the confidence, contentment and assurance of personal peace is also a function of the recognition of a true relationship with reality, which moves us beyond a reliance on falsehood or pretence? This connection between truth, non-violence and justice was also highlighted by Mahatma Gandhi, who held that *satyagraha*, the quiet and irresistible spiritual force that pursues the truth (*satya*), requires both non-violence (*ahimsa*) and self-sacrifice (Hick, 1999: ch. 21). It has been said of this position:

> Nonviolence is necessary because no one possesses absolute truth, only fragments of truth, and thus no one is allowed to force his or her partial truth on others. Nonviolence is capable of instituting community because it participates in the power of truth, a power greater than all violence ... Nonviolent resistance and voluntary suffering break the logic of suspicion, condemnation, self-justification, and make it possible for conflicts to be carried on within the domain of discourse. (Hodgson, 1994: 311)

For Gandhi, selfless action precluded violent action (in his view, against *all* living things). In the famous 'Salt March' of 1930, organized to protest against the British government's salt laws, hundreds were bloodily beaten as they staged a silent demonstration. Their example of non-violence attracted the attention and sympathy of the world to the Indians' claims for independence, and was instrumental in achieving peaceful political change. For Gandhi (who believed that 'God is Truth'), non-violence and truth were two sides of the same coin: there was no way to find truth except through non-violence.

The Christian theologian Peter Hodgson interprets this as an appeal to 'the power of the Spirit, not the power of weapons and wealth'. Others might offer a more psychological interpretation of the effectiveness of non-violence in converting the violent and unjust, while acknowledging that God's Spirit creates and sustains our human psychology. Whatever the process, we may accept that evil and hatred can sometimes be 'absorbed' and 'neutralized' by one who receives them passively, without retaliation. So the mother holding the violent child takes his blows until they metamorphose into hugs. She knows 'the truth of the matter', and has the confidence and courage to stand by her insights into what her child *truly* wants and needs. And that truth, in the end, prevails, as her inner peace creates an outer peace. In an analogous way, the behaviour of a Nelson Mandela, in treating his prison guards with respect and kindness over many years and positively modelling reconciliation with his enemies in many other ways, has undeniably had a worldwide effect. Such actions may be said to embody a truth about the reality of human relationships and human nature that violence distorts or rejects: they capture something of Parker Palmer's concern for our 'obedience to truth' (Palmer, 1993).

Process peace

Before leaving this theme, I want to draw attention to one arresting illustration of these psychological and spiritual claims, in a metaphysical account that also links peace with truth. Process philosophy and theology offer a speculative metaphysics that takes our experience of ourselves as a model for all reality, as demanded by Alfred North Whitehead's 'reformed subjectivist principle'. In his book *Adventures of Ideas*, Whitehead discusses peace as a quality of mind, an active state or 'positive feeling' that 'crowns the "life and motion" of the soul'. He resists the negative conception of peace that is based on an ignorance of – or a lack of feeling towards – the suffering of the world, in favour of a fundamental trust in 'the efficacy of Beauty': the 'intuition of permanence' that 'tragedy was not in vain' (1933: 285–6). Here, peace is 'not the absence of war or violence, but the presence of other relationships ("a broadening of feeling") with the wider world' (Moore, 2004: 9).

'The attainment of Truth', Whitehead wrote, 'belongs to the essence of Peace': the conformance of Appearance to Reality. In his philosophy the factor that constitutes the general drive towards such an end is the persuasion or 'lure' that realizes perfection ('a Harmony of Harmonies') out of the events that make up the world, which is experienced as the sense of Peace (1933: 292, 296). In process thought, persuasion is always and fundamentally more effective than coercion: hence God influences the world by his love, without determining it or controlling it through his power. And peace is an ideal that is encountered through God, which 'pulls the individual and the world towards its finest' (Moore, 2004: 8).

Whatever our view of this theistic metaphysics, we may find in the account an illustration of where true effectiveness is to be found in interpersonal relationships.

Ordinary theology, peace and religious education

In this last section, I want to pick up the two main foci of this essay and suggest their relevance for religious education.

Religious education and ordinary theology

Whether or not we treat the ordinary beliefs of ordinary believers (and of non-believers too) as significant, they will inevitably be taken seriously by the people who have them. It is necessarily the case that your theology is always more significant to you than is any other theology, whether mine or St Paul's or Moltmann's. In conversation with another theology, your own may change, indeed you may be converted to its view, but only as and when it becomes *your* theology. And the sort of person you are will always define what is going to be significant for you, in theology as in life.

These are general truths about people, but they are particularly apposite when applied to the young. All learners, whether in church or school, come to religious education with some form of religious belief. Sometimes it will be highly developed, even weighty, or it may be nothing more than 'a hotchpotch of confused and contradictory ideas'; it may include religious affirmations or 'a belief in the falsity or meaningless irrelevance' of religion (Wright, 1993: 94). Whatever the nature of this belief, religious education must help the learners to reflect on it and to understand it better. It is a grave mistake to dismiss it as irrelevant. We must particularly encourage children to reflect on their own broad 'ordinary theology' of deeply held moral and spiritual concerns and insights, whether or not these are explicitly articulated in religious belief or expressed in overt religious belonging.

As I have noted elsewhere, writing in the context of school religious education (RE) in Britain:

> This concern for personal believing has traditionally been reflected in the often-disparaged 'Personal Quest' approach to RE, with its focus on 'an unrestricted personal quest for meaning in life in terms of actual experience' and on those human experiences and attitudes whose 'significance for religion is implied, rather than directly referred to', in contrast to the study of explicit religious phenomena. This quest for a faith to live by has been labelled the 'architectonic role' of RE. Its survival in RE programmes indicates a continuing appreciation of the value of reflection on – and indeed development of – the learner's own life-stance and meaning-system. I believe that we should be willing to label this 'quest' a form of theology, for in principle it involves more real 'doing' of theology than most of what goes on even in theological seminaries. In practice, however, it needs to be *more* theological, in the sense of more critical, reflective, systematic and *intellectual* than it often is. (Astley, 1996: 71–2; cf. Wright, 2000b)

In the context of this claim, I argued for a greater emphasis in religious education on this element of personal reflection on the part of pupils: a reflection that may properly and naturally be designated (or at least may develop into) a form of theological reflection. This should include reflection on their understanding of 'peace'.

Education for peace

The entry under the heading 'education for peace' in *Harper's Encyclopaedia of Religious Education* (Stassen, 1990) dismisses a focus in religious education purely on achieving religiousness as a 'private peace of mind'. G. H. Stassen argues that that would be teaching 'unhealthy denial' in a world that is continually threatened by war and wastes millions on defence. He claims that is also unbiblical: 'peace does not refer to an internal state of mind, but [to] a relationship of wholeness, fulfillment, justice, and freedom in community with God, neighbors, nature, and oneself.'

I see the biblical data and the educational need rather differently, but in any case Stassen goes on to deny any either/or claim, affirming that 'there must be both an inward journey and an outward journey' (ibid.: 475). Interestingly, he argues that the sinful bondage or addiction to power that leads to war should be tackled as if it were a form of alcoholism, advocating 'a group process of sharing and mutual support' which follows 'specific steps of inner spiritual recovery and other change in behavior' (ibid.: 477). Apparently, spiritual healing and formation *can* create peacemakers.

Educational processes, sometimes bordering on the therapeutic, may be used to induct learners into an attitude and disposition of personal peace. Those who understand religious education in its confessional (evangelistic, nurturing) form, as including *spiritual formation*, may be quite happy to embrace such methods (see Robson and Lonsdale, n.d.; Cottingham, 2005: 75–8, 145–9). The same methods might also be adopted by those who include formation in certain spiritual values, or the 'provocation of spiritual insight' (Holley, 1978: 141) or of spiritual experience, as an integral part of non-confessional religious education – and even of dimensions of the secular curriculum (see Best, 1996; Wright, 1998, 1999, 2000a; Mott-Thornton, 1998; Thatcher, 1999).

A major aspect of this form of education may be described as the education of the learner's *vision* or *onlooks*, which brings me back to my concern for ordinary theology (Astley, 2002: 82–6). I believe that it is this dimension of our interpretative experience – that is, the way we look on things – that best captures the difference between those who are religious or spiritual, and those who are not. Religion and spirituality do not necessarily involve seeing different things, but they always involve seeing the same things differently. And this difference of perception flows from our character and nature. As William Blake put it, in the less inclusive language of the eighteenth century: 'As a man is, so he sees' (Blake, 1799). Once this vision has been enabled, it flows back into character, leading to and catalyzing further change and learning. Learning to have a certain attitude or emotion towards something is often a function of learning to see things in certain ways (Hamlyn, 1978: 124).

It seems to me that a great deal of education is involved in directing children's attention, widening their horizons, and 'opening their eyes' to things that we believe are always there, but that the learners have not yet seen. Religious formation cannot do without it. Let me put this in Christian terms. 'Surely this man was a Son of God', says the centurion when he *sees* how Jesus dies (Mark 15: 39): he has embarked, not on an inference from unambiguous facts, but on a shift of perspective. A religious person is one who is able to recognize this, that and the other act, event or situation as God's rule, hand and intention. To be a Christian is to be someone who is able to see the 'signs of the kingdom' in this way, in the way that Jesus did – in the widow's mite and the child set in the midst of the disciples. And in order to see the kingdom's signs, one must be a sign of the kingdom oneself. The ability to see the kingdom is a distinguishing mark of those who are already part of it (see Astley, 2007).

We may make the same point about the ability to see what Jesus calls, in his lament over Jerusalem, 'the things that make for peace' (Luke 19: 42). To be able to see the elements that make up, and those that obstruct, peacemaking, one must *be* a person of peace.

In peace education, as elsewhere, values both flow from vision and also give rise to vision. The two cannot be separated. Therefore, forming the peaceful child and adult, as people whose personal peace will overflow into overt peacemaking, is partly a matter of shedding light on and bringing into focus aspects of reality and of human experience that are too frequently obscured. In a word, it is a rendering of a deeper truth about life. In another word, it is an education in peaceable perception.

References

Argyle, M. (1987). *The Psychology of Happiness*, London, Routledge.

Astley, J. (1994). *The Philosophy of Christian Religious Education*, Birmingham, AL, Religious Education Press.

Astley, J. (1996). 'Theology for the untheological? Theology, philosophy and the classroom', in J. Astley and L. J. Francis (eds), *Christian Theology and Religious Education: Connections and Contradictions*, London, SPCK, pp. 60–77.

Astley, J. (2002). *Ordinary Theology: Looking, Listening and Learning in Theology*, Aldershot, Ashgate.

Astley, J. (2007). *Christ of the Everyday*, London, SPCK.

Augustine (1961). *Confessions*, ET Harmondsworth, Penguin.

Best, R. (ed.) (1996). *Education, Spirituality and the Whole Child*, London, Cassell.

Blake, W. (1799). Letter to the Revd Dr J. Trusler, in *Poetry and Prose of William Blake*, ed. G. Keynes, London, Nonesuch, 1961, p. 84.

Browning, D. S. (1991). *A Fundamental Practical Theology*, Minneapolis, MN, Fortress.

Brümmer, V. (1981). *Theology and Philosophical Inquiry: An Introduction*, London, Macmillan.

Cottingham, J. (2005). *The Spiritual Dimension: Religion, Philosophy, and Human Value*, Cambridge, Cambridge University Press.
Cupitt, D. (1999a). *The New Religion of Life in Everyday Speech*, London, SCM.
Cupitt, D. (1999b). *The Meaning of It All in Everyday Speech*, London, SCM.
Cupitt, D. (2000). *Kingdom Come in Everyday Speech*, London, SCM.
Cupitt, D. (2001a). *Reforming Christianity*, Santa Rosa, CA, Polebridge.
Cupitt, D. (2001b). *Emptiness and Brightness*, Santa Rosa, CA, Polebridge.
Cupitt, D. (2003). *Life, Life*, Santa Rosa, CA, Polebridge.
Cupitt, D. (2005). *The Great Questions of Life*, Santa Rosa, CA, Polebridge.
Erikson, E. (1977). *Childhood and Society*, London, Triad/Granada.
Evans, D. (1979). *Struggle and Fulfillment: The Inner Dynamics of Religion and Morality*, Cleveland, Collins.
Evans, D. (1993). *Spirituality and Human Nature*, Albany, NY, State University of New York Press.
Evans, D. D. (1963). *The Logic of Self-Involvement: A Theological Study of Everyday Language with Special Reference to the Christian Use of Language about God as Creator*, London, SCM.
Faber, H. (1976). *Psychology of Religion*, ET London, SCM.
Farley, E. (1996). 'Can church education be theological education?', reprinted in J. Astley, L. J. Francis and C. Crowder (eds), *Theological Perspectives on Christian Formation: A Reader in Theology and Christian Education*, Leominster, Gracewing and Grand Rapids, MI, Eerdmans, pp. 31–44.
Frei, H. (1992). *Types of Christian Theology*, ed. George Hunsinger and William C. Placher, New Haven, CT, Yale University Press.
Greeley, A. M. (1975). *The Sociology of the Paranormal: A Reconnaissance*, London, Sage.
Hamlyn, D. W. (1978). *Experience and the Growth of Understanding*, London, Routledge & Kegan Paul.
Hardy, A. (1979). *The Spiritual Nature of Man: A Study of Contemporary Religious Experience*, Oxford, Clarendon.
Hauerwas, S. (1983). *The Peaceable Kingdom: A Primer in Christian Ethics*, London, SCM.
Hick, J. (1999). *The Fifth Dimension: An Exploration of the Spiritual Realm*, Oxford, Oneworld.
Hodgson, P. C. (1994). *Winds of the Spirit: A Constructive Christian Theology*, London, SCM.
Holley, R. (1978). *Religious Education and Religious Understanding*, London, Routledge & Kegan Paul.
Hull, J. M. (1985). *What Prevents Christian Adults from Learning?*, London, SCM.

Hull, J. M. (1999). 'Bargaining with God, religious development and economic socialization', *Journal of Psychology and Theology*, 27, 3, 241–9.

Hyde, K. E. (1990). *Religion in Childhood and Adolescence: A Comprehensive Review of the Research*, Birmingham, AL, Religious Education Press.

Kelsey, D. H. (1992). *To Understand God Truly: What's Theological about a Theological School*, Louisville, KY, Westminster/John Knox.

Kittel, G. (1964). *Theological Dictionary of the New Testament*, ET Grand Rapids, MI, Eerdmans.

Lebacqz, K. (1998). 'Social ethics', in B. Hoose (ed.), *Christian Ethics: An Introduction*, London, Cassell, 163–72.

McDonald, J. I. H. (1990), 'Towards a theology of peace', in D. B. Forrester (ed.), *Theology and Practice*, London, Epworth, pp. 39–53.

McGhee, M. (2000). *Transformations of Mind: Philosophy as Spiritual Practice*, Cambridge, Cambridge University Press.

Martin, D. (1967). *A Sociology of English Religion*, London, Heinemann.

Maslow, A. (1976). *The Farther Reaches of Human Nature*, Harmondsworth, Penguin.

Moore, M. E. M. (2004). 'Imagine peace: knowing the real – imagining the impossible', *Process Papers*, 8, 5–25.

Mott-Thornton, K. (1998). *Common Faith: Education, Spirituality and the State*, Aldershot, Ashgate.

Osmer, R. R. (1990). 'Teaching as practical theology', in J. L. Seymour and D. E. Miller (eds), *Theological Approaches to Christian Education*, Nashville, TN, Abingdon, pp. 216–38.

Ottley, R. L. (1917). 'Peace', in J. Hastings, J. A. Selbie and L. H. Gray (eds), *Encyclopaedia of Religion and Ethics*, vol. IX, Edinburgh, T. and T. Clark, pp. 700–1.

Palmer, P. J. (1993). *To Know as We are Known: Education as a Spiritual Journey*, San Francisco, CA, HarperSanFrancisco.

Robson, J. and Lonsdale, D. (eds) (n.d.). *Can Spirituality be Taught?*, London, ACCT and BCC.

Selby, P. (1997). *Grace and Mortgage: The Language of Faith and the Debt of the World*, London, Darton, Longman and Todd.

Solomon, R. C. (1983). *The Passions*, Notre Dame, IN, University of Notre Dame Press.

Stace, W. T. (1960). *Mysticism and Philosophy*, London, Macmillan.

Stassen, G. H. (1990). 'Peace, Education for', in I. V. Cully and K. B. Cully (eds), *Harper's Encyclopaedia of Religious Education*, San Francisco, CA, Harper & Row, pp. 475–8.

Thatcher, A. (ed.) (1999). *Spirituality and the Curriculum*, London, Cassell.

Thomson, J. B. (2006). 'Pew theology', *Theology*, CIX, 848, 111–18.

Towler, R. (n.d.). *Conventional and Common Religion in Great Britain*, Leeds, University of Leeds.

Whitehead, A. N. (1933). *Adventures of Ideas*, New York, Free Press.
Williams, R. (1983). *The Truce of God*, London, Collins.
Wolterstorff, N. (2004). *Educating for Shalom: Essays on Christian Higher Education*, Grand Rapids, MI, Eerdmans.
Woodhead, L. (2004). 'Theology, the trouble it's in', in G. Hyman (ed.), *New Directions in Philosophical Theology: Essays in Honour of Don Cupitt*, Aldershot, Ashgate, pp. 173–86.
Wright, A. (1993). *Religious Education in the Secondary School: Prospects for Religious Literacy*, London, David Fulton.
Wright, A. (1998). *Spiritual Pedagogy: A Survey, Critique and Reconstruction of Contemporary Spiritual Education in England and Wales*, Abingdon, Culham College Institute.
Wright, A. (1999). *Discerning the Spirit: Teaching Spirituality in the Religious Education Classroom*, Abingdon, Culham College Institute.
Wright, A. (2000a). *Spirituality and Education*. London, RoutledgeFalmer.
Wright, A. (2000b). 'The spiritual education project: cultivating spiritual and religious literacy through a critical pedagogy of religious education', in M. Grimmitt (ed.), *Pedagogies of Religious Education: Case Studies in the Research and Development of Good Pedagogic Practice in RE*, Great Wakering, McCrimmons, pp. 170–87.
Wulff, D. M. (1995). 'Phenomenological psychology and religious experience', in R. W. Hood, Jr. (ed.), *Handbook of Religious Experience*, Birmingham, AL, Religious Education Press, pp. 183–99.

10
Violence for political purposes: the case of the London bombings

WILLIAM K. KAY

Introduction

On 7 July 2005, four young men detonated bombs within the London transport system. In the blast that followed, the bombers themselves died, and subsequent evidence strongly suggests that this was by deliberate act of self-destruction (House of Commons, 2006: para. 35). All the suspected bombers came from, or were on the fringes of, the Muslim community in Britain.[1] A BBC TV Panorama programme (21 August 2005) questioned the effectiveness of the leadership given to the Muslim community by the Muslim Council of Britain. One of the things the programme showed is that there are younger Muslim leaders who are prepared to confront the attempts by radical groups to turn Islam into an ideology of terror, but there were suggestions that some older Muslim leaders in Britain were too complacent in the face of political extremism. Others, however, were absolutely clear that suicide bombing against civilians is *haram*, forbidden in Islam.

Exactly two weeks later, on 21 July, an almost identical attack on the transport system of London was attempted and, again, the perpetrators appear to have been young Muslims. What was particularly horrific about both the attack and the attempted attack was that the bombers, or alleged bombers, were British subjects. In other words, these young men had been assimilated into British culture, indeed, at least one was granted asylum in Britain at the age of twelve, and had grown up in the country and received a normal education and other benefits.[2] To all intents and purposes, these young men, particularly the first group of bombers, appeared to be fully adjusted to a British way of life (Home Office, 2006). There is no evidence that the two attacks were connected (House of Commons, 2006: para. 42).

As the police investigation proceeded and more and more information became available about what happened, attention was turned to the Islamic community and the apparent failure of some sections of it to confront its most radical elements. Equally, questions were asked of the British government about its apparent failure to act decisively against extremists who, sheltering under the cover of Islamic ideals, appear to embrace an ideology of hatred. However, when the government *did* introduce legislation to curb the glorification of terrorism, libertarian arguments in favour of free speech were quickly raised. For instance, Dr Mohammed Naseem, chairman of the Birmingham Central Mosque, compared the government powers and proposals with those taken by Hitler when he demonized Jews;[3] and Shami Chakrabarti, director of the civil rights group Liberty, said 'Mr Blair has attacked key human rights and would jeopardise national unity'.[4]

The events in London in July 2005 have had repercussions in other parts of Europe and may eventually threaten the liberal consensus across the EU. Even if this consensus is maintained, the question arises: how many British young people are prepared to use violence for political purposes? Or, to put this issue in another way: how widespread among young people, both religious and secular, is the willingness to embrace political violence – even if this violence does not include a simultaneous willingness to commit suicide? For, although suicide bombers have in recent years arisen in places where the Islamic community is engaged in a violent struggle, the concept of suicide bombing certainly includes the mid-century kamikaze fighter pilots of Japan and those who more recently have, from a Buddhist background, fought within Sri Lanka. As Bendle (2006) argues, suicide bombing may also be directed into attacks against civil society itself. Civil society is seen as an evil, 'as the realm of corruption and evil, as the place where the battle for purity and the realization of God's will must be carried out', and it is this that justifies the indiscriminate nature of the killing.

The issues of the use of violence for political purposes and of suicide bombing are, of course, separate and distinct, but there is an overlap between them. Suicide bombing turns violence against the perpetrator, as well as against the people who are its targets; whereas violence for political purposes is turned only against the targets (although this discussion recognizes that violence for political purposes may be perpetrated against buildings, objects and animals).

For these reasons it is logical to treat suicide bombers as a subset of the larger set of those who are prepared to use violence for political purposes.

It has not been possible to discover any studies that have specifically investigated the prevalence of violence carried out for political purposes. Studies have focused on criminal acts using violence, and Home Office studies (for example Graham and Bowling, 1995) found that no less than 12% of 14- to 17-year-old males and 7% of 14- to 17-year-old females in a nationally representative sample admitted to such crimes. The inference here is that crimes of this type that are motivated by specifically political considerations would have registered lower percentages.

It is also logical to treat suicide bombers as a subset of the larger set of those who commit suicide. One can make the assumption that suicide bombers share some of the psychological characteristics of those who commit suicide without taking the lives of other people, and we can do this because those who commit suicide expect to have an impact upon those they leave behind – which is why they write explanatory notes for those who find them. Suicide, in other words, is rarely without reference to the social world of the person who dies, as an analysis of suicide notes confirms (Williams, 1997).

The assumption that suicide bombers belong to the same set of those who commit suicide is challenged by Hassan (2005) who compiled a database of more than 200 Muslim suicide bombers.[5] From interviews with failed or prospective suicide bombers, she argues that they do not conform to the classic psychological profile of potential suicides. On the contrary, these were educated and adjusted young people (they ranged in age from 18 to 38) who were motivated by religious idealism and moral certitude. In most cases, they were male – a finding that continues the link between maleness and violence (see Austin, 1980).

While this essay does not reject Hassan's findings, it is reasonable to argue that suicide bombers will not necessarily display the same psychological profile in different parts of the world. Where there is some kind of social pressure, even glorification of suicide bombing, the potential bomber is likely to be a rather different person from one who occupies a culture where suicide bombing is treated with horror and, even, contempt: there is a clear contrast between Gaza and London. Robert Baer (2005) reports seeing 'official certificates of martyrdom' being given out in Gaza mosques 'like graduation diplomas to families of suicide bombers', something which would be unthinkable in London. Moreover, if suicide bombers belong to networks (Flint, 2003, quoting Arquilla, Ronfeldt and Zanini, 1999; Arquilla and Ronfeldt, 2001; Hoffman et al., 2001), they will be able to create the social support necessary for them to act counter-culturally.

Suicide

In Britain, suicide is reported to be the second most common cause of death among young people, male and female, after motor vehicle accidents (Williams, 1997: 20). In April 2002, the Department of Health issued a consultation document, *National Suicide Prevention Strategy for England*, which begins with the words:

> Suicide is a major public health issue. Around 5000 people take their own lives in England every year. In the last 20 years or so, suicide rates have fallen in older men and women, but risen in younger men. The majority of suicides now occur in young adult males. In men under 35, suicide is the most common cause of death.

Williams (1997: 41) confirms that the high rate of suicides, especially among young males, began to climb from the 1980s onwards, particularly in industrialized countries like the United States and Japan. In the United States, in the 15 to 24 age group, suicides among white males have risen by 163% in the period between 1960 and 1987, and by 214% among black males in the same period (Berman and Jobes, 1991: 19). By each method and in each country, suicide among males is higher than it is among females. However, it should be noted that official statistics among both sexes almost certainly *under*count cases of suicide because, among many religious groups, suicide is stigmatized.[6]

Sociological theories
Ever since the work of Durkheim (1897), suicide rates have been a matter of academic concern, and his masterly analysis of international statistics, as well as his original approach to causation,

allowed him to identify four different forms of suicide, each of which depended upon a different relationship between the individual and society (Lukes, 1975). Since his approach was sociological and deliberately avoided attempts to pry into the interior consciousness of completed[7] or attempted suicides, Durkheim was able to advance the view that the individual who is totally submerged within society may lack autonomy, and so be excessively vulnerable to social pressures. Equally vulnerable at the other end of the scale is the individual who is isolated from society, and so lacks the sense of meaning and purpose which collective activity can give. It is this kind of individual who, in a modern urban and mass society, is most likely to be in danger. A similar situation arises when society itself is changing very rapidly and when norms and values are in perpetual flux. Here, an individual is in danger of being unable to integrate within society, despite efforts to do so. The chaotic nature of this sort of society is itself alienating to those unable to keep pace with change. Finally, societies that are static, prescriptive and controlling may produce the opposite effect. Here, the individual lacks freedom to act and is trapped by the demands of a rigid social code. In these circumstances, suicide may be seen as a way of escape.

Durkheim's analysis also took account of the value-systems provided by monotheistic religions, so that he contended that differences in suicide rates in European countries with similar social fabrics might be attributable to the Protestant doctrine of individual responsibility, or individual faith for salvation. Here, then, he anticipated that Protestant countries would have higher suicide rates, as indeed they do, than Roman Catholic countries.

This analysis of suicide statistics has been translated into a number of risk factors that are now routinely considered in any study of the subject. Where social isolation has been caused by divorce or bereavement among the young or by the illnesses of extreme old age, suicide risk is raised. Conversely, where a person is a member of a team, group, trade union, close family, supportive marriage, community, congregation or club, suicide risk is lowered (Kay and Francis, 2006).

Further academic reflection on Durkheim's findings has attempted to refine his theory. Stengel (1965: 25) points out that 'suicide rates among Roman Catholics in predominantly Protestant countries have been found to be below the national average. The same applies to orthodox Jews and Moslems.' He argues that it is 'religious devoutness rather than a specific religious faith which is decisive'.

Psychological theories
Psychiatric data link suicide risk with mental illness. Among young people, 'acute, severe mental disorder and chronic disorder of behaviour' (Appleby et al., 1999) are implicated. Indeed, according to Harris and Barraclough (1997), 'all mental disorders have an increased risk of suicide excepting mental retardation and dementia'. In Freudian theory, suicide is the turning of hostility against the self, or 'retroflexed rage' (Berman and Jobes, 1991: 41). The mental illness most specifically linked with suicide is schizophrenia. At any one time, up to one per cent of the population suffers from schizophrenia, and of this group 30 to 40 per cent have attempted suicide at least once (Williams, 1997: 54; Jamison, 2000: 120). Schizophrenics may hear voices commanding them to carry out dangerous actions. They may also be subject to hallucinations, some of which can be frightening.

Most commentators argue that suicide, or the depression leading to suicide, is likely to be the result of a combination of factors, some of which are sociological or, at any rate, external to the sufferer, while others are linked with internal or psychodynamic predispositions. So an interactive model is seen as being most fruitful in terms of prediction and, therefore, of prevention. Indeed, it is common for a range of variables, some sociological and some psychiatric or psychological, to be entered into multiple regression equations together, where the dependent variable is propensity for suicidal acts (see, for example, Schapira et al., 2001).

Cognitive psychology has dealt with the impact of depression on mental functioning. A distinction can be drawn between the impact on mental functioning of anxiety and the impact of depression. Depression certainly leads to impairment in the performance of tasks, and the theoretical explanation for this is found in a resource-allocation theory. In this theory, the depressed person is bound up with inner attention to thoughts and feelings, and as a result has less mental resource available for carrying out tasks. The distinction between depression and anxiety finds that depression tends to follow loss events (such as bereavement), while anxiety tends to follow danger events. Depressed individuals focus on the past, particularly their losses, while anxious individuals focus on the present and future, particularly on possible forthcoming dangers. The relevant distinction in relation to suicide is that depressives tend to interpret neutral events more negatively (Eysenck and Keane, 1995: 452).

Personality theories constructed within the behaviourist paradigm have already been used to identify propensity for suicidal ideation. McCulloch and Philip (1972: 50–1) report on findings derived from the Sixteen Personality Factor Questionnaire (16PF) developed by Cattell (1965). Among men and women who had attempted self-harm by poisoning, they found a disposition to perpetual anxiety linked with poor tolerance of frustration, fearfulness and a tendency to introversion. Taking a variety of studies into account, they profiled the male personality type of the attempted suicide as 'a loner who pays little heed to the needs and expectations of society ... is emotionally volatile, and is prone to be extra-punitive'. The female is apprehensive, guilt-prone and dissatisfied with life.

Method

The foregoing theoretical considerations point to the importance of both personality variables and social variables within any modern study of suicide and violence. The personality variables in this instance will provide evidence of stability and give some indication, through psychoticism, of social integration. The social variables will provide an indication of the respondents' perceptions of the key agencies by which societal values are mediated. The agencies selected relate to human rights groups (not only because suicide bombing violates the human rights of those who are killed and injured, but also because it is intended to assert the human rights of those who have been victimized by the perceived aggressor), political parties (because these may or may not promulgate violence), the courts (since these are the dispensers of justice and stand in contrast to politically motivated violence) and the police (since these are the enforcement agents of the state). People rejecting the courts and the police show themselves to be suffering profound alienation.

Attitudinal variables are connected with personality, and four scales were included here to tap into the value-systems of young people. *Xenophobia* is indicative of ethnocentrism: suicide bombers are not known for attacking their own ethnic group. *Nihilism* registers whether or not young people have any positive values: suicide bombers would be expected to reject nihilism in the light of their anticipated glorification beyond death. The *humanity* scale registers care for other human beings: suicide bombers and those who use political violence might be anticipated to argue that they are acting precisely because they do care for other human beings, despite the damage they cause their targets. *Autonomy* is selected as a variable here since, according to Durkheimian research, suicide is an autonomous act: likewise one could hypothesize that violent political acts would be perpetrated by those who have considered carefully the purpose and outcome of their proposed acts. Finally, the *family* remains important, and one may hypothesize either that ethnocentrism is an extension of family loyalty or that sociopathic behaviour will be linked with rejection of the family.

To investigate these issues empirically, a database of British pupils was analysed. The questionnaire that generated the database contained a series of items and scales, including a version of the Eysenck Personality Questionnaire (EPQR-A; see Francis, Brown and Philipchalk, 1992); a five-point measure of trust placed by individuals in institutions like the police, churches and political parties; a five-point measure of the importance of relationships with family members; and scales by which respondents assessed the importance to them of humanitarian values, xenophobia, autonomy, nihilism and family orientation (see Appendix). The questionnaire also asked respondents whether they 'would use violence for political purposes' and gave them the option of replying 'have done', 'would consider', 'would refuse to do'.

Sample

The data were collected in 2003 and 2004 from pupils from schools in England and Wales. All the questionnaires were distributed by class teachers during ordinary lessons and completed anonymously. Schools were approached on a random basis in the first instance, though, when some schools recommended others to participate in the project, an element of snowball sampling also occurred. The schools approached were those with pupils up to the age of 19 and in urban areas.

The sample was drawn from fifteen schools in England, made up of six types: comprehensive (ages 11–18), sixth form college

(16–18), Church of England voluntary controlled comprehensive (11–18), Church of England voluntary aided grammar (11–18), Roman Catholic sixth form (16–18) and Roman Catholic voluntary aided comprehensive (11–18). Pupils from church-affiliated schools made up 57% of the sample, which totalled 1083 pupils, aged between 14 and 20 years of age. Because the project attracted church schools, this sample has a higher proportion of church-affiliated pupils than would be found in the general population. The two largest groups were aged 16 (30.8%) and 17 (34.3%); 13.6% were aged 18 and only 0.8% were 19 or over. The majority were female (56.6%).

Seventy-six per cent of pupils said that they belonged to a church or religious group; thus 24% belonged to no religious group. As many as 30% of pupils said they belonged to the Roman Catholic Church, and 27.8% to the Church of England. The sample also comprised 3.7% Methodists, 3.5% religious Muslims and 0.5% non-religious Muslims. The remainder included Greek Orthodox, Seventh Day Adventist, Pentecostal, Mormons, Rastafarian, pagan, Sikh, Buddhist and Jewish, who all contributed pupils, each amounting to less than 0.5% of the total. Fifty-seven per cent of pupils never or only once or twice a year attended a place of worship, while 25.8% attended once a month or more. The remainder attended 'sometimes'.

Results

Table 1 shows the responses of young people in the sample concerning the use of violence for political purposes, crosstabulated against religious affiliation. Two points stand out strongly: 4.5% of these pupils claim that they *already* have used violence for political purposes; and religious affiliation, or non-affiliation, does not significantly affect the propensity for violence when Muslim pupils are compared with Roman Catholics, Anglicans or those of no religious affiliation. In fact, it is pupils of no religious affiliation who show the highest percentage (6.2%) of having already used violence. (It is worth emphasizing that none of the young people in this sample is from Northern Ireland.)

Table 2 shows an analysis of variance of significant differences in levels of trust placed by young people in key social agencies.

Table 1 Cross-tabulation: use violence for political purposes, by religious group

Use of violence for political purposes	Religious group				Total
	None %	Muslim (religious) %	R.C. %	C. of E. %	
Would refuse to do	82.4	88.5	74.3	87.2	81.7
Would consider	11.4	7.7	21.4	9.3	13.7
Have done	6.2	3.8	4.4	3.5	4.6
Total	193	26	206	226	651

Note: Bonferroni post hoc tests showed significant differences between Roman Catholic and Church of England groups ($p<.036$) but not between any of the other combinations.

Numerous other religious groups have been omitted because their sample sizes are all very small.

Table 2 One-way analysis of variance: trust in meso-level social agencies, by uses of violence for political purposes

Trust in . . .	F	Sig.
Courts	5.100	.006
Human rights groups (e.g. Amnesty International)	4.444	.012
Political parties	3.608	.028
Police	4.325	.014

The post hoc comparisons show that, in general, those who reject the use of violence trust these agencies more than those who have considered the use of violence or actually used violence. The one exception to this concerns trust in political parties. Here, surprisingly, those who *have* used violence for political purposes trust political parties more than those who refuse political violence. This implies that such violence was inspired, or partially inspired, by these political parties.

Further Bonferroni post hoc comparisons showed that:

(i) those who refused to use violence for political purposes trusted the courts more than those who would consider such violence ($p<.004$);
(ii) those who refused to use violence for political purposes trusted human rights groups more than those who would consider such violence ($p<.012$);
(iii) those who refused to use violence for political purposes trusted the police more than those who would consider such violence ($p<.011$);
(iv) those who have used violence for political purposes trusted political parties more than those who refused to consider such violence ($p<.023$).

Table 3 shows an analysis of variance of significant differences in scores on personality and attitude scales. The post hoc comparisons demonstrated that those who would consider the use of violence or have used violence are more xenophobic, more psychotic, less inspired by humanitarian motives, less autonomous, less oriented to the family and more oriented to nihilism than those who would refuse to use violence. They are, however, no more or less neurotic than those who would not use violence.

Table 3 One-way analysis of variance: social attitudes and personality, by uses of violence for political purposes

Scale	F	Sig.
Xenophobia	6.172	.002
Neuroticism (EPQR-A)	.673	NS
Extroversion (EPQR-A)	.419	NS
Psychoticism (EPQR-A)	40.694	.000
Humanity	36.310	.000
Autonomy	31.176	.000
Family orientation	12.702	.000
Nihilism	13.195	.022

Further Bonferroni post hoc comparisons showed that:

(i) those who would consider using violence for political purposes showed higher xenophobia scores than those who would refuse to use violence in this way ($p<.004$);
(ii) those who refused to use violence for political purposes showed higher humanity scores than those who have used or would consider using violence for political purposes ($p<.000$);
(iii) those who refused to use violence for political purposes showed higher autonomy scores than those who have used or would consider using violence for political purposes ($p<.000$);
(iv) those who refused to use violence for political purposes showed higher family orientation scores than those who have used or would consider using violence for political purposes ($p<.000$ or $p<.016$);
(v) those who refused to use violence for political purposes showed lower nihilism scores than those who have used or would consider using violence for political purposes ($p<.000$ or $p<.042$).

Table 4 shows an analysis of variance of the importance of family members in relation to the possible use of violence for political purposes. In each case, those who rejected the use of violence rated

Table 4 One-way analysis of variance: importance of family members by uses of violence for political purposes

How important are the following people in your life?	F	Sig.
Father	1.469	NS
Mother	7.568	.001
Brother(s)	5.087	.006
Sister(s)	7.744	.000

Note: Bonferroni post hoc comparisons showed that those who would refuse the use of violence for political purposes rated family members (with the exception of the father) as significantly more important to them than did those who would consider using or have used violence for political purposes.

family members as more important than did those who considered the use of violence or had used violence. The only exception here concerned the father. The father's importance was the same for those who accepted and those who rejected violence.

Discussion

Sociological

The number of young people who have already, at this relatively early stage of life, engaged in violence for political purposes is surprisingly high, but, given the figure quoted earlier that as many as 12% of males have committed 'violent offences', it seems credible. The data-gathering process does not reveal what kind of violence was used and what kind of political purposes were in view. These young people may have supported animal rights activists, demonstrated violently in local elections, engaged in racially motivated behaviour or been active in a variety of other situations. The comparisons in Table 1 demonstrate that this type of violence is neither enhanced nor diminished by religious affiliation or its lack. In other words, within the sample we cannot blame religion, agnosticism or atheism for inciting violence, and the only significant difference revealed by post hoc tests is that between Roman Catholics and Anglicans, more Roman Catholics than Anglicans would consider the use of violence for political purposes. The repeated reassurance that Islam in a western context is a religion of peace is supported by these figures.

There is evidence here that those who are prepared to use violence for political purposes are inclined to be alienated from the enforcement agencies of the state. The courts and the police are less well trusted by them and they have less time for human rights groups. Instead, and surprisingly, those who are prepared to use political violence have a trust in political parties, which would suggest that some of this preparedness for violence is stimulated by political agencies. It may be, for instance, that far-right political parties are attractive to pupils who have already used violence or are prepared to use it. This indicates that the kind of violence being considered by these young people is politically motivated, rather than religiously motivated. This is especially so since the young people who are prepared to use violence are less autonomous than others. We might expect that the use of violence for political purposes required greater autonomy, a capacity to think carefully through the issues and to depart from social norms, but the data here indicate the opposite of this. Young people who are prepared to use violence are, in some sense, being led into it by others.[8] This finding is more eloquently put by the novelist Salman Rushdie (2006):

> one of the things I discovered was a kind of bizarre class differential between the warriors and the suicide bombers. Strapping on a suicide belt is looked down upon by some who think it is more manly to kill face to face with a knife. Fighting is manly. Suicide bombing is cheap.
> Those drawn into the act of suicide are malleable personalities. Hezbollah, for example, has developed a quite detailed psychological profile of the kind of person who can be persuaded to be a suicide bomber. You have to be a weak personality to be a suicide bomber. You have to accept the abnegation of the self. (2006: 7)

Such people are then in a position to shift the blame for their actions from themselves to the authority to which they have submitted. As Maikovich puts it:

> researchers have repeatedly shown that individuals tend to act more violently when a legitimate authority source accepts responsibility for their actions (Diener, 1977; Milgram, 1974). Tilker (1970) found that displacement of responsibility lessens concern about the well-being of others who are being mistreated, and also lessens the moral restraints one feels on one's own actions. (2005: 391(2))

Psychological

Beyond the sociological factors, there are a range of psychological and personal factors that bear on the issues at stake here. The highly significant association between psychoticism and a willingness to use political violence indicates that political violence may be a reflection of inner personality dynamics. The Eysenckian conception of psychoticism is of a form of behaviour related either to male sex hormones or to the more rudimentary functions of the human brain (Funder, 1997). Psychotics by this definition are asocial, glacial and often cruel. The psychotic lacks empathy, and it is this lack that facilitates the infliction of pain on other human beings without any corresponding sense of guilt. When psychoticism is coupled with xenophobia, with little or no orientation to the family, and also with nihilism, pieces of a meaningful jigsaw puzzle begin to fall into place. Those who are prepared to use violence for political ends appear to have little or no conception of the impact of that violence on the emotions of other people, and they have no sense of restraint stemming from family bonds. The nihilistic orientation may take the form of allowing young people to see meaning created by violent acts: violence can become a kind of political language.[9] Moreover, in Maikovich's words (2005), 'violent individuals grew up ... and some were likely born with genetic predispositions for impulsive and aggressive personalities. For many violent individuals, then, violence is a reasonable conflict-reducing strategy that does not cause any dissonance whatsoever.'

The sharp contrast between those to whom mothers, brothers and sisters are important and those to whom they are less important is reflected in their acceptance of violence for political purposes. In other words, those to whom mothers, brothers and sisters are rated as highly important are much less likely to see violence as a legitimate tool. This implies that, conversely, those who accept the legitimacy of violence are also those for whom family members are much less important. Or, to put this bluntly, if you do not care whether you kill a member of your own family, then you can indulge more easily in indiscriminate violence. We could go further than this and speculate that young people who focus on violence as a political tool are likely to have dysfunctional relationships in the home.

These considerations, however, need to be read against the non-significance in Table 4 of the importance of the father. We could interpret the distinction between the father and other members of the family in two ways: either, the lack of statistical difference in relation to the father arises from the fact that some political violence is encouraged by the father, and that there is no contrast between those who reject violence and who have a good relationship with the father and those who accept violence and also have a good relationship with their father – in both cases the father is important, but important in different ways. Alternatively, the non-significance of the father may arise from the fact that the father simply does not appear on the horizon of the young people who accept the use of violence. The father is a nonentity and insignificant, because he is absent.

The use or rejection of violence needs now to be placed alongside data on suicide. The initial sociological and psychological perspectives on suicide suggest that suicide is performed by isolated people who do not have the support of a good social group and who may be suffering from depression or various mental conditions. The evidence provided by the data analysed here shows that those who are prepared to use physical violence may be socially isolated in one respect, isolated from their families and partially alienated from the meso-level agencies within society, while, at the same time, they may be politically motivated, even by nihilism. In terms of psychological factors, the lack of any significance of the neuroticism variable (Table 3) points away from depression (since depression and neuroticism are correlated: Eysenck, 1978).

Nevertheless, the most general conclusion from these data is that there are young people within British society who are prepared to use non-democratic means to attain political ends and who are, in this sense, already radicalized. It is not difficult to imagine that young people of this disposition are vulnerable to the recruitment approaches of religiously motivated terrorists, but, equally, it would not be correct simply to attribute the creation of a pool of potential suicide bombers to a range of religious factors. As has been shown (Table 1), non-religious young people contribute the largest percentage of those who have already, by their own admission, committed acts of violence for political purposes. The thesis of this essay, which is supported by these figures and this discussion, is that psychotic and conformist (that is, less autonomous) young people who are alienated from their families and in other ways nihilistic in outlook are susceptible to political and religious manipulators, even those who set up cells of suicide bombers.

Appendix

Xenophobia

Item	Item-scale r
Foreigners who turn to crime in my country should be deported immediately.	.6022
The foreigners take away jobs from the natives because they work for less money.	.7217
A lot of foreigners have it too good in this country.	.7782
Foreigners who don't want to conform to this country shouldn't stay here.	.6571
The economy would do a lot better in this country if there were fewer foreigners.	.7614
People from this country should not marry foreigners.	.5689
Most politicians in this country care too much about foreigners, and not enough about the people who have always lived here.	.7170
There are too many foreigners in this country.	.7979
Foreigners shouldn't act so provocatively in public.	.7071
I try to stay away from foreign young people.	.5341
Alpha level .9146	

Nihilism

Item	Item-scale r
In my opinion, life has very little meaning.	.6134
In my opinion, life is meaningless.	.6526
There is no reason for life to exist.	.5560
Alpha level .7720	

Humanity

Item	Item-scale r
Be ready to help others.	.6477
Share with others, and be able to give from yourself.	.6576
Accept every person the way he or she is.	.5455
Do something for society.	.5228
Alpha level .7823	

Family orientation

Item	Item-scale r
Have a happy partnership.	.5857
Have children.	.5858
Build a family of your own where you feel comfortable.	.6792
Later build a comfortable home.	.6105
Alpha level .7979	

Autonomy

Item	Item-scale r
Think and act independently.	.4652
Not get depressed over unpleasant issues.	.3335
Hold on to one's personal opinion, even if it goes against the majority.	.4313
Having the courage to say 'no'.	.5389
Alpha level .6540	

Notes

1 Three of the four bombers were British nationals (*http://news.bbc.co.uk/1/hi/uk/4676861.stm*, 6 August 2005): Hasib Hussain, Mohammad Sidique Khan and Shehzad Tanweer.
2 Of the men who are alleged to have attempted bombings on 21 July, Yasin Hassan Omar arrived in Britain as a 12-year-old refugee from Somalia, Muktar Said Ibrahim arrived from Eritrea at about the same age in 1992, and Osmar Hussein (also called Hamdi Isaac) also had a British passport. (*http://news.bbc.co.uk/1/hi/uk/4721645.stm*, 6 August 2005.)
3 *http://news.bbc.co.uk/1/hi/England/west_midlands/4126688.stm*, 6 August 2005. Meanwhile, 'Blair vows hard line on fanatics' (6 August 2005).
4 *http://news.bbc.co.uk/1/hi/uk_politics/4747573.stm*.
5 Hassan does not specify where her sample comes from, but they operate in the Gaza area, are Arabic-speaking and inspired by Hamas. In other words, they do not seem to be acculturated to the west.
6 Husain's death in battle at the hands of Umayyad soldiers in 680 CE was martyrdom, not a suicide, and his death is generally deplored by

both Sunni and Shi'ite Muslims. Its re-enactment by Imami Shi'ites may serve to glorify martyrdom in general, however.
7   The mental state of completed suicides is investigated by psychological autopsy.
8   See Post, 2005: 'The survival of the group is paramount because of the sense of identity it provides. *Terrorists* whose only *sense of significance* comes from *being terrorists* cannot *be forced to give up terrorism*, for *to do so would be to lose their very reason for being*' (original italics).
9   See, for instance, Third World Youth Festival, Forum of Cultures, Barcelona (UNESCO), 2004: *http://www.unesco.org/youth/background todebates.doc*, 18 August 2005.

References

Appleby, L., Cooper, J., Amos, T. and Faragher, B. (1999). 'Psychological autopsy study of suicides by people aged under 35', *British Journal of Psychiatry*, 175, 168–74.

Arquilla, J. and Ronfeldt, D. (2001). 'Osama bin Laden and the advent of netwar', *New Perspectives Quarterly*, 18, 4, 23–33.

Arquilla, J., Ronfeldt, D. and Zanini, M. (1999). 'Networks, netwar, and information-age terrorism', in I. O. Lesser, B. Hoffman, J. Arquilla, D. Ronfeldt and M. Zanini (eds), *Countering the New Terrorism*, Santa Monica, CA, RAND, pp. 39–84.

Austin, R. L. (1980). 'Subcultures of violence', *Sociological Quarterly*, 21, 545–61.

Baer, R. (2005). 'This deadly virus', *Observer*, 7 August, 25.

Bendle, M. F. (2006). 'Existential terrorism: civil society and its enemies', *Australian Journal of Politics and History*, 52, 1, 115–30.

Berman, A. L. and Jobes, D. A. (1991). *Adolescent Suicide: Assessment and Prevention*, Washington, American Psychological Association.

Cattell, R. B. (1965). *The Scientific Analysis of Personality*, Harmondsworth, Penguin.

Department of Health (2002). *National Suicide Prevention Strategy for England: Consultation Document*, London, Department of Health Publications.

Durkheim, É. (1897). *Le Suicide: Étude de Sociology*, Paris, Alcan.

Eysenck, H. J. (1978). *You and Neurosis*, Glasgow, Fontana.

Eysenck, M. W. and Keane, M. T. (1995). *Cognitive Psychology* (3rd edn), Hove, UK, Lawrence Erlbaum Associates.

Flint, C. (2003). 'Terrorism and counterterrorism: geographic research questions and agendas', *Professional Geographer*, 55, 2, 161–9.

Francis, L. J., Brown, L. B. and Philipchalk, R. (1992). 'The development of an abbreviated form of the Revised Eysenck Personality Questionnaire (EPQR-A): its use among students in England, Canada, the USA and Australia', *Personality and Individual Differences*, 13, 443–9.

Funder, D. C. (1997). *The Personality Puzzle*, London, W. W. Norton and Co.

Graham, J. and Bowling, B. (1995). *Young People and Crime*, London, Home Office Research and Statistics Department Research Findings (No. 24).

Harris, E. C. and Barraclough, B. (1997). 'Suicide as an outcome for mental disorders', *British Journal of Psychiatry*, 170, 205–28.

Hassan, N. (2005). 'Are you ready? Tomorrow you will be in Paradise', *The Times*, 14 July.

Hoffman, B., Arquilla, J., Ronfeldt, D. and Zanini, M. (2001). 'Change and continuity in terrorism', *Studies in Conflict and Terrorism*, 24, 5, 417–28.

Home Office (2006). *Report of the Official Account of the Bombings in London on 7th July 2005*, London, The Stationery Office.

House of Commons (2006). *Intelligence and Security Committee Report into the London Terrorist Attacks on 7 July 2005* (Cm. 6785), London, The Stationery Office.

Jamison, K. R. (2000). *Night Falls Fast: Understanding Suicide*, London, Picador.

Kay, W. K. and Francis, L. J. (2006). 'Suicidal ideation among young people in the UK: churchgoing as an inhibitory influence, *Mental Health, Religion and Culture*, 9, 2, 127–40.

Lukes, S. (1975). *Émile Durkheim: His Life and Work*, Harmondsworth, Penguin.

McCulloch, J. W. and Philip, A. E. (1972). *Suicidal Behaviour*, Oxford, Pergamon Press.

Maikovich, A. K. (2005). 'A new understanding of terrorism using cognitive dissonance principles', *Journal for the Theory of Social Behaviour*, 35, 4, 373–97.

Milgram S. (1974). *Obedience to Authority: An Experimental View*, New York, Harper & Row.

Post, J. M. (2005). 'When hatred is bred in the bone: psycho-cultural foundations of contemporary terrorism', *Political Psychology*, 26, 4, 615–36.

Rushdie, S. (2006). 'Inside the mind of jihadists', *New Perspectives Quarterly*, Winter, 7–11.

Tilker, H. A. (1970). 'Socially responsible behavior as a function of observer responsibility and victim feedback', *Journal of Personality and Social Psychology*, 14, 95–100.

Schapira, K., Linsley, K. R., Linsley, J. A., Kelly, T. P. and Kay, D. W. K. (2001). 'Relationship of suicide rates to social factors and availability of lethal methods', *British Journal of Psychiatry*, 178, 458–64.

Stengel, E. (1965). *Suicide and Attempted Suicide: A Clinician's Guide to Evaluation and Treatment*, London, MacGibbon & Kee.

Williams, M. (1997). *Cry of Pain: Understanding Suicide and Self-Harm*, Harmondsworth, Penguin.

11
Education for peaceful coexistence in the Israeli state Jewish school system

YAACOV J. KATZ

Israeli society comprises numerous heterogeneous ethnic and national groupings, and also different religious sectors. As a result, peaceful coexistence, tolerance, inter-group understanding and inter-group skills are key issues addressed by the Israeli educational system in an attempt to promote cohesion and coherence in Israeli society. Much has been done to promote peaceful coexistence among the two major Jewish sectors in the Israeli state education system: pupils attending state religious and those attending state secular schools. Pupils belonging to these two sectors participate in programmes designed to promote peaceful coexistence, tolerance and understanding between religious and secular pupils, as part and parcel of their routine school activities. However, little has been done as yet to promote coexistence between pupils belonging to the two major Jewish sectors in the school population and those belonging to the minority Arab Moslem, Christian and Druze population groups. While much still needs to be done on this score, the educational system is determined to promote those values vital for cohesion and coherence across Israeli society.

State education in Israel

Prior to the establishment of the state of Israel in 1948, the educational system was semi-private and partisan, and catered for the different population groups on the basis of ideological affiliation. The different political parties established school streams congruent with their political ideology without any central authority monitoring the different systems (Bar-Lev and Katz, 1991). Immediately after the establishment of the state of Israel, the different educational streams functioned under the control of the Israeli Ministry of Education and Culture, but the political parties served as 'supervizing committees' of each of the streams. In this turbulent period (from 1948 to 1953), which faced the state as a result of the mass influx of immigrants from Europe, North Africa and the Middle East, inter-stream competition led to much bitterness and a waste of precious resources. In addition, it was thought untenable by many that the state should shoulder the responsibility for the educational system without having any real say in the running of the different educational streams.

The first Prime Minister of Israel, David Ben-Gurion, led the struggle against the stream system. In 1953, after lengthy negotiations, he succeeded in convincing the members of the different political parties to support the call to do away with the stream system and to form a united state educational system. This system, as portrayed in the 1953 State Education Act, is based on state secular and state religious elementary and high schools, which are subordinate to the Israeli Ministry of Education and Culture.

School principals are subordinate to state inspectors of education, who oversee the implementation of state educational policies and curricula throughout the system. The Israeli school system, comprising the elementary school, which offers a wide spectrum basic education to pupils aged 6 to 12 (first grade through to sixth grade), and the secondary school, which offers pupils a more specialized academic and technological education (seventh grade through to twelfth grade), has two major goals. The first goal deals with scholastic achievement, and the second focuses on the social and personal development of pupils. In state religious schools, this social and personal development emphasizes the inculcation of religious belief, morals and values based on age-old Jewish tradition. In state secular schools, social and personal development accentuates culture, good citizenship and social values based on universal humanistic philosophy (Katz, 1998).

According to Katz (2004), there are a number of sectors in the educational system. The two major sectors in the school-going population may be described as the state religious educational sector, which comprises approximately 20%, and the state secular sector, which includes about 52% of the school-going population. These are the two sectors dealt with in the present chapter. The remaining 28% of pupils belong to the ultra-orthodox Jewish, Arab Moslem, Arab Christian and Druze educational sectors.

The aims of state religious education in Israel

Volbe (1986) stated that the major idea behind religious high school education in modern times is to inculcate in the pupil religious belief and knowledge of the Jewish law, in addition to fostering the individual's responsibility towards the public and the needs of others. Urbach (1986) added that the study of the Torah in the religious high school should address problems of religious belief as well as morality and society. The religious high school pupils, at the completion of their formal studies, should be God-fearing persons positively integrated into modern society. Bar-Lev (1985a) noted that religious high school education gravitates towards the internalization of Jewish religious belief, tradition and morality, and prepares the pupil for public duties and the fulfilment of the needs of society.

Lichtenstein (1983) proposed that the typical modern-day religious high school, especially one catering to the modern orthodox sector in the Israeli population, seeks to develop spiritual perspectives, such as belief, in addition to the ethical and moral values that serve as the basis for a radical critique of the secularly oriented state and society. Lichtenstein added that the religious high school is designed to reconcile the conflicting claims of spirituality and secularity, of personal growth and public service.

In a succinct summary of the aims of the state religious school system, Bar-Lev (1985b) described the modern-day religious high school as educating towards embracing religious belief and deportment as well as towards the acceptance of the morals, values and ethics that are based on Jewish tradition. In addition, the religious school aims to promote the fulfilment of national and civic responsibilities. The element of contribution to society through public service is intrinsic to the philosophy of the modern religious high school. The clear-cut educational mode of promoting a new type of society-oriented and religious citizen who participates fully in all walks of Israeli life characterizes the modern religious high school.

Parents choose this sector mainly because of their particular religious persuasion. This is usually modern orthodox. In this sector, the emphasis is placed on achievement in the different subjects offered to the pupils, in addition to a range of religious subjects that are taught from a clear modern orthodox point of view. Values that are concurrent with modern orthodox Judaism are imparted to the pupils, and teachers are aware of the centrality of orthodox Judaism in the values presented to the pupils. Therefore, teachers are intent on inculcating an orthodox Jewish mode of values education in general, and education for peaceful coexistence and tolerance in particular, in their pupils, and view western civilization and citizenship through the Jewish orthodox prism.

The aims of state secular education in Israel

Aloni (1997) examined the ethos of the state secular education system in Israel and proposed that values and morals, as well as good citizenship, are part and parcel of the development of an indigenous Israeli culture. He presented a sociological definition of the term 'culture', which in his view represents a system of values, objectives, knowledge, skills and feelings constituting the societal norms specific to an individual society. According to Aloni, cultural education is defined as the aspect of the educational process that is concerned with the feelings, values, beliefs, attitudes and emotional well-being of pupils. Thus, the secular term 'culture' in the state secular school system displaces the term 'religious belief and deportment' in the state religious school.

Eisenberg (1989) discussed three major value-concepts that characterize the state secular school in Israel. The concepts 'acquired truth', 'freedom of thought' and 'modern' represent the driving forces behind secular education in Israel. Truth is acquired through knowledge, which in turn is acquired through the freedom of thought processes and originality of thought: the study of the modern versus the traditional leads the pupil to the establishment of a value-system congruent with a humanistic perception of the world. Religious belief is considered by the state secular school system to be anachronistic, and it is the spirit of free inquiry which leads to the development of values and morals.

Katz (1998) stated that Israeli society is at the crossroads of a moral and ethical crisis. Social abuses and delinquency increasingly characterize the pre-adolescent school-going community. As a result, the educational authorities have given high priority to the emphasis on moral and ethical development in the educational process. In the state secular school system, this moral and ethical education is based on universal humanistic values. An emphasis on moral and ethical reasoning, coming to terms with moral issues, and the provision of a healthy moral and ethical atmosphere are major elements in values education in the state secular school. The presentation of real-life ethical and moral problems to pupils and their attempts to provide suitable solutions to these dilemmas are integral features of moral and ethical education. Democracy, human rights, racial, religious and ethnic equality and harmony, and good citizenship are just some of the issues that come to the fore in this aspect of education.

Parents choose this sector mainly because they have no particular religious commitment and wish their children to experience an all-round education that emphasizes academic achievement as well as humanistic values and citizenship. In this sector, the different subjects are taught from a pluralistic and secular values point of view that does not seek to impart to the pupils any particular ideology, apart from the humanistic and democratic values that characterize western civilization. Thus, education for peaceful coexistence, tolerance and understanding is inculcated in the pupils in the secular educational sector from a humanistic and universal standpoint, without alluding to Jewish religious sources or traditions.

Education for peaceful coexistence and tolerance

Chatfield (1986) proposed that education for peace and peaceful coexistence should include three major components: judicial order, associated with the Latin word 'pax'; ethical social relationships, conveyed by the Greek word 'irene'; and well-being that flows from spiritual wholeness, intimated by the Hebrew word 'shalom'. Thus, peace education must include learning and instruction that allude to the upholding of law and order, the promotion of positive social relationships, and the development of psychological and spiritual well-being. Vriens (2003) described education for peaceful coexistence as resembling in its methodology other forms of problem-oriented education, such as development education, environment education and human rights education. According to Vriens, education for peaceful coexistence, tolerance and understanding needs careful justification, and must be legitimized as an integral part of the school curriculum by pointing out its importance for the lives of pupils in the school setting, as well as in the wider society. As a part of values education, peace education must be imparted in the affective domain by experiential learning and instruction that appeals to the pupils' feelings and to their authentic daily needs, rather than to their rational and cognitive judgements.

Iram (2001) described education for peace and tolerance as an integral part of multicultural education in heterogeneous societies, where different population groups live together and interact. Thus, peace education deals, first and foremost, with the prevention of racism, discrimination, inequality, unfairness and segregation. After preventative measures have been implemented in the peace education programmes of heterogeneous societies, positive measures – such as the promotion of equality, understanding, tolerance, coexistence and peace – can be added to the peace education curriculum. Steiner-Khamsi (2003) advocates that, in sectoral societies, peace education must move away from educational approaches that tend to see each pupil as a representative of a specific nation, race, ethnicity or religion. Instead, peace education must emphasize multicultural settings based on communality of values, identity, equality and inter-group cooperation and understanding.

According to Grossman et al. (1997), increasing pro-social actions undertaken within the school in order to promote friendships, coexistence, tolerance, conflict resolution and inter-group understanding can bring about the prevention of negative behaviour. Educators agree that inter-group communication and understanding need to be included in the school programme to address the problem of inter-group alienation and friction, which can lead to frustration, a breakdown of discipline, and even classroom upheaval and violence. De Jong (1994) concluded that researchers agree that interventions that stress the value of peaceful coexistence, tolerance, conflict resolution and inter-group skills can lead to understanding and empathy between heterogeneous groups of pupils. Educational administrators and policy-makers insist that any educational programme that promotes peaceful coexistence and conflict resolution between groups of pupils should emphasize prevention (Giuliano, 1994).

Thus, there seems to be agreement between researchers who have studied the different aspects of education for peaceful coexistence that carefully prepared educational interventions, designed to promote tolerance and understanding, are important for the promotion of peace education within the school system. Prevention can be achieved by implementing suitable peace education programmes, and different pupil groups can be taught to come to terms with each other through these educational means.

Education for peaceful coexistence and tolerance in Israeli schools

Katz and Yablon (2003) indicated that one of the major goals of Israeli society is to do its utmost to bridge inter-group, inter-ethnic and inter-cultural gaps between different sectors in the population, and to generate peaceful coexistence, tolerance and inter-group understanding. Official documents of the Israeli Ministry of Education Culture and Sport concerned with values education adopt a list of goals that include peace education, coexistence, democracy, emotional well-being, equality, integrity, respect, rule of law, tolerance and understanding. Over the years, the educational system in Israel has made gradual progress in an attempt to implement and internalize these values. The perception of peace education in Israel is that it is consistent with the notion that Israel is a Jewish and democratic state, and that education must contribute substantially to the closing of gaps between the different population groups, and most especially between the different Jewish sectoral groups, in order to facilitate peaceful coexistence, tolerance and understanding, as is expected in a normative Jewish and democratic state.

In the years immediately after the establishment of the state and during its initial decades, peace education in Israel focused on nation building. This was an immediate necessity in a country that numbered approximately 600,000 citizens in 1948, the year the country became independent, and grew sixfold in the first fifty years of its existence as result of immigration from all corners of the globe. During these years, peace and other humanistic and democratic values, as stand-alone concepts, were only marginally emphasized in the curriculum (Ichilov, 1993). This was because of the perceived urgent need to impart to the mainly immigrant pupil population the normative societal values that were deemed to be vital in the young Jewish and democratic state. In 1976, peace and values education was added for the first time as a separate, mandatory subject of study in Jewish high schools. The content taught in each of the two Jewish educational sectors was slightly different, being adapted to the special needs of each sector. In general, these programmes included peace education, education for coexistence, understanding and tolerance, and the inculcation of universal humanistic and democratic values that were considered normative in a Jewish democratic state.

Concerns about the less than satisfactory understanding of the importance of education for peaceful coexistence and understanding between Jewish religious and secular sectors in the population began gradually to be heard in Israeli society. Influential academics and public figures often criticized the state educational system for neglecting the social gaps in Israeli society, and especially the gap between pupils attending state religious and those attending state secular schools, regarding the need to emphasize peaceful coexistence, tolerance and understanding between the two sectors. This led to a reassessment of the situation by the relevant authorities in the Ministry of Education, Culture and Sport, and to a strengthening of peace and values education in the educational system. In 1985, a Unit for Values Education was established in the Ministry of Education, Culture and Sport. This unit was responsible for peace and values education programmes of study. In the following years, the unit's status and roles were gradually changed and enhanced, and at a certain point the unit was enlarged and given the responsibility for the study of both peace and values education, and Jewish heritage and values, in both state educational sectors. The unit was charged with implementing the study of both Jewish and democratic values in the school system, and a large amount of resources was invested in order to achieve an improvement in this area. Although pupils then participated in peace and values education programmes, after some years the authorities felt that the results were still unsatisfactory and needed to be improved. As a result the unit was shut down completely in 1999 (Pedatzur and Perliger, 2004), and peace and values education was subordinated to the Pedagogic Secretariat at the Ministry, a powerful body responsible for strategic pedagogical planning and formal curricula and content taught at all levels in the school system.

The Pedagogic Secretariat initiated the compilation of a new peace and values education programme and published a new textbook, to be used by both state religious and state secular schools. The new textbook deals with peace education, values education and citizenship in a Jewish and democratic state. More specifically, it addresses peace and coexistence, inter-group tolerance and understanding, human rights and democracy within Israeli society. The textbook deals especially with the problematic social schisms in Israeli society, and in particular with the schisms between religious and non-religious Jews, consensually recognized as a glaring weakness of Israeli Jewish society. In addition to the theoretical study of peace and values education, as reflected in the new textbook, experiential activities, such as ongoing face-to-face meetings between pupils from state religious and state secular schools, take place from time to time. During these activities, which are usually structured workshops and discussions, issues considered to be of importance to both religious and secular sectors are discussed. Workshop leaders usually use conflict resolution with the pupils in order to bridge gaps and to increase inter-group understanding. School principals and teachers of pupils in both sectors also meet from time to time in order to discuss ways and means of bridging gaps between the two sectors, and the Pedagogic Secretariat provides ongoing in-service training, designed to equip both principals and teachers with the necessary know-how and tools to engage in peace and values education with their pupils.

Pinson (2005) indicated that the new peace and values education programme has not significantly achieved its aim of becoming a platform for developing a common peace and values code for both religious and secular Jewish citizens of Israel. In her analysis of the situation, much still needs to be done to close the peace, coexistence, understanding and tolerance gaps that exist between the religious and secular population sectors in the country. Barak (2005) added that, although there is a significant improvement in the content of the new peace and values education programme, this has not yet been accompanied by an increase in the number of classroom hours needed to implement the programme adequately. In light of the programme being based on the definition of Israel as a Jewish and democratic state, it emphasizes the particular issues that typify those characteristics of Israel as a unique Jewish and democratic state, without adequately addressing the universal aspects of peace and values education.

Despite the perceived shortcomings of the peace and values education programme of the Israeli school curriculum, the Israeli core curriculum, designed in 2002 and implemented in 2003, has added further impetus to the inculcation of peaceful coexistence and understanding between the two major Jewish population sectors in the educational system (Katz, 2002). All classes in the elementary and junior high schools (grades 1 to 9) are now obliged to study a peace and values education programme which includes intensive references to peaceful coexistence, tolerance, inter-group understanding, civil rights, democracy, emotional well-being, equality, integrity, respect and rule of law in the Jewish and democratic state (Katz, 2005). In addition, the mandatory core curriculum calls for the inculcation of universal humanistic values as an integral part of the peace and values education programme, and this aspect of the programme has been adopted by schools in formal lessons and activities. The core curriculum promotes education for peaceful coexistence, tolerance, inter-group understanding and cooperation by emphasizing the common denominators of the Jewish and democratic state. Values such as rule of law, democracy, equality of opportunity in all domains and intersector dialogue form the basis of peace and values education in the core curriculum. However, controversial issues that may impede the acceptance of the common denominator of values (such as the superiority of the secular legal system over the rabbinic legal code, the religious basis for secular Zionism, the involvement of religious parties in the Israeli parliamentary system, and religious legislation and the resulting limitation of certain aspects of personal freedoms) are not included in the peace and tolerance education programmes.

According to Wahrman (2003), the omission of these controversial topics and issues that cause conflict in Israeli society limits the scope of the peace education programme and does not contribute to the health of a sectoral society. Nevertheless, the educational authorities mirror the wishes of Israeli society in general, and, although aware of these limitations, ensure that the foundations of the peace education programme emphasize the issues that are accepted as vital for coexistence, tolerance and intergroup understanding in the Israeli school system. Thus, the peace and values education programme has been limited in its scope consciously in order to reflect consensus and agreement, in the hope that progress will be made in fostering peaceful coexistence between religious and secular Israeli pupils and citizens.

In summary, it is apparent that both state religious and state secular schools in Israel are involved in serious attempts to implement constructive and effective peace, coexistence, tolerance and inter-group understanding education programmes as part of their integral curricula. Progress has been made over the years, and the topic has been made central to the educational agenda of these educational sectors, in the hope that the gap between religious and secular pupils will be bridged and narrowed. Much still needs to be done, and the educational authorities responsible for peace education should review the present situation in order to decide on the improvements that are necessary for implementation in the state religious and state secular peace education programmes.

Mention should be made of the fact that peace education for other sectors in the educational system, including the ultra-orthodox Jewish sector, the Arab Moslem sector, the Arab Christian sector and the Druze sector, needs to be overhauled and reconsidered in order to bring it up to a par with the programme implemented in the state religious and state secular Jewish schools. This aspect of peace education is now a prime goal of the Pedagogic Secretariat, which has mooted a programme entitled 'Common Citizenship', in which Jewish, Moslem, Christian and Druze pupils study common values that characterize modern democratic society, and meet from time to time in order to discuss the implementation of common informal projects, such as the production of joint plays on issues of common interest, the establishment of joint sports teams, the establishment of joint music and dancing troupes, and participation in joint field trips.

Thus, peace education for other sectors in the Israeli school population, especially those comprised of ethnic minorities, has become an additional educational consideration of paramount importance for Israeli society in general and the Israeli educational system in particular, in the hope that increased peaceful coexistence, tolerance and inter-group understanding will better characterize the heterogeneous Israeli society.

References

Aloni, N. (1997). 'Cultural education in a multi-cultural society', *Matzav Ha'Inyanim*, 7, 3–6 (Hebrew).

Barak, M. (2005). 'Civics education in Israel', *Adalah's Newsletter*, 18, September (Hebrew).
Bar-Lev, M. (1985a). 'The cultural conflict of youth in yeshiva high schools', *Niv Hamidrashia*, 242–8 (Hebrew).
Bar-Lev, M. (1985b). 'Yeshiva educational institutions in Israel', in W. Ackerman, A. Carmon and D. Zucker (eds), *Education in an Evolving Society*, Jerusalem, Van Leer Institute, pp. 407–45 (Hebrew).
Bar-Lev, M. and Katz, Y. J. (1991). 'State religious education in Israel: a unique ideological system', *Panorama: International Journal for Comparative Religious Education*, 3, 2, 94–105.
Chatfield, C. (1986). 'Concepts of peace in history', *Peace and Change*, 11, 2, 11–21.
De Jong, W. (1994). 'School-based conflict resolution: give educators more credit', *Journal of Health Affairs*, 13, 4, 163–4.
Eisenberg, Y. (1989). 'On three tensions in religious education', *Dapim*, 8, 38–40 (Hebrew).
Grossman, D. C., Neekerman, H. J., Koepsell, T. D., Liu, P. Y., Asher, K. N., Beland, K., Frey, K. and Rivara, I. P. (1997). 'Effectiveness of a violence prevention curriculum among children in elementary school', *Journal of the American Medical Association*, 277, 20, 1605–11.
Giuliano, J. D. (1994). 'A peer education program to promote the use of conflict resolution skills among at-risk school age males', *Public Health Reports*, 109, 2, 158–61.
Ichilov, O. (1993). *Education for Citizenship in a Changing World*, Tel Aviv, Sifriat Hapoalim (Hebrew).
Iram, Y. (2001). 'Education for democracy in pluralistic societies: the case of Israel', in L. Limage (ed.), *Democratizing Education and Educating Democratic Citizens: International and Historical Perspectives*, New York, RoutledgeFalmer, pp. 213–26.
Katz, Y. J. (1998). 'Affective education in Israeli elementary schools: principles and practice', in P. L. F. Lang, Y. J. Katz and I. Menezes (eds), *Affective Education: A Comparative View*, London, Cassell, pp. 145–52.
Katz, Y. J. (2002). 'A values based core curriculum: the Israeli perspective', *Panorama: International Journal for Comparative Religious Education*, 14, 1, 117–24.
Katz, Y. J. (2004). 'State religious education in Israel: developmental trends in the Zionist era', in Z. Gross and Y. Dror (eds), *Education as a Social Challenge*, Tel Aviv, Ramot Publishing House/Tel Aviv University, pp. 73–83 (Hebrew).
Katz, Y. J. (2005). 'The Israeli school core curriculum and matriculation examinations: an attempt to set standards for a national educational system', *Educational Practice and Theory*, 27, 1, 67–82.

Katz, Y. J. and Yablon, Y. B. (2003). 'Can internet technology promote inter-group attitudes towards equality, understanding, tolerance and coexistence?', in Y. Iram and H. Wahrman (eds), *Education of Minorities and Peace Education in Pluralistic Societies*, Westport, CT, Praeger Publishers, pp. 169–79.

Lichtenstein, A. (1983). 'The ideology of hesder', *Alon Shevut*, 100, 9–22 (Hebrew).

Pedatzur, A. and Perliger, A. (2004). 'The inherent paradox of civic education in Israel', *Megamot*, 43, 1, 64–83 (Hebrew).

Pinson, H. (2005). 'Between a Jewish and democratic state: contradictions and tensions in the civic education curriculum', *Politika*, 14, Summer, 9–24 (Hebrew).

Steiner-Khamsi, G. (2003). 'Cultural recognition or social redistribution: predicaments of minority education', in Y. Iram and H. Wahrman (eds), *Education of Minorities and Peace Education in Pluralistic Societies*, Westport, CT, Praeger Publishers, pp. 15–28.

Urbach, E. E. (1986). 'On Judaism and education', in M. Bar-Lev (ed.), *Religious Education in Israeli Society*, Jerusalem, Hebrew University, pp. 131–46 (Hebrew).

Volbe, S. (1986). 'The modern theological academy (yeshiva)', in M. Bar-Lev (ed.), *Religious Education in Israeli Society*, Jerusalem, Hebrew University, pp. 125–8 (Hebrew).

Vriens, L. (2003). 'Education for peace: concepts, contexts and challenges', in Y. Iram and H. Wahrman (eds), *Education of Minorities and Peace Education in Pluralistic Societies*, Westport, CT, Praeger Publishers, pp. 57–74.

Wahrman, H. (2003). 'Is silencing conflicts a peace education strategy? The case of the "Jewish State" topic in Israeli civics textbooks', in Y. Iram and H. Wahrman (eds), *Education of Minorities and Peace Education in Pluralistic Societies*, Westport, CT, Praeger Publishers, pp. 229–54.

Name index

Abraham 22, 59
Aguilar, M. I. 97, 109
Albright, W. F. 20–1, 27
Al-Khattar, A. M. 50–1, 61
Almond, G. A. 49, 61
Aloni, N. 198, 205
Amin, I. 33
Amos 26
Amos, T. 192
Annas, J. 107–9
Appleby, L. 179, 192
Appleby, R. S. 61–2, 47, 49, 57, 59
Arafat, Y. 10
arap Moi, D. T. 100
Arendt, H. 19
Argyle, M. 160, 170
Armstrong, K. 39–41, 45, 53, 61
Arndt, E. M. 113
Arquilla, J. 177, 192–3
Asher, K. N. 206
Astley, J. vii, ix, 1–5, 79, 151–73
Atatürk 36–7, 45
Augustine, St 159, 170
Austin, R. L. 176, 192
Axelrod, R. 125–6, 129

Babic, M. 55, 61
Baer, R. 177, 192
Barak, M. 203, 206
Barash, D. 123, 129
Bar-Lev, M. 195, 197, 206–7
Barraclough, B. 179, 193
Barry, B. 66, 72, 78
Baumfield, V. 60–1

Beckham, D. 46
Beland, K. 206
Ben Gurion, D. 16, 196
Bendle, M. F. 175, 192
Berman, A. L. 177, 179, 192
Best, R. 79, 169–70
Bharathi, K. S. 99, 106, 108–9
Blair, T. 175, 191
Blake, W. 169–70
Boesak, A. 7, 10, 28
Bourdieu, P. 3, 131–46, 148–9
Bowling, B. 176, 193
Boyer, P. 18, 28
Bretherton, L. 72, 78
Brown, D. 5
Brown, L. B. 181, 193
Browning, D. S. 154, 170
Brümmer, V. 153, 170

Cantor, N. 22, 28
Carr, C. 86, 89
Carter, J. 19, 36
Cattell, R. B. 180, 192
Chakrabarti, S. 175
Charles I 31
Chatfield, C. 199, 206
Clements, R. E. 12, 28
Clines, D. J. A. 24, 28
Clinton, B. 10–12
Comenius, J. A. 112, 129
Constantine 31
Cooper, J. 192
Cosin, J. 162
Cottingham, J. 169, 171
Cupitt, D. 154–6, 171, 173

Daly, M. 116, 129
Darwin, C. 114, 129
Davies, E. W. 26, 28
Davies, O. 69, 74, 78
De Jong, A. J. 103, 109
De Jong, W. 200, 206
Deidun, T. 27–8
Deist, F. E. 8, 26, 28
Deutsch, R. D. 114, 129
Dewey, J. 81, 89
Drury, J. 65, 78
Durkheim, É. 177–8, 192–3

Eibl-Eibesfeldt, I. 118, 129
Eisenberg, Y. 198, 206
Eliot, T. S. 161
Ellis, M. 19, 28
Erasmus 110, 130
Erikson, E. 162, 171
Esau 13
Etzion, Y. 17
Evans, D. 152–3, 161, 163, 171
Eysenck, H. J. 189, 192
Eysenck, M. W. 180, 192
Ezekiel 16, 18, 44

Faber, H. 162, 171
Fallaci, O. 123
Falwell, J. 18
Faragher, B. 192
Farley, E. 151, 154, 171
Ferguson, A. 61
Ferguson, N. 61
Fichte, J. G. 113
Finkelstein, I. 21, 28
Fiorenza, E. S. 25, 28
Flint, C. 177, 192
Foerster, F. W. 112
Ford, D. 68, 78
Francis, L. J. vii, ix, 79, 170–1, 178, 181, 193
Franck, S. 112
Frei, H. 154, 171
Freire, P. 111, 118
Freud, S. 162
Frey, K. 206
Frey, S. 123, 129
Fries, J. F. 121

Funder, D. C. 187, 193
Fuoss-Bühler, S. 119–20, 129

Galileo 41, 45
Galston, W. A. 72, 79
Gandhi, M. 45, 106, 109, 127, 165
Gay, P. 114–15, 129
Gebara, I. 104, 108–9
Girard, R. 52, 61
Giuliano, J. D. 200, 206
Goldstein, B. 14–15
Gordon, N. 86, 89
Gottwald, N. K. 22, 28
Graham, J. 176, 193
Greeley, A. M. 163, 171
Greenleaf, R. K. 106, 109
Grimmitt, M. 60–1, 173
Grossman, D. C. 200, 206

Haakedal, E. vii, 3, 131–50
Hahn, K. 117
Halisch, F. 123, 129
Hamlyn, D. W. 169, 171
Hansen, H. B. 92, 109
Hardy, A. 162, 171
Harries, R. 50
Harris, E. C. 179, 193
Hassan, N. 176, 193
Hauerwas, S. 48, 61, 164, 171
Heimbrock, H.-G. 60, 62, 149–50
Henry VIII 31
Herzl, T. 15, 29
Hess, Y. 16
Hick, J. 165, 171
Hill, C. 47, 62
Hitler, A. 35–7, 110, 175
Hobbes, T. 66, 120
Hodgkin, R. 44–5
Hodgson, P. 165, 171
Hoffman, B. 177, 192–3
Holley, R. 162, 169, 171
Hughes, T. 117
Hull, J. M. vii, 2, 46–63, 66–7, 79, 130, 155, 163, 171–2
Hussain, H. 191

Name index

Hussein, O. 191
Hyde, K. E. 162, 172

Ibrahim, M. S. 191
Ichilov, O. 201, 206
Iram, Y. 200, 206–7
Isaac, H. 191

Jackson, R. 34, 45, 60, 62, 149
James, W. 49, 62, 117
Jamison, K. R. 179, 193
Jean Paul *see* Richter, J. P. F.
Jeffner, A. 138, 149
Job 26
Jobes, D. A. 177, 179, 192
Joel 48
John the Divine 44
Jonah 26, 42, 44
Jones, G. L. viii, 1, 6–29
Joshua 11–16, 20–3, 29
Josiah 22–3
Juergensmeyer, M. 48, 62

Kagan, R. 82–3, 89
Kamaara, E. K. vii, 3, 90–109
Kant, I. 112, 121
Katz, Y. J. vi, vii, 4, 195–207
Kay, D. W. K. 194
Kay, W. K. vii, 4, 174–94
Keane, M. T. 180, 192
Kelly, T. P. 194
Kelsey, D. H. 154, 172
Kenyatta, M. J. 100
Kepel, G. 52, 56, 62
Khan, G. 37
Khan, M. S. 191
Kierkegaard, S. 32, 35, 138
King, M. L. 45, 106, 127
Kittel, G. 158–9, 172
Koepsell, T. D. 206
Kohlrausch, F. 113
Kung, H. 47, 62
Kurtén, T. 133, 138–41, 144–5, 147–9
Kymlicka, W. 72, 79

Landau, D. 16–17, 28
Lazarus 105

Le Guin, U. 43, 45
Lebacqz, K. 158, 172
Leganger-Krogstad, H. 147, 149
Lemche, N. P. 21, 28
Levinas, E. 68–71, 74, 78–9
Lichtenstein, A. 197, 207
Lindner, R. 56, 62
Lindsey, H. 18–19, 28
Linsley, J. A. 194
Linsley, K. R. 194
Liu, P. Y. 206
Locke, J. 64–6, 75–6, 79
Lonsdale, D. 169, 172
Lopez, G. 86, 89
Lötzsch, F. 121, 130
Loubser, J. A. 7, 28
Lukes, S. 178, 193
Luyken, J. 162

MacCrone, I. D. 10, 28
McCulloch, J. W. 180, 193
McDonald, J. I. H. 163, 172
MacDonald, R. 117
McGhee, M. 165, 172
Mackie, J. L. 116, 130
Maikovich, A. K. 187–8, 193
Mairson, A. 17, 28
Mandela, N. 166
Marion, J.-L. 70, 79
Martin, D. 152, 172
Marty, M. E. 47, 61–2
Mary 32, 50, 52
Masalha, N. 16, 29
Maslow, A. 162–3, 172
Mather, C. 13–14, 29
Milgram S. 187, 193
Miller, F. D. 109
Milton, J. 44
Mofokeng, T. A. 24–5, 29
Mokrosch, R. 129–30
Moltmann, J. 47, 62, 104, 109, 167
Moore, M. E. M. 166–7, 172
Moran, G. viii, 3, 81–9
Moses 7, 11, 16, 18
Mott-Thornton, K. 169, 172
Mwesigwa, F. S. 33–5, 38, 43, 45

Name index

Napoleon I 113
Naseem, M. 175
Naugle, D. K. 138, 149
Neekerman, H. J. 206
Nicolaisen, T. 147, 149
Nipkow, K. E. viii, 3, 5, 110–30
Noll, M. A. 13, 29
Nye, J. 83, 89

O'Dea, J. A. 99, 109
O'Dea, T. F. 99, 109
Ogot, B. A. 92, 96, 109
Omar, Y. H. 191
Osmer, R. R. 154, 172
Ottley, R. L. 164, 172

Palmer, P. J. 166, 172
Parekh, B. 72, 79
Parsons, W. S. 37, 45
Pascal, B. 160
Passeron, J.-C. 131, 133–5, 149
Patai, R. 15, 29
Patrick, D. 12, 29
Paul, E. F. 109
Paul, J. 109
Paul, St 31, 43, 128, 167
Pedatzur, A. 202, 207
Peperzak, A. 68, 70, 79
Perliger, A. 202, 207
Perlmutter, D. 50, 62
Perrin, J. 14–15
Philip, A. E. 180, 193
Philipchalk, R. 181, 193
Phillips, D. Z. 138
Phinehas 48
Pinson, H. 203, 207
Pol Pot 35
Post, J. M. 192–3
Potter, Harry 43–4
Priestley, J. G. viii, 2, 30–45
Prior, M. 23, 29
Pullman, P. 42, 44–5

Rabin, Y. 10
Rawls, J. 66
Richman, C. 17
Richter, J. P. F. 112, 121, 130

Rivara, I. P. 206
Robbins, M. viii, ix, 79
Robson, J. 169, 172
Ronfeldt, D. 177, 192–3
Rowlett, L. L. 22, 29
Rudin, J. 51, 62
Runcie, R. 32
Rushdie, S. 44–5, 187, 193

Sacks, J. 14–15
Said, E. 67–8, 79
Salomon, G. 17
Sampson, F. E. 44–5
Samuel 16, 158
Saul 16
Schapira, K. 179, 194
Scheilke, C. 62, 149, 150
Schreiner, P. 62, 149–50
Schweitzer, A. 108
Selby, P. 155, 172
Shaw, R. P. 115–16, 119, 130
Silberman, N. A. 21, 28
Silberschmidt, M. 94, 109
Silverman, K. 13–14, 29
Sinaga, D. 109
Sivan, E. 49, 61
Skeie, G. 131, 138, 149
Smith, H. W. 48, 62
Smith, M. 84, 89
Smith, N. 47, 62
Sobel, D. 41, 45
Solomon, N. 15, 29
Solomon, R. C. 160, 172
Spellman, W. M. 64, 79
Spencer, H. 114
Spero, M. H. 48, 63
Stace, W. T. 161, 172
Stalin, J. 35
Stassen, G. H. 168, 172
Steiner-Khamsi, G. 200, 207
Stengel, E. 178, 194
Stern, P. D. 12, 29
Stoll, D. 54, 63
Streib, H. 147, 150
Strom, M. S. 37, 45

Tanweer, S. 191
Taylor, C. 72, 79

Name index

Temple, W. 117
Teresa of Calcutta, Mother 106
Thatcher, A. 169, 172
Thatcher, M. 32
Theissen, G. 126–7, 130
Thompson, T. 53, 63
Thompson, T. L. 21, 29
Thomson, J. B. 151, 172
Tiger, L. 113
Tilker, H. A. 187, 193
Tolkien, J. R. R. 42, 44–5
Towler, R. 152, 172
Trivers, R. L. 124
Tzu, S. 165

Urbach, E. E. 197, 207

Van Gogh, V. 49
van Seters, J. 21, 29
Vidler, A. R. 32, 45
Vogel, C. 116, 130
Volbe, S. 197, 207
von Rad, G. 158
von Schiller, F. 64
Vriens, L. 199, 207

Wacquant, L. J. D. 133–4, 140, 142, 149

Wahrman, H. 204, 207
Wamalwa, K. 108
Warrior, R. A. 25, 29
Weinfeld, M. 7, 29
Weymar, E. 113, 130
Whitehead, A. N. 166, 173
Whitelam, K. W. 21, 29
Wickler, W. 123, 130
Wilhelm II 112
Williams, M. 176–7, 179, 194
Williams, R. 32, 160, 173
Wilson, M. 116, 129
Wittgenstein, L. 42, 45, 138
Wolterstorff, N. 160, 173
Wong, Y. 115–16, 119, 130
Woodhead, L. 146, 150, 154, 173
Wright, A. viii, 2, 64–80, 167–9, 173
Wright, N. T. 77, 80
Wulf, C. 129–30
Wulff, D. M. 163, 173
Wyschogrod, M. 8, 29

Yablon, Y. B. 201, 207
Yancey, P. 105, 109
Young, I. 72, 80

Zanini, M. 177, 192–3

Subject index

9/11 *see* Twin Towers
acceptance 26, 71, 127, 155, 159–61, 163, 187, 190
Africa/Africans 3, 6–10, 24, 28–9, 33, 90–109, 119–21
Afrikaners 7, 9
aggression 49, 68, 71, 95, 110–29, 180, 188
ahimsa 165
Allah 47, 50, 67
  see also God
alterity *see* difference
altruism 120, 124–6, 129
  see also self-interest; self-sacrifice
Amalek/Amalekites 13–14, 16
amity 115
Anglicans 44, 46, 162, 186
  schools 182–3
anthropology 3, 55, 59, 110, 133–4, 138, 141, 142, 145
anti-Judaism/anti-Semitism 25, 121
  see also Israelis/Israel; Jews/Judaism
anti-violence *see* violence
anxiety 116, 120, 159, 179–80
apartheid 7–10, 28
apocalyptic 53–4
apostasy 12
Arabs 4, 14, 16, 19, 33, 40, 89, 117, 191, 195–6, 205
Armageddon 41, 53
Armenians 35, 37, 45
assassin/assassination 14, 50, 88
assimilation, social 121, 132, 174
Assyria 22–3
atheology 153

attitudes 1–2, 21, 35–6, 39, 47, 50–1, 61, 66, 96, 98, 100–1, 103, 105–7, 113, 118, 120, 122, 138–9, 153, 158, 161–73, 184, 198, 207
Australia 193
autonomy 72, 93, 178, 181, 184–91
axial period 56

basic proposition 133, 138–45
basic trust 133, 139, 147–8, 162
Bible 6–9, 11, 13, 16, 18, 19–29, 41, 54, 103, 110, 122
  see also Hebrew Bible
bombing 83, 87, 123
  see also London bombings; suicide bombings
Boston 13, 38
Boy Scout movement 117
Britain/British 9–10, 31, 33–4, 46, 117, 155, 165, 168, 172, 174–5, 177, 181, 189, 191
brood care 118
Buddhists/Buddhism 45, 67, 175, 182
Burundi 92

Calvinism 8–9
Canaan/Canaanites 2, 7, 9–13, 20–3, 25–6, 28–9
Canada 29, 116, 193
capital 134–6, 142, 146–7
care 70, 88, 95, 100, 105, 107, 116, 118, 125, 181, 188
  see also love
charity *see* love

Christians/Christianity 1, 3, 4, 6, 10, 14, 17–19, 27, 31–3, 38–45, 47, 50–1, 54, 57, 59–62, 65, 67, 78, 88, 90–109, 113, 121, 126, 129, 151–73, 195–6, 205
Christ-like 100, 103
Church Mission Society 33
CIA 87
citizenship 58, 79, 112–13, 122, 149, 196–9, 203, 205–6
civic concerns/education 73, 91, 102, 107, 197, 206–7
class 96–7, 114, 124, 128, 135, 187, 204
coercion 83, 89, 167
cognition 2, 51, 113–16, 121–2, 131, 138, 152, 200
  cognitive psychology 179, 192
  cognitive therapy 60
  see also reason
colonialism/imperialism 2, 6, 21, 23, 25, 29, 33, 67, 69, 71, 73, 76, 79, 91–2, 98, 100, 109, 120, 111, 114
common good 65–6
compassion 19, 55, 59, 72, 78, 117, 121, 123
competition 4, 52, 56, 91, 96–8, 101, 114, 116, 130, 132–3, 136, 141–2, 145–8, 196
concern *see* care
conflict 3, 31–6, 38–42, 45, 81–2, 85, 88–9, 90–2, 95, 99, 101, 114, 120, 122–3, 127, 132, 143, 155, 158, 164, 165, 193, 204, 206–7
  of beliefs 26, 64–80, 193
  ethnic 96–7
  see also ethnic cleansing
  gender 92–5, 98, 104–5, 109
  of interests 145
  -reducing strategies 164–6, 188, 200, 203, 206–7
  religious 1, 99, 111
  resolution 200, 203, 206
Congo 90
consistency 54, 56

contamination *see* purity
contemplation 161–2
contentment 74, 160–5
contextuality 133, 136, 151–2
conversion 6, 54, 56, 128
cooperation 58, 85, 91, 124–6, 129–30, 145, 200, 204
Council of Europe 58, 62, 64
critical (dialectical) convergence 111
critical openness 147
critical peace education 129
critical public 112–13, 122
critical religious belief/understanding 24–7, 57, 60, 65, 111, 121, 152–4, 168
  see also religious education; Scripture/sacred scriptures; self-criticism
critical theory 141
crucifixion/cross 31, 104–5, 109, 160
Crusades 31

deception 165
  see also self-deception
delight 160
democracy 37, 40, 68, 79, 80, 87, 100–2, 109, 111–13, 120, 131–2, 135, 137, 143–4, 189, 199, 201–7
  democratic theology 154
Denmark 138
depression 179–80
depth 44, 70, 109, 153
detachment 34–5, 161
Deuteronomy 7–8, 11–12, 16, 18, 22, 26–9
development issues 8–10, 91, 94–5, 98, 108, 199
  see also economic issues
dialogue/dialectic 59, 109, 111, 145–7, 149, 204
  see also hermeneutics
difference 2, 33, 60, 64, 66–80, 92, 102, 114, 120, 123, 133, 143
  difference-blindness 66–7, 69–70
  gender difference 116–18, 150
  religions of 146

dignity 103, 119, 122, 124, 160
discrimination 9, 62, 92, 99, 128, 200
disinterestedness 71, 135
see also love
Dome of the Rock 17–18
doxa 135–6, 139
Druze 4, 195–6, 205
Dutch Reformed Church (DRC) 7–9

economic issues 55, 90, 92–7, 100–1, 108–9, 114, 124–6, 134–6, 142–3, 172, 190
see also development issues
education for peace *see* peace education
eirene 158
elect/election (political) 45, 101, 107–8, 186
elect/election (religious) 8–9, 13–14, 21, 29
emotion 39, 47–8, 52, 86, 105, 108, 113–14, 116–20, 122–3, 156, 159–61, 164, 169, 180, 188, 198, 201, 204
empathy 7, 46, 66, 123, 129, 141, 143, 187, 200
enemy 7–8, 14, 31, 84, 87–8, 114–15, 122, 127–9, 166
England 12, 31, 33, 36, 47, 59, 114, 117, 173, 177, 181, 192, 193
Enlightenment, the 35, 65, 68–9, 72–8, 112
enmity 115
epistemology 3, 131, 133, 138, 140–1, 147
equality 9, 66, 72, 78, 119–22, 164, 199–204, 207
Eritrea 191
ethics 2, 13, 16, 19–21, 24, 27–9, 43, 48, 52, 58, 60, 64, 65, 67, 70–9, 81–2, 84, 89, 90, 108, 110, 115–17, 120–1, 124–6, 128, 130, 133, 139, 141–5, 147–9, 153–5, 161, 163, 167, 174, 187, 196–9

evolutionary ethics 124–6
see also responsibility, moral
ethnic cleansing 2, 7–12, 21–3
ethnocentrism 180–1
ethos 3, 90–109
definition of 103
Europe 9, 15, 35–6, 62, 83, 113–15, 120–1, 129, 149–50, 175, 178
see also Council of Europe; European Union
European schooling 124, 131
European Union 81
evil 14–15, 21, 43, 76, 84, 104–6, 109, 110, 142, 152, 175
absorption/neutralization of 166
evolutionary psychology 110, 115, 124–6
existentialism 138, 143, 148, 192
Eysenck Personality Questionnaire 181, 187–9, 192–3

faith 10, 24, 34, 47–61, 65, 67, 74, 121, 152, 159, 168, 178–9
faith development 54
faith schools *see* religious schools
family 4, 60, 90, 92–4, 109, 115–16, 118–20, 125, 135, 156–7, 163, 178, 181, 184–8, 191
family semantic 118–19, 125
fan 46–7, 57
fanaticism/fanatic 2, 46–63, 191
definition of 46–7
education of 56–61
fantasy 40–3
femininity 94, 98, 135–6, 146, 148, 177, 180
feminism 25, 104, 150
see also femininity; patriarchy; women
field 34, 132, 134–7, 140, 142, 146–8
fighting 13, 32, 85, 97, 113, 115, 187
for peace 31–2, 156

flourishing, human 72, 75–7, 160–2
force 3, 65, 81–9, 108, 127, 128, 134, 164–5, 180, 186, 192
foreigners 7, 9, 23, 26, 48, 68–9, 114
France 114, 119, 135–6, 148, 190
freedom 67, 71–6, 82, 118, 127, 143, 159, 164, 168, 178, 204
    freedom of belief 62, 65, 198
    psychological 159
fundamentalists/fundamentalism 17–19, 28, 32, 39–42, 44–5, 47–9, 54, 61–2, 68, 71–2, 113

game theory 125
Gaza 177, 191
gender discrimination/violence 3, 92–5, 98, 104–5, 109
    see also femininity; masculinity; patriarchy
gender fields 135–6, 148
gender programmes 94, 98
genes 55–6, 118–19, 130, 188
Genesis, book of 9, 16, 18, 21, 40, 44
Geneva Conventions 88
genocide 6, 11–12, 14, 16, 19, 21, 31, 35, 109
Germany 111–12, 114–15, 117, 128, 148
global village 64
God 6–16, 19, 27, 50, 53, 55, 59, 67, 69, 99, 103–5, 109, 113, 127–8, 114, 152–3, 155, 158–9, 162, 164–5, 167–9
    God-talkers 151
Golden Rule, the 125
Gordonstoun School 117
Great Trek 10
Gush Emunim 16

habitus 134–7, 140, 143
hajj 38
Hamas 191
happiness 73, 76, 155, 160–2, 170, 191
haram 174
head-hunting 122–3

Hebrew Bible 1, 6–29, 48, 110, 158
Hebron 14
hermeneutics 26, 52–3, 60, 110, 154
    see also dialogue; Scripture/sacred scriptures
heroes 14, 113
hidden curriculum 112, 144
Hindus/Hinduism 59, 102, 165
history teaching 36–8
Holocaust/holocausts 15, 35–6, 45
Holy War 10–14, 16, 193
    see also war
home/at home 18, 74–5, 156, 159–60, 162, 188, 191
homicide 14, 116, 123, 129
hospitality 2–3, 64–80
hostages 123
human nature 3, 76, 99, 110–30
humanism 77, 143–4, 196
humanistic *see* values, humanistic
humility 32, 100, 103–4, 128, 152, 162
hunting 55, 117
Hutu 92, 97
hypocrisy 30, 115

identity, human 52, 66, 69–72, 86, 101, 149, 200
    collective 92, 115, 118, 192
ideology 23, 25–7, 55–6, 111, 114, 116–18, 122, 195, 206
idolatry/idols 12, 48, 55, 61, 70
image/imagery 31–2, 40, 43, 45, 104, 113–14, 120, 126, 129, 160
immigration *see* migration
imperialism *see* colonialism
India 165
indirect communication 41
indoctrination 110, 114, 118, 122, 129–30
infanticide 116
integration, social 124, 132, 178, 180, 197

International Seminar on Religious Education and Values ix, 1, 126
interpretation (of scripture) *see* Scripture/sacred scriptures
interrelatedness 133, 137
Iraq 32, 35–7, 81, 83, 88–9
Islam *see* Muslims/Islam
Israelis/Israel 1, 2, 4, 6–26, 28–9, 30, 40, 42, 48, 87, 89, 128, 195–207
  education in Israel 4, 195–207
  see also Hebrew Bible; Jews/Judaism

Japan 87, 175, 177
Jerusalem 18, 22, 28, 71, 105, 128, 170
Jesus Christ 17–18, 45, 47–8, 50, 52–4, 57, 65, 67, 100, 103–9, 117, 126–9, 158–9, 169–70
Jews/Judaism 1, 14, 17, 25, 29, 35, 39, 45, 51, 62, 70, 113, 117, 121, 198, 207
  orthodox/ultra-orthodox 14–18, 179, 196–8, 205
  see also Hebrew Bible; Israelis/Israel
jihad 193
  see also Holy War
joy 64, 159–60, 162
judgement/justice 3, 5, 19, 24, 27, 55, 57, 59, 66, 72–3, 76, 80, 94, 96–9, 102–8, 110, 119–24, 143, 156, 158, 164–8, 180
just war 88
justification for violence 6–29, 50–1

Kaaba 48
Kalenjin 97
kamikaze pilots 175
KANU 101–2
Kenya 3, 90–4, 97, 99–102, 107–9
Kikuyu 91, 93, 96–7, 106
Kingdom of God 30, 126, 155, 158–60, 170–1
Korea 36

language 4, 31, 44, 54, 59, 96, 99, 103, 118–19, 123, 126, 131–2, 138–47, 153–6, 171–2, 188
  of family 118–19
  of orthodoxy 144, 146
  of peace 4, 31–2, 151–60
  of power/force/violence 3, 31–2, 81–9
  see also image/imagery
leadership 3, 11, 17, 22, 51, 54, 56–7, 97, 100–7, 136, 145, 174, 203
  servant-leadership 106, 109
learning/learners 6, 13, 37, 39, 66, 70, 73–4, 82, 89, 113–30, 167–71, 199
  context of 151
  experiential 36–9, 168–70, 200
  student-guests 74–5
Lebanon 30
Lebensraum 11–12
liberal/liberalism 64–8, 71–9, 83, 114, 142, 175
  hard/soft liberalism 73
liberation 11, 25, 28–9, 100–1, 104–6, 113
Liberia 90
life-view 133, 137–45, 147–8
life-worlds 60, 69, 147
listening 77, 84, 139, 141, 154–5, 170
logos 39
London bombings 4, 174–7, 191, 193
love 3, 25, 65, 72, 78, 84, 100, 102–8, 116, 118, 121–2, 125, 127–9, 143, 145, 160–7
  education for 121
Lutherans 112, 137, 143–4

Maasai 91
marriage 9, 121, 178
martyrdom 14, 104, 177, 191–2
masculinity 98, 105, 114, 116–18, 122, 134, 149, 176–7, 187–8
maturity 60, 102, 130
meaningfulness of life 168, 171, 178, 188, 190

mental illness 179–80
mercy 8, 16, 37, 59, 123
Methodists 182
Middle East 19, 123, 196
  see also Israelis/Israel; Lebanon; Palestine
migration 93, 112, 117, 121, 132, 201
model syllabuses 59
Molucca Islands 122–3
moral education 100, 196–9, 202, 204 *and passim*
  see also ethics
morals/morality see ethics
Moral Majority 18
Muhammad 45, 48
multicultural 66, 72, 78–9, 124, 200, 205
multi-ethnic 115
multi-party politics 92, 97, 101
murder see homicide
Muslim Council of Britain 174
Muslims/Islam 4, 14, 17, 19, 31, 45, 33–4, 38–40, 50–1, 54, 59–62, 67, 102, 113, 121, 174–6, 182–3, 186, 192
  British Muslims 4, 174
myth/mythos 20, 22–3, 39, 53

National Rainbow Coalition (NARC) 98, 102
nationalism 15, 66, 79, 109, 110, 113, 115, 122, 129–30
Nazis 35, 38, 110, 117
neutrality 34–5, 73, 111, 154
New England 13
Nigeria 99
nihilism 139, 181, 184–5, 188–9, 190
nonconformists 46
non-violence see violence
North America 12–13, 106
  Native Americans 13, 25
North of England Institute for Christian Education ix
Northern Ireland 50, 99, 182
Norway 132, 136–7, 141, 143–4, 146

Old Testament see Hebrew Bible
omnipotence 103, 105
onlooks 152–3, 169–70
oppression 7, 9, 20, 22–5, 127–8
orthodoxy 22, 60–1, 66, 144
  see also Jews/Judaism, orthodox/ultra-orthodox
Other, the 2, 52, 64–80, 82, 119, 126–7
outsider 7, 23, 48, 55
  see also stranger
Outward Bound Schools 117

pacifism 31
Palestine 9–10, 15–19, 29
parable 41, 70
paradox intervention 127–8
passivity 26, 83–4, 127, 163, 166
patriarchy 92–3, 99
  see also masculinity
patriotism 115, 130
peace 1–5, 11, 15, 30–45, 57, 59, 71, 76, 91, 95, 99–103, 110–30, 151–73, 186, 195, 198–207
  biblical 158–9, 168
  fighting for 31–2, 156
  inner 156–60, 166, 168
  language of 4, 31–2, 151–60
  of mind 155–7, 160, 168
  outer 166
  peaceful coexistence 4, 76, 195–207
  peace process 16, 156
  personal 4, 156–70
  and process philosophy/theology 30, 166–7, 172
  public 4, 155–7, 163–6
  spiritual 158–63, 169
  Stoic 159
  vision/perception 169–70
peace education 3, 59, 76, 64–80, 110–30, 168–70, 172, 199–205, 207
  education in peaceable perception 170
peacemaking 4, 31, 127, 163–4, 169, 170

Peace Studies 36, 155
  see also peace education
peak experience 162–3
persecution 52, 56, 159
  religious 9, 12
personality 4, 49, 55–6, 60, 180–1, 184, 187, 192–3
persuasion 118, 122, 166–7, 187
Pharaoh's law 121
pilgrimage 14, 38
Poland 37
politics/political 3–4, 11, 21, 24–8, 33–4, 39, 47, 49, 51, 55, 57, 62, 64, 68, 73, 79, 82, 86–8, 90–150, 156, 163, 165, 174–207
politics of difference 66, 72, 80
postmodern/postmodernity 68, 76–7, 141, 155
power 3, 28, 33, 37, 50, 52–4, 68, 76, 81–9, 92–109, 125, 132, 134, 136–7, 140, 142, 144, 146, 164–8
  hard/soft 83
  spiritual powers 43
praxis 77, 163
privatization of religion 58, 65–8, 136, 146
process thought 166–7
promised land 7, 10–16
Protestants 33, 46, 178
psychoanalysis/ psychotherapy 49, 56, 62–3, 111, 114–15, 162, 179
psychology 39, 166, 170
  cognitive 179, 192
  of religion 4, 59, 160–3, 171–3
  social 111, 113, 123
Puritans 12–14
purity 8, 10, 12, 14, 20–1, 51, 175

Quakers 44
Qur'ān 11, 44, 53, 59, 67

rabbis 16, 39
racism 10, 21, 58, 110, 113–14, 124, 200

reason 65, 69, 120–2, 142–5
receptivity 83–4, 161
reciprocity 93, 124–6, 143
reconciliation 19, 61, 95, 101, 103, 116, 120, 122, 128, 158, 160, 164, 166
redemption *see* salvation
religionism 66–7
religions of difference 146
religions of humanity 146
religious affiliation 56, 182, 186, 195
religious education 1–4, 32–6, 38–42, 45, 56–62, 64–80, 99–102, 111, 126–7, 129, 131–50, 167–73, 196, 197–8, 206–7
  architectonic role 168
  Christian education 3, 98–108, 130, 158–60
  classroom as a home 74
  confessional/non-confessional 169, 196–9
  contextual 137, 147
  inner-religious 58
  intra-religious 58–9
  inter-religious 58–9, 67, 120, 124, 150
  Jewish education 195–207
  multi-faith 34
  Personal Quest approach 2, 30, 59, 168
  and thinking skills 60
  see also critical religious belief/understanding; dialogue/dialectic; model syllabuses; respect
religious experience 29, 60, 62, 162–3, 171, 173
Religious Right 17
religious schools 58, 60, 196–8
religious studies 1, 111
  see also religious education
respect 2, 19, 34, 48, 57, 60–1, 71, 74–5, 103, 132, 144, 146–7, 164, 166, 201, 204
  for religious belief/understanding 57, 60

responsibility, moral 57–8, 70–1, 74, 94–5, 145, 178, 187, 197
retaliation 119, 125–8, 166
Rift Valley Province 92, 97
rights, animal 186
rights, human 15, 19, 62, 66, 72, 94, 100–3, 120–2, 175, 180, 199, 203
  collective 72
  groups 180–6
  minority 79
  Roman Catholics 33, 39, 102, 178, 186
  schools 182–3
Rwanda 31, 35, 92, 97, 109

sacralization 99
sacrifice 17, 59, 100, 108
  see also self-sacrifice
safety 11, 71, 86
saint 14, 18, 49
St George's Chapel, Windsor 31–2
salaam 30
Salem 117
Salt March 165
salvation 17, 56, 65, 73, 75–8, 99–100, 104–5, 109, 158–9, 178
sameness 2–3, 64, 68–78
sanctity/sanctification 8, 121–2
satisfaction 101, 113, 159–62, 180
satya 165
satyagraha 165
Scandinavia 138
Scripture/sacred scriptures 1, 2, 4, 6–29, 31–2, 52–3, 59, 153, 158
  authority of 6, 17, 20, 22, 25–7
  see also fundamentalists/ fundamentalism
  canon of 58
  ethical criticism of 23–7
  historical criticism of 8, 20–4, 41, 43
  reader-response approach to 23
secular/secularists/ secularization 4, 30, 34–5, 40, 48, 52, 57–8, 61, 64, 72, 74–5, 77, 106, 136–9, 141, 144, 146, 155, 169, 174, 195–9, 202–5
security 54, 69, 71, 74, 85, 87, 107, 158, 162
self-acceptance 163
self-actualization 163
self-criticism 55, 154
self-deception 55, 165
self-destruction 174
self-esteem 52, 94
  see also identity, human
self-evident 138–9
self-harm 194
self-interest 84–5, 90, 107
self-involvement 152, 171
self-justification 165
self-preoccupation 161, 163
self-reflexivity 140–1
self-restraint 164, 187–8
self-sacrifice 125, 165
self-transcendence 59, 161
self-understanding 2, 36–9, 67, 69–74
separation/separatism 7–10, 122, 132
  separation of church and state 40
  see also apartheid
Serbia 87
serenity 156, 159
shalom 30, 74, 158, 160, 199
Sikhs/Sikhism 182
Six Day War 18
slavery 7, 9–11, 25, 33, 84, 103
social and personal development 196
  see also learn/learners, experiential
social psychology 111, 113–14, 123
socialization 112, 131, 135, 138, 172
society 1, 4, 6, 8, 10, 21, 23–4, 34, 48, 49, 52, 53, 55–8, 64–6, 71, 75, 77, 92, 96, 99, 114, 118, 120, 122, 124, 144, 146, 155, 163, 175, 178, 180, 189–90, 192, 195, 197–8, 200–7
solidarity 64, 66, 68–9, 75, 119–22, 124–5, 143

Somalia 90, 191
South Africa 6–10, 24, 28–9
Spain 40
Spirit, Holy 59, 165–6, 171
spiritual/spirituality 4, 8, 30, 41, 43–4, 52, 57–60, 62, 64, 67, 73, 77, 79, 83, 107–8, 113, 124, 146, 152, 155–6, 158–73, 197, 199
  formation 169
  insight 169–70
  powers 43
  vision 169–70
sport 46, 116–17
stranger 66, 70–4, 106, 114, 120
  see also outsider
strife/striving 30, 32, 67, 75, 101, 143, 151
Sudan 90
suicide 174–94
  risk factors 178–9
  suicide bombings 4, 174–7, 180–1, 187, 189, 191, 193
superpower 112
surrendering the will *see* acceptance
symbolic actions 127–8
symbolic competition 4, 132
symbolic consumption 52
symbolic violence 3, 43, 131–50
sympathy 123, 165
syncretism 12
Syria 87

teachers/teaching 1–2, 9, 12, 26–7, 32, 34, 38–9, 42–5, 57–60, 74–5, 100, 103, 105–6, 127, 132–7, 140–8, 168, 172–3, 181, 198, 203
  teacher-hosts 75
temple 17–19, 46, 48
Temple Institute 17
terror/terrorism 1, 3, 4, 43, 49, 50–2, 55, 61–2, 85, 86, 87–9, 90, 124, 174–5, 189, 192–3
  war on 3, 43, 85–6, 88–9
theological listening 154–5, 170

theological reflection 168
theology 2, 7, 8, 10, 16, 18–19, 24, 27, 52, 59–60, 65–7, 73, 77, 88, 90, 101, 104, 111–13, 133, 138, 145, 165, 170–3
  academic 1, 151–2, 207
  church 46
  contextual 145, 152
  critical 154
  of the cross 104
  defined 151
  democratic 154
  descriptive 154
  empirical 151–73
  feminist 25, 104
  kneeling 152
  liberation 25
  normative 154
  onlook 152–3
  ordinary 4, 151–7, 159–73
  peace theology 110
  process 166–7
  subterranean 152
thug 50
Tit for Tat 125–6
tolerance 3, 7, 23, 34, 40, 51, 57–8, 62, 65–7, 71, 73, 77, 105, 132, 143, 146, 180, 195, 198–207
Torah 8, 11, 14–19, 26, 197
torture 87–8
totality 68–9, 79, 104, 138
tranquillity 31, 157–9
transcendent 53–4, 59, 73, 121, 128, 139
travellers 106
tribalism 31, 66–7, 92, 115, 118
trust 123, 133, 138–9, 143–8, 161–2, 166, 181–6
  see also basic trust; faith
truth 38, 40–1, 44, 53, 55, 59–60, 71, 73, 77–8, 141, 144, 148, 163–7, 170, 198
  conflicting religious 66–7, 71, 77–8
  power of 164–6
Turkey 35, 45
Tutsi 92, 97
Twin Towers 31, 33

Subject index

Uganda 33–5, 43, 45, 90, 109
ultimate concern 47
United Nations 30, 58, 66, 85, 90, 112
United States of America 29, 36, 50, 81, 83, 85, 87–8, 177
utopia 7, 76, 78

values
  education/inculcation of 100, 196–9, 202, 204 *and passim*
  humanistic 7, 58, 65, 143, 198–9, 201–4
  see also ethics
Vietnam 36, 123, 129
violence 1, 6–29, 33, 36, 38, 40, 43–5, 50–2, 54, 56, 61–2, 64–150, 164–6, 174–94
virus of 107, 192
Virgin Mary 50,
virtue *see* ethics
vision 18, 70, 124, 161, 169–70

Wales 59, 173, 181
war/warfare 1, 10–14, 16, 18–19, 25, 27, 30, 35–6, 81–9, 90, 110–30, 155, 158, 165–8
  Holy War 10–14, 16, 193
  world war 19, 35–6, 35–6, 81
  see also terror/terrorism, war on
weakness 37, 54, 82–4, 103–4, 107
well-being 69, 72, 74, 158, 162–3, 187, 198–201, 204
Welsh National Centre for Religious Education ix
West, the 21, 25, 35, 37, 42, 50, 64, 68–9, 72–4, 120–1, 142, 191, 198–9
West Bank 16, 18
Western Wall 38
women 3, 37, 90, 92–5, 98, 99, 104, 109, 116, 132, 135–6, 146–7
  see also femininity; feminism
women's development *see* gender programmes
world-view 69–78, 138

xenophobia 6–10, 26, 180–90

Youth for Understanding 124

Zionism 15–18, 204, 206
Zivilcourage 128